Projecting State and Local Populations

Projecting State and Local Populations

Donald B. Pittenger

Population Studies Division,
Office of Program Planning and Fiscal Management
State of Washington

Ballinger Publishing Company ● Cambridge, Mass.
A Subsidiary of J.B. Lippincott Company

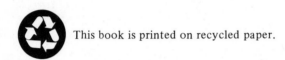

Copyright © 1976 by Ballinger Publishing Company. All rights reserved. No part of this publication may be reproduced, stored in a retrieval system, or transmitted in any form or by any means, electronic mechanical photocopy, recording or otherwise, without the prior written consent of the publisher.

International Standard Book Number: 0–88410–356–0

Library of Congress Catalog Card Number: 75–38694

Printed in the United States of America

Library of Congress Cataloging in Publication Data

Pittenger, Donald B
  Projecting state and local populations.

  Bibliography: p.
  1. Population forecasting—United States.
2. Population forecasting. I. Title.
HB3505.P57   301.32'01'82   75–38694
ISBN 0–88410–356–0

Contents

Chapter Eight
Projecting Population by Age and Sex:
The Migration Component

Chapter Nine
Projecting Populations by Age and Sex:
The Complete Model

Chapter Ten
Practical Considerations   217

List of Figures

List of Tables

List of Exhibits

☆ ☆

☆ ☆

Note: Within the text a star line denotes the beginning and end of an exhibit.

Preface

There has been a gap in the demographic literature with respect to small area demographic projections. Several monographs exist on the projection of national populations, but these are of limited use for the analyst interested in projecting state and local populations because the subject of migration is either ignored or downplayed in such works. On the other hand, a good many state and local population projections have been made in the last few decades using a variety of techniques, yet more than ten years have elapsed since even a booklet-sized discussion of projection methodologies has appeared. Consequently, this writer—who is a trained demographer—spent many months learning to make projections "on the job." And what of the analyst who is not a demographer? Where is he to turn besides a widely scattered literature comprised largely of official publications by state and local governments and occasional journal articles?

The book before you is an attempt to fill the gap mentioned above. While it does not cover every possible topic related to local population projections, it does treat the heart of the subject. This writer believes that the material contained in this book provides the technical basis for an industrious analyst to create population projections at the state of the art practiced in the mid-1970s. Most speculative or otherwise untried methods are given little coverage; our emphasis is on what has actually been done by practicing analysts.

Of course, this book will have its limitations. Part of this is unavoidable because the potential users of the book run the gamut from skilled analysts who are interested in technical solutions to forecasting problems, to administrators who seek a little exposure to the subject matter. Therefore, the book may seem too elementary to some and too esoteric to others.

Although the book may be of use as a supplemental text in certain courses in demography, planning, and geography, it lacks exercises; these must be supplied by the instructor.

Computational examples are held to what the writer feels are essentials for projection work. Detailed accounts of data smoothing and adjusting are not provided because they can prove to be lengthy and can distract the reader from problems specific to projection creation. References to works that treat such subjects are provided in the text.

Should this book prove successful enough to warrant more editions, the writer would welcome constructive criticisms from readers of the present edition. He would especially welcome examples of projection techniques that are new or that otherwise were not covered in the present work.

D.B.P.
Olympia, Washington
October, 1975

Acknowledgements

Material for this book was gathered by this writer over a period of several years while the project moved from a notion to a contractual commitment. A major reference source for local projections was the New York State Office of Planning Services Library, Pam Daniels, librarian. Many of the recent state projections were generously furnished by state officials in response to a request by this writer. Journal references and pre-1965 federal sources were located at the University of Washington Library in Seattle and the Washington State Library in Olympia.

Portions of the book were reviewed by Joan Gentili, Theresa Lowe, and Christopher Cluett, but any omissions or factual errors are the responsibility of the author. Credit for typing the manuscript goes to Carolyn Hunt who had to contend with deadline pressures.

General acknowledgements must go to some present and former associates. Foremost is John E. Smith of New York State, who got the writer into the forecasting business. Judith K. Van Voorhis programed the New York projection model and forced the writer to clarify his thinking on a number of occasions. This writer's leaders—Charles R. Guinn of New York State and John R. Walker of Washington State—shared their philosophies on projections and forecasts with the writer.

Geoffrey S. Gunn of Ballinger Publishing Company must be acknowledged for accepting the concept of this book and causing it to be published.

Finally, the writer's wife Jeanne deserves special mention because she was tolerant and supportive of the project even though she "lost" her husband for two or three hours an evening over a six month period while the book was being written.

Chapter One

Introduction

INTENT OF THE STUDY

This study is intended to serve as a reference and guide for persons who are charged with the task of making state and local population projections. Its primary target is the analyst who actually must create the projections. However, the study can be profitably read by such persons as project supervisors or planners who may not themselves create the projections, yet who have the need to know how the work can be done. The study also may be used as a text in demography, planning, and economics courses that touch on population forecasting.

From what has just been stated, it is apparent that this is not intended as light reading. Nor is it a highly esoteric work designed to appeal only to population projection experts. We are assuming that the reader has had one or two years of college, because that is about the basic level of training required for coping with the mathematical concepts that will be discussed. A master's degree should be the readership norm, however, for the bureaucratic reason that research analysts charged with doing such projects usually are of an organizational level which has the MA or MS degree as the entrance requirement. We also assume the typical reader has had little or no formal training in demography. Therefore, we have included a chapter on basic demographic rates and concepts that should serve as a sufficient introduction to demography for those who only wish to do projections.

SCOPE OF THE STUDY

The present writer has made no effort to produce an encyclopedic study of population projection. Instead, the present work is focused on the task of creating population projections for subnational areas—primarily states and counties, but also other areas with relatively fixed boundaries such as townships or even census tracts.

Professional demographers have tended to expend their efforts on national projections because the relatively small impact of migration at that level permits the simplification of the problem of age-sex group projection to a coherent body of theory and mathematics [1]. The presence of practically unrestricted geographic mobility between subareas of nations complicates matters greatly. This is partly because migration is itself difficult to predict and partly because the effect of migration is also latent in historical mortality and fertility data, making it difficult indeed to sort out the pure effect of each component of population change.

Even within the small area focus of this study there are a few omissions. For instance, highly technical parameter estimation procedures used in fitting certain mathematical functions are referenced, but not described in detail. We instead present more simple procedures that can be worked out using desk or pocket calculators which illustrate the results of the fitting procedures. We assume the interested analyst can go to the technical reference if he wishes to pursue the matter. Another area of omission is urban modeling, results of which may include population projections for segments of cities or metropolitan areas. Some projection procedures covered in this study may be used for metropolitan subareas, but the subject of urban modeling is not treated directly. Once again, the reader is directed to the specialized literature.

We shall deal with the techniques of population projection that have been used in the United States, with emphasis on the techniques used since 1960 for official state and county projections. Not every technique that has ever been used is included in the discussions, partly because some were judged not to be of general applicability and partly because some may have been overlooked when materials were gathered for the study. However, this writer is confident that virtually all significant techniques are included.

There is no one ideal method for projecting population. Each technique has strengths and weaknesses—inflexibility being a weakness common to nearly all methods. These strengths and weaknesses are noted in the discussions of the methods. In a very few instances, examples are presented that the writer regards as being almost entirely inappropriate techniques. These counterexamples should allow the reader to sharpen his judgment for the time when a projection method is to be selected.

Another feature of this study is the use of empirical population data in the computation examples. The 1964 monograph on projection techniques by Stanbery [2] used simplified, fictitious data. Such simple data serve to illustrate quantitative concepts more clearly than do empirical data. But empirical data, which are seldom very tidy, are what the projection analyst must work with. Therefore, the empirical examples used in the present study should also serve to sensitize the inexperienced analyst to what he may expect when he begins actual data manipulations.

CONCEPTS AND DEFINITIONS

Three terms must be defined at the outset of this study. These terms are *estimate*, *projection*, and *forecast*. The definitions that follow are those of the present writer, and other authorities may disagree on some of the points. However, this writer believes that the definitions are both logical and valid.

An *estimate* is an indirect measure of a condition that *exists* or *has existed*, and which, in principle, could be or could have been measured directly. Estimates are therefore made because direct measurement data are not yet available or because it is (or was) impractical to collect such data. For example, suppose one wants to know the population of a county at the present moment or perhaps at a given date in the past. If it is deemed too expensive to census the present population or if a census had not been taken as of the given past date, the only means of determining the number of persons is to infer it using the best available methods and symptomatic data. Another example would be an instance where a census had been taken, but it would be several months before the data could be completely tabulated; in the absence of the census data, an estimate might have to suffice. In most demographic work, estimation techniques differ from projection techniques because symptomatic data are used. If symptomatic data were not available, the estimate might have to be made using projection methods. In any event, the key distinction between estimates and forecasts is temporal.

A *projection* is the exact measurement of a *future* condition that would exist if the rules and assumptions embodied in the projection method proved to be empirically valid in the future. Projections may assume continuations of past conditions, present conditions, or trended changes in historical conditions. They also may assume entirely new transition rates. The point is, given the method and the assumptions, *a projection is always correct if the operations of the projection method are carried out without error.* The number of possible projections for any given population is therefore infinitely large.

A *forecast* is a projection that is also a *judgmental statement* concerning the expected measurement of future conditions; it is a *prediction*. In other words, *all forecasts are projections, but not all projections are forecasts.* Most demographers refer to their forecasts as projections, perhaps to protect themselves from being proved wrong. Keyfitz correctly notes that economists feel few qualms about calling their statements of future conditions forecasts and that meteorologists "are less certain that tomorrow will bring rain than demographers are that next year's population will be larger than this year's in the United States" [3]. The present study will tend to use the terms *forecast* and *projection* interchangeably and the reader should bear in mind that the distinction between the two is conceptual rather than operational.

Two subspecies of forecasts mentioned by Keyfitz that are worth passing along are "counterpredictions" and "normative predictions" [4]. The latter is a goal or target value such as population capacity of an area given certain zoning constraints. The former is a prediction of what cannot happen—for example, that the U.S. population will double in the next ten years. These forecasts will not be given further treatment in this study.

Other terms and concepts will be defined as they are encountered in the presentation of the subject matter.

PLAN OF THE STUDY

The reader does not have to read this study in the sequence in which it is presented. However, later chapters assume knowledge of what was covered previously and the earlier chapters present methods that are computationally more simple than techniques covered toward the end. It might be useful to skim the final chapter first, because it contains a practical overview of the forecast creation process. The chapter should be reread more carefully after the entire study has been read.

Chapter Two contains a summary treatment of demographic methods and measures that are of use to the projection analyst. Professional demographers may skip this chapter; all other readers are urged to at least skim it, and persons unfamiliar with demography should read it carefully.

Chapters Three and Four deal with methods for projecting population totals and thereby form a self-contained block of material. Chapter Three concerns direct projections of population size, whereas Chapter Four has to do with indirect projections.

Chapters Five through Nine treat the projection of populations disaggregated by age and .sex and, implicitly, any other age-sex–related status such as race or ethnicity. This block of chapters is also relatively self-contained. Chapter Five introduces the concept of age-sex–specific projections by components of demographic change. Chapters Six, Seven, and Eight respectively deal with techniques for projecting mortality, fertility, and migration. Chapter Nine indicates how the component projections may be combined into a cohort-component projection model.

As was mentioned above, Chapter Ten presents practical considerations for population forecasters.

NOTES TO CHAPTER ONE

1. United Nations, *Methods for Population Projections by Age and Sex,* Manuals on Methods of Estimating Population, Manual III, Population Studies, no. 25 (New York, 1956), chs. I and II.

2. Van Buren Stanbery, *Population Forecasting Methods*, revision prepared by Frank V. Hermann, U.S. Department of Transportation (Washington, D.C.: Government Printing Office, 1964).

3. Nathan Keyfitz, "On Future Population," *Journal of the American Statistical Association* 67, 338 (1972):353.

4. Ibid., p. 357.

Chapter Two

Summary of Basic Demographic
Measures and Concepts

INTRODUCTION

The purpose of this chapter is to summarize the demographic concepts and measures necessary for comprehension of the remainder of this study. The presentation will be concise, so the reader seeking more detailed discussions of these topics should refer to such standard works as Barclay [1] and Shryock and Siegel [2].

SIMPLE MEASURES OF POPULATION CHANGE

This section treats measures of population change that are called "crude" or "unrefined." Both terms are relative, but demographers tend to consider as "crude" any measure that does not include age detail.

Total Change

The most simple way of looking at population change is to compare population counts taken at two or more dates. If P_t is the total population of an area at one date—usually a census date— and P_{t+1} is the total population of the same area one unit of time later—at the next census, a one decade unit in the United States—then we may express change as

$$\Delta(P_{t,\,t+1}) = P_{t+1} - P_t \tag{2.1}$$

$$\%\Delta(P_{t,\,t+1}) = [(P_{t+1} - P_t)/P_t] \cdot 100 \tag{2.2}$$

$$R(P_{t,\,t+1}) = P_{t+1}/P_t \tag{2.3}$$

where $\Delta(P_{t, t+1})$ is numerical change in the population, $\%\Delta(P_{t, t+1})$ is the percent change, and $R(P_{t, t+1})$ is the change ratio. Using 1960–1970 data for King County, Washington (Seattle and its environs), we present the following numerical examples:

$$\Delta(P_{t, t+1}) = 1{,}159{,}375 - 935{,}014 = 224{,}361$$

$$\%\Delta(P_{t, t+1}) = (224{,}361/935{,}014) \cdot 100 = 24.0$$

$$R(P_{t, t+1}) = 1{,}159{,}375/935{,}014 = 1.23995 \quad .$$

Note that $\%\Delta(P_{t, t+1}) = [R(P_{t, t+1})] - 1.0 \quad .$

Crude Birth Rate

Population change can be expressed in terms of the fundamental components of demographic change—fertility, mortality, and migration. That is,

$$P_{t+1} = P_t + B_{t, t+1} - D_{t, t+1} + M_{t, t+1};$$

$$M_{t, t+1} = I_{t, t+1} - O_{t, t+1} \tag{2.4}$$

where $B_{t, t+1}$ is live births during the interval, $D_{t, t+1}$ is deaths, $M_{t, t+1}$ is net migration, $I_{t, t+1}$ is inmigration, and $O_{t, t+1}$ is outmigration. Often, only data on net migration are available and the in and out flows must be regarded as latent processes. Birth and death data are assumed to be recorded by place of residence in this and all other references in this study. The rate of change for the population as a whole can be decomposed into component rates of change, so long as the same denominator is used in calculating the rates. We will begin by discussing the crude birth rate *(CBR)*.

The *CBR* may be expressed

$$CBR = (B_t/P_t) \cdot k \tag{2.5}$$

where k is a constant that permits the rate to be expressed as births per k persons. Conventionally, k is set at 1,000. Birth rates are usually calculated for a period of one year, and the denominator population is the number of man-years lived by the population during the measurement period. Except where the population increases or decreases by more than about a third during the interval, an estimate of the population at the interval midpoint may be used [3]. Below is a numerical example using King County, Washington, data for the year 1964.

$$CBR = (18{,}305/1{,}030{,}367) \cdot 1{,}000 = 17.77$$

The 1964 population of King County was estimated by assuming that 1960–1970 population change was linear—i.e., that it changed by the same number of persons each year. Since July 1, 1964, is 17 out of a possible 40 quarters into the intercensal decade, the population as of that date is estimated as

$$17/40 \cdot \Delta(P_{t,\,t+1}) + P_t = 0.425 \cdot 224{,}361 + 935{,}014$$

$$= 95{,}353 + 935{,}014 = 1{,}030{,}367 \cdot$$

Other methods of interpolation such as geometric change may be used. See Shryock and Siegel [4] or Chapter Three of this book for details.

Crude Death Rate

The crude death rate *(CDR)* is analogous to the *CBR* and may be expressed

$$CDR = (D_t/P_t) \cdot k \ . \tag{2.6}$$

Again, we use 1964 King County data for the numerical example:

$$CDR = (9{,}149/1{,}030{,}367) \cdot 1{,}000 = 8.88 \ .$$

Rate of Natural Increase

The rate of natural increase *(RNI)* is the net growth of a population due to the difference between births and deaths. Net migration is ignored. The *RNI* can assume either positive or negative values, and may be written

$$RNI = [(B_t - D_t)/P_t] \cdot k \ . \tag{2.7}$$

Alternatively, it can be expressed *RNI* = *CBR* − *CDR*. Using the King County data, we obtain

$$RNI = (9{,}156/1{,}030{,}367) \cdot 1{,}000 = 8.89 \ .$$

Crude Net Migration Rate

As will be discussed below, migration cannot always be measured directly. Sometimes, it can be inferred from other data. For instance, equation (2.4) may be rearranged

$$M_{t,\,t+1} = P_{t+1} - P_t - B_{t,\,t+1} + D_{t,\,t+1} \cdot \tag{2.8}$$

Once net migration has been estimated, its crude rate may be calculated in a manner analogous to the *CBR*, the *CDR*, and the *RNI*. If the annual growth of King County is assumed to be equal to

$$(P_{t+1} - P_t)/10$$

and annual net migration is equal to

$$M_{t,\,t+1}/10,$$

then the 1964 crude net migration rate *(CNMR)* is estimated as

$$CNMR = [(M_{t,\,t+1}/10)/P_{1964}] \cdot k \ .$$

For King County,

$$CNMR = (11{,}970/1{,}030{,}367) \cdot 1{,}000 = 11.62 \ .$$

For projection purposes, this rate is usually not multiplied by k.

A NOTE ON AGE GROUPING

Census data and vital statistics data are often presented by age group. In some instances the group may be a single year of age. Otherwise, five year and ten year age groupings are common. We shall discuss the groupings used in the United States. Most other nations follow the same logic, but the reader is advised to confirm this before proceeding with an analysis.

Persons classified as being in a single year age group in census reports are persons who were that age at their last birthday. The census schedule asks for the respondent's date of birth, which is compared by a computer to the date of the census. A person born October 31, 1939, would have been 30 years old on April 1, 1970, the day of the census. A person born March 31, 1939, would have been 31 years old, and a person born April 1, 1939, would have been 30, since the census is taken as of midnight, March 31–April 1. Thus, a person reported as being age 30 in the 1970 census would have completed at least 30 years of life at the time of the census, but less than 31 years.

Multiple year age groups categorize persons in an analogous way. For instance, age group 30–34 includes persons who are more than 30 years old, but are less than 35 years old.

Vital statistics data are usually reported on a calendar year basis, and age is reported as of the individual's last birthday. Accordingly, there is a disparity between census and vital statistics data when rates are to be calculated. The usual solution to this problem is to assume that all of the events that occur over a calendar year are treated as if they occurred at the midpoint of the year. The population "at risk" to that event must be established for that same point. As an illustration, let us say that we want to know the birth rate for females in age group 25–29 in the year 1970. Vital statistics data provide the number of births during 1970 to women who were in the 25–29 age range at the exact time the birth took place. That is, if a woman who turned 30 on January 3, 1970, gave birth on January 2, the birth would have been recorded in the 25–29 group. The same would be true for a woman turning 25 on December 29, 1970, who gave birth two days later. The use of an estimated July 1, 1970, female population aged 25–29 as the rate denominator is an attempt to indicate an average number of females who were in the 25–29 age range during 1970. It is possible to refine the denominator value so as to more accurately capture the true "at risk" population, but such refinement is more properly the subject of a book on formal demography.

THE AGE STRUCTURE

A population's age structure—the number of persons or the proportion of the population in each age and sex group—is an important demographic reality. This is because values of crude demographic rates change when the age structure changes (see Chapter Five for examples). Therefore, it is useful to tie component change rates to comparatively small age groups in order to minimize the age structure distortion factor. "Refined" rates based on age groups will be presented in following sections of this chapter.

An important demographic fact is that the age structure at any given time reflects the history of each birth cohort that is part of the composition of that population. That is, the male population in a county aged 40–44 in 1970 represents male births in that county from April 1, 1925, to March 31, 1930, plus all inmigrants to the county and minus all decedents in the county and outmigrants from the county who were males born during that interval. It follows that future populations also must result from births and subsequent cumulative effects of mortality and migration. If age-specific rates of fertility and mortality were constant for a length of time longer than the longest human life span, and assuming that no migration occurred, a population would assume a fixed proportional age structure. This is what demographers call a "stable population," which is an important element in demographic theory and in national population estimates and projections in many parts of the world. A useful reference is Bourgeois–Pichat's United Nations manual on stable population theory [5].

The concept that a population's demographic history is mirrored in the character of its age structure is conveniently illustrated by the "population pyramid" which essentially is two sets of bar graphs laid back to back. Each set represents age groups for one sex. Examples of population pyramids are shown in Figure 2–1. These pyramids indicate the *share* of the total population held by each age group 0–4, 5–9, . . . , 70–74, 75+ for Washington State and five of its counties. An alternative presentation would have been to indicate the *number* of persons in each category; such a presentation would not have been practical in this case because the state population is more than a thousand times as large as that of the smallest county illustrated. By convention, the male population comprises the left-hand side of the pyramid and the female population is on the right.

The "Coke bottle" pattern assumed by the state is typical of the age structure found in most parts of the United States in 1970. The pinched waist of the structure represents the result of the low birth rates that prevailed during the 1930s. The lower bulge is the cohort born during the baby boom that lasted from the end of World War II until the early 1960s, and the contraction under the bulge is indicative of the decline in births during that decade.

The county pyramids were selected to illustrate some variations that can be found in localities. Garfield County is an agricultural county in the southeast corner of the state. Its age pattern reflects high birth rates and substantial net outmigration of young adults. Pierce County includes the city of Tacoma as well as large military populations in Fort Lewis and McChord Air Force Base. The presence of the military is reflected in the large proportions of young males. San Juan County encompasses a group of islands to the north of Puget Sound. The county is becoming a popular retirement area, as is indicated by the shares of the population over age 50. Snohomish County is a suburbanizing county to the north of Seattle. It attracts numerous migrants in their early thirties, and this migration largely offset the low depression births in the age pattern. Whitman

Figure 2–1. Population Pyramids: Washington State and Selected Counties, 1970

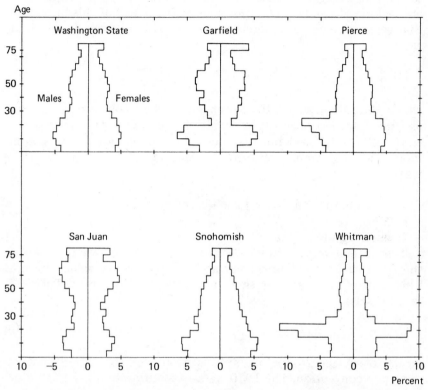

Source: U.S. Bureau of the Census, *Census of Population: 1970 General Population Charac-teristics*, Final Report PC(1)–B49, Washington (Washington, D.C.: Government Printing Office, 1971), Table 35.

County is wheat farming country south of Spokane. It also contains a land-grant university and the large proportions of college students in the county are clearly shown.

The projection analyst is advised to become familiar with the age structures of the populations he is to project.

REFINED FERTILITY MEASURES

Since changes in the age structure of a population can alter the values of crude demographic measures while instantaneous age-specific rates remain constant, it follows that the greater the refinement of age detail in demographic rates, the less will be the age structure distor-tion of those rates. We begin this discussion with simple refinements and then move on to more detailed fertility measures.

Child-Woman Ratio

This is an index of fertility that is used where a census has been taken, but where vital statistics data on births are of poor quality or are lacking altogether. One problem with the use of this measure is that censuses tend to undercount very young children. The formula is

$$C\text{-}WR = (_{0-4}P_t/_{15-44}{}^fP_t) \cdot k \tag{2.9}$$

where the subscripts on the lower left of the letters are age groups, and the f in the upper left designates females. Other age groups such as $15-49$ may be used, but the ones indicated here are the most common. The child-woman ratio for Nassau County, New York, in 1970 was

$$C\text{-}WR = (98,105/299,707) \cdot 1,000 = 327.3 \ .$$

General Fertility Rate

The general fertility rate *(GFR)* is used to refine the *CBR* where the age structure is known, but age-specific fertility values are not. This is often the case for small areas such as townships. The *GFR* may be written

$$GFR = (B_t/_{15-44}{}^fP_t) \cdot k \ . \tag{2.10}$$

Again, other age groups might have been used, but $15-44$ has become the convention. The 1970 Nassau County rate is

$$GFR = (17,336/300,227) \cdot 1,000 = 57.7 \ .$$

The July 1, 1970, population was estimated using a procedure that is simple, but not necessarily the best available. Each five year age group in the childbearing age range in 1970 was compared to the same age group in 1960 and the population difference was taken. These differences were extended ahead three months from the census by multiplying them by the ratio $41/40 = 1.025$. The ratio denominator is the 40 quarters in the 1960–1970 decade, and the numerator is the 41 quarters from April 1, 1960, to July 1, 1970. A numerical example using age group $25-29$ is $36,651 - 35,933 = 718 \times 1.025 = 736 + 35,933 = 36,669$. An alternative procedure would have been to trend birth cohorts—for example, age group $15-19$ in 1960 which becomes age group $25-29$ in 1970—three months beyond the census, but then an adjustment would have been needed because about one-twentieth of the cohort would be in age group 30–34 on July 1. Given the relatively short interval between April and July, there is little advantage in using a complicated method.

Age-Specific Fertility Rates

Age-specific fertility rates *(ASFRs)* may be calculated for any age group, although five year and one year groupings are most commonly used. The rate is

$$ASFR\ (a)\ =\ (_aB_t\ /\ _a{}^fP_t)\ \cdot\ k \tag{2.11}$$

where *a* is an age group for the female population and the maternal age group for the births. The 1970 *ASFR* for age group 25–29 in Nassau County is

$$ASFR\ (25-29)\ =\ (6{,}018/36{,}669)\ \cdot\ 1{,}000\ =\ 164.1\ \ .$$

Cumulative, Total, and Completed Fertility Rates

The sum of all *ASFRs* in the childbearing age range for a given year, adjusted for the width of the age range, is the total fertility rate *(TFR)*. The *TFR* is the number of births per *k* women that would be attained if a hypothetical cohort of women reproduced at the various *ASFR* levels over the ages of fertility. The formula can be expressed

$$TFR\ =\ W\ \cdot\ \left\{ \sum_{a=i}^{N}\ [(_aB_t\ /\ _a{}^fP_t)\ \cdot\ k]\right\} \tag{2.12}$$

where *a* stands for age, and the letter sigma (Σ) refers to a summation beginning with the value below the Σ and ending with the value above it. The letter *i* designates the initial age of fertility and the *N* denotes the final age; these ages are usually assumed to be 15 and 44 respectively. The sum is multiplied by *W*—in this case 5—to expand single year values into five year rates, making the results consistent with the span of the age group. The Nassau County *TFR* for 1970 may be calculated:

Age	*Births*	*Females*	*ASFR*		
15–19	1,268	73,739	17.2		
20–24	5,294	47,334	111.8		
25–29	6,021	36,669	164.2		
30–34	2,996	37,310	80.3		*ASFR*
35–39	1,351	45,680	29.6		409.9
40–44	406	59,495	6.8		× 5
			409.9	*TFR* =	2,049.5

Births to females less than 15 years old and 45 years old and older were added to the nearest age group listed above.

The cumulative fertility rate *(CFR)* is a partial *TFR*, being the sums of *ASFR*s from the initial age of fertility to any given age less than the final age of fertility, adjusted for age group width. It may be written

$$CFR = W \cdot \left\{ \sum_{a=i}^{n} [({_a}B_t / {^f}P_t) \cdot k] \right\} \qquad (2.13)$$

where $n < N$. The 1970 Nassau County *CFR*s are

Age	ASFR	Cum.	× 5 = CFR
15–19	17.2	17.2	86.0
20–24	111.8	129.0	645.0
25–29	164.2	293.2	1,466.0
30–34	80.3	373.5	1,867.5
35–39	29.6	403.1	2,015.5

The completed cohort fertility rate *(CCFR)* is analogous to the *TFR*, except that the rate is built up from data for a single birth cohort of women over their childbearing years rather than using data taken from a number of birth cohorts at one year to form a "synthetic cohort." The difficulty with the *CCFR* is that it cannot be calculated until a cohort's childbearing is completed, and therefore it tells us nothing directly about future fertility. Cumulative fertility rates may also be calculated for birth cohorts; their use is explained in the chapter on projecting fertility rates.

Gross and Net Reproduction Rates

The gross reproduction rate *(GRR)* and the net reproduction rate *(NRR)* are measures of the degree to which women reproduce the next generation of women. The *GRR* can be written

$$GRR = W \cdot \left\{ \sum_{a=i}^{N} [({_a}{^f}B_t / {_a}{^f}P_t) \cdot k] \right\} \ . \qquad (2.14)$$

It is identical to the *TFR* except that only female births are used. The *NRR* may be expressed

$$NRR = W \cdot \sum_{a=i}^{N} \left\{ [({_a}{^f}B_t / {_a}{^f}P_t) \cdot k] \, {_a}{^f}S_t \right\} \qquad (2.15)$$

where ${_a}S$ is the ratio of survivors in age group a to the number born.

The value of S may be obtained from a suitable life table (see the next section). The NRR refines the GRR by taking into account the mortality of potential mothers. The Nassau County GRR and NRR for 1970 are calculated as follows, with 1970 U.S. white female life table data supplying the survivorship ratio:

Age	Female Births	Females	Female ASFR	$_aS$	Female ASFR·S
15–19	603	73,739	8.78	0.97759	8.58
20–24	2,563	47,334	54.15	0.97454	52.77
25–29	2,870	36,669	78.27	0.97119	76.02
30–34	1,452	37,310	38.92	0.96713	37.64
35–39	659	45,680	14.43	0.96128	13.87
40–44	190	59,495	3.19	0.95228	3.04
			197.74		191.92
			× 5		× 5
			$GRR = 988.7$		$NRR = 959.6$

Other Refinements

It is possible to examine fertility of married women by computing an age-specific marital fertility rate. This rate is analogous to the *ASFR* except that legitimate births appear in the numerator and married women comprise the denominator.

Birth rates may also be calculated by birth order and by parity status. Parity is the number of live births a woman has given; each woman may be assigned a parity, including parity zero. Birth rates by parity would be the ratio of women of parity n who progress to parity $n + 1$ in a given year. Birth order refers to the sequential value assigned to each of a woman's children in terms of their date of birth. The ratio of third births in a given year to the number of women of childbearing age would be a birth order fertility rate. These and similar refinements will be considered in the chapter on fertility projection.

REFINED MORTALITY MEASURES

Most mortality measures that make use of age, sex, and racial detail are summarized by the various elements of the life table. For this reason, most of this section will deal with life tables.

Age-Specific Death Rates

Death data can be refined by classification by age, sex, and race through age-specific death rates *(ASDR)*. These rates are analogous to the *ASFR*, above, and may be written

$$ASDR = (\,_aD_t/\,_aP_t) \cdot k \tag{2.16}$$

where D is deaths. The data necessary to calculate $ASDRs$ may also be used to construct life tables, which provide a more comprehensive picture of mortality.

The Life Table

Life tables are actuarial or demographic decrement tables that are usually constructed for "synthetic cohorts"—a cross-section of persons in all ages at a given time. They make use of death data classified by age, sex, and, sometimes, race. Population counts by the same categories are used as denominators for calculation of the basic life table death rates, which differ slightly from the $ASDR$ just described in that deaths are related to persons alive at the start of a period of time. Given a set of death rates for all age groups, the remainder of the life table may be readily constructed. Introductions to life table construction may be found in Barclay and in Shryock and Siegel [6].

Life tables are standardized to the mortality experience of a hypothetical birth cohort whose initial size—or radix—is usually taken to be 100,000 persons. The death rates are applied so as to diminish the size of the cohort as it ages. During the calculation process, other information can be derived and included in the table. This can best be illustrated by reference to an actual life table, so segments of the 1959–1961 United States life tables for white females are presented in Table 2–1. Examination of the table indicates that the following relationships obtain:

$$l_{x+t} = \,_tq_x \cdot l_x \tag{2.17}$$

$$_td_x = l_x - l_{x+t} = l_x - (\,_tq_x \cdot l_x) \tag{2.18}$$

$$L_x = (l_x + l_{x+t})/2 \quad , \; t + 1, \text{usually;} \tag{2.19}$$

$$T_x = \sum_{x}^{\omega} L_x \quad , \text{where } \omega = \text{final age;} \tag{2.20}$$

$$^o e_x = T_x / l_x \quad , \text{approximately.} \tag{2.21}$$

Note that the basic life table data treat populations as of a birthday—i.e., exact age four, exact age five, and so forth. Census data deal with populations in an age range and these populations are often

Table 2–1. Portions of the 1959–1961 United States Life Table For White Females

Age Interval	Proportion Dying	Of 100,000 Born Alive		Stationary Population		Average Remaining Lifetime
Period of Life Between Two Ages	*Proportion of Persons Alive at Beginning of Age Interval Dying During Interval*	*Number Living at Beginning of Age Interval*	*Number Dying During Age Interval*	*In the Age Interval*	*In This and All Subsequent Age Intervals*	*Average Number of Years of Life Remaining at Beginning of Age Interval*
x to $x+t$	$_t q_x$	l_x	$_t d_x$	$_t L_x$	T_x	$°e_x$
0–1	0.01964	100,000	1,964	98,319	7,419,159	74.19
1–2	0.00135	98,036	132	97,970	7,320,840	74.68
2–3	0.00081	97,904	80	97,864	7,222,870	73.78
3–4	0.00063	97,824	62	97,793	7,125,006	72.83
4–5	0.00055	97,762	53	97,735	7,027,213	71.81
5–6	0.00047	97,709	46	97,686	6,929,478	70.92
6–7	0.00041	97,663	41	97,643	6,831,792	69.95
7–8	0.00037	97,622	36	97,604	6,734,149	68.98
8–9	0.00033	97,586	32	97,570	6,636,545	68.01
9–10	0.00030	97,554	29	97,540	6,538,975	67.03
105–106	0.47662	16	7	12	25	1.53
106–107	0.49378	9	5	7	13	1.46
107–108	0.51095	4	2	3	6	1.40
108–109	0.52810	2	1	2	3	1.35
109–110	0.54519	1	1	0	1	1.29

Source: U.S. National Center for Health Statistics, *United States Life Tables: 1959–61*, vol. 1, no. 1, (Washington, 1964), Table 6.

treated as being concentrated at the midpoint of the age range. Hence, the L_x values are equivalent to census age population values and a life table survival rate to be used with census data would be of the form

$$_tS_x = {}_tL_{x+t}/{}_tL_x = {}_{a,\,a+n}S_t \tag{2.22}$$

the term on the right being in the notation used in previous sections. Death rates would be

$$ASDR = (l_x - l_{x+t})/{}_tL_x \quad . \tag{2.23}$$

We shall occasionally make use of life table data in this study.

Census Survival Rates

Another means of measuring mortality is to compare the population in a cohort at one census with the same cohort population enumerated in a later census. Symbolically,

$$_{a,\,a+n}S_{t,\,t+n} = ({}_{a+n}P_{t+n})/({}_aP_t) \tag{2.24}$$

is the ratio of survivors at a later census to those alive at an earlier census. Since censuses tend to miscount persons to different degrees for different age groups, the survival rate in (2.24) is likely to be different from that of (2.22), even if the latter is from a cohort life table. Census survival can only be used to approximate mortality for a population that is relatively closed to migration—typically, this would be the native-born population of a nation. The main use of measures of census survival is in the calculation of rates of net migration.

AGE-SPECIFIC NET MIGRATION RATES

There are problems related to the measurement of migration that were absent when birth and death rates were calculated. In the first place, migration seldom can be measured completely. Second, there is lack of agreement as to the choice of denominator values for rate computations. Finally, even the net number of migrants may fluctuate depending on the estimation technique used. The aim of the discussion that follows is to present information about net migration that will be of use to the population projection analyst. Constraints imposed by the above-mentioned problems will be treated in light of the constraints inherent to projection techniques.

Definition of Migrant

The U.S. Bureau of the Census defines two categories of persons who change their usual place of residence. *Movers* are all persons changing residence and *migrants* are those whose residential change involves the crossing of a county boundary. The population projection analyst may choose to regard anyone who moves into or out of the area being projected as a migrant, even if that area is a subarea of a county.

A time element is also involved. Except in certain countries that maintain continuous population registers, migration is measured in terms of persons who either were not in an area on one date but were in the area on a second date, or those who were in the area on the first date and not in the area on the second date. These dates typically are five or ten years apart, which implies that many moves are missed. For example, this writer was enumerated as living in Seattle, Washington, on April 1, 1960. On April 1, 1965, he also lived in Seattle. Between those dates, he was in military service in California, New York State, Pennsylvania, Maryland, and Korea. On April 1, 1970, he was enumerated in Seattle again. But in the interim, he lived nearly three years in Philadelphia while attending graduate school. In none of the usual measures based on U.S. census data would this writer have been classified as a "migrant."

Data from the Social Security Continuous Work History Sample and the Census Bureau's Current Population Survey do provide information for intervals smaller than five years but these data seldom have been used as the basis for population projections for reasons discussed below.

Direct Migration Measures

There are three ways of directly measuring migration. One way is through continuous population registers. These exist in only a few countries, so we shall ignore them in this discussion other than to note that they provide the best possible source of migration data.

A second means of measuring migration is from public records that are not registers yet which do provide some migration information. Data collected for U.S. Social Security purposes include a individual's employer and, often, place of employment. Employment changes are reported in these records and migration between job market areas may be inferred for the work force covered by social security. Unfortunately, place of work is not recorded uniformly, which creates some biases. (An example would be a man living in Chicago who quits a job to go to work in the Chicago branch of a company headquartered in New York. The company is not required to report the place of work of the employee, and if it does not make such a report the man would be reported as working at the corporate headquarters. This means that he would be recorded as a Chicago to New York migrant when he in fact never left Chicago.) Also, the fact that not all workers are covered by social security should caution the analyst not to hastily generalize these results to all American migrants.

Another source of migration data from administrative records in the United States is Internal Revenue Service income tax returns. Tax forms contain information on location of family residence and these records have been compared over time for purposes of population estimation. Again, these records are incomplete in their coverage and are otherwise subject to response biases such as failure to indicate county of usual residence.

Finally, migration data may be obtained by directly questioning individuals. The Census Bureau asks persons where they lived on April 1 five years prior to the current census and this answer is compared to their census date residence. Analogous queries are made in the Current Population Survey. The main problem with this kind of data, aside from missing intervening moves and return moves, is that memory is fallible and the reported data are not necessarily accurate. However, this is still a very useful source of migration data for the projection analyst because the five year interval is the same as is used for most cohort-component projections and because directional flow data by age, sex, and other characteristics may be obtained.

Indirect Migration Measures
Indirect measures of migration only get at net numbers of migrants—not directional flows. This is because these measures operate on a residual basis: Beginning populations are compared to final populations on a cohort basis with natural change taken into account and any differences are imputed to net migration. See equations (2.5) and (2.8) and the discussion in the accompanying text for the general logic; for cohorts older than ten years at the end of the measurement period references to fertility can be ignored.

Vital Statistics Method.   Where vital statistics data are complete and available it is possible to build up cumulative natural change data over the measurement period to arrive at an expected population to which the enumerated population can be compared and net migration estimated. This task can be laborious if age and sex detail are used, and the results are not free from bias. For instance, numbers of births and deaths are "contaminated" by migration in that net migration, depending on its direction, either adds or subtracts births and deaths from what would have occurred in the absence of migration. In other words, net inmigration brings in extra people, some of whom will die and be included in the death count and some of whom will give birth, adding to the birth tally. Also, this method's results can be distorted by age-related census enumeration error. Very young persons are usually undercounted more than other children. This means that differences in accuracy of age-specific enumeration of a cohort over two censuses will result in a gain in the reported number of teenagers which is due to the better count but which would be attributed to positive net migration.

The vital statistics method is almost always used to estimate net migration for the total population or race and sex group totals rather than by age. Sometimes these total net values are used as a control for the sum of age-specific net values obtained by other methods. In any event, the migration contamination factor would still be present, although the census enumeration error effect would be lessened because of the aggregation of the age data.

Life Table Survival Rate Method. Net migration between censuses can also be estimated by surviving the initial population and intercensal births to provide the expected population for comparison to the population enumerated at the second census. Symbolically,

$$_{a,\,a+10}M_{t,\,t+10} = {}_{a+10}P_{t+10} - ({}_{a}P_{t} \cdot {}_{a,\,a+10}S_{t,\,t+10}) \tag{2.25}$$

where the subscript a refers to an age group, including births during the first and second halves of the intercensal decade, and S is a survival rate. In the present case, survival rates are obtained from life tables as was shown in equation (2.22). The subscripts differ, and $_{t}S_{x}$ in the life table notation is equivalent to $_{a,\,a+10}S_{t,\,t+10}$ in the present notation, where $_{a,\,a+10}$ and $_{t,\,t+10}$ represent change over one decade.

Selection of suitable life tables is one difficulty inherent to this method. It usually takes about two years from the date of a census before all the necessary death data are available for state and regional life table construction. This means a quick postcensal reading on migration is not possible if the analyst wishes to interpolate between accurate life table values based on census population data. Alternative techniques include the use without modification of the life table based on the earlier census or the use of current national life table data adjusted to historical local age-specific variations from national mortality.

Another problem with the life table method is the census enumeration biases mentioned in the previous section. The raw survival rates implicitly assume no census bias and resulting net migration values would have to include the census error effects with actual migration effects. Rough corrections for census error may tend to reduce this bias, although it should immediately be emphasized that little is known about the magnitude of census errors for specific localities.

The main theoretical advantage of the life table method is that local survival rates can be applied to the local population and that the distortion effect on mortality from net migration during the decade does not appear.

Census Survival Rate Method.   The census survival rate method of net migration estimation operates in the exact manner expressed in equation (2.25). The only difference is the survival rate used; the present application uses the survival rate from equation (2.24).

Census survival rates are useful because they include the effect of enumeration error as well as the effect of mortality. One shaky assumption underlying the method is that mortality and census error have little local variation from the nationwide factors that form the survival rate values.

A variation on this method is called the reverse census survival technique, and the relevant equations are:

$$_{a+10,\,a}S_{t+10,\,t} = {}_aP_t \,/\, _{a+10}P_{t+10} = 1 \,/\, _{a,\,a+10}S_{t,\,t+10} \qquad (2.26)$$

$$_{a+10,\,a}M_{t+10,\,t} = \left(_{a+10}P_{t+10} \cdot {}_{a+10,\,a}S_{t+10,\,t} \right) - {}_aP_t \cdot \qquad (2.26)$$

The reverse method takes the population at the second census, creates the expected numbers of persons alive at the first census, and then compares the expected with the actual population at the first census to arrive at the net migration estimate. The relationship between the migration values derived from the two methods is

$$_{a+10,\,a}M_{t+10,\,t} = \left(_{a,\,a+10}M_{t,\,t+10} \right) / \left(_{a,\,a+10}S_{t,\,t+10} \right) \cdot \qquad (2.27)$$

This implies that, since the survival rate in the expression is usually less than unity, the reverse method tends to generate more migrants than does the basic or "forward" method. The difference has to do with the implicit treatment of mortality, and the interested reader may refer to Lee et al. [7] for a detailed explanation. Siegel and Hamilton [8] also discuss both methods and present an intermediate method. An example of the forward method appears in Chapter Eight of the present study.

Both the census survival and the life table survival method results may be forced to vital statistics-derived control totals, as was done by Bowles and Tarver [9].

Rate Denominators

Once the net numbers of migrants have been calculated, they must be turned into rates. The choice of a denominator population requires some thought on the part of the analyst. Hamilton [10] suggests five mathematical-logical and four practical considerations in the selection process. The mathematical-logical considerations are: "a logical relationship between the numerator and the denominator, compatibility with natural increase rate formulas, stability for use in statistical analysis, a procedure for handling the time factor, and adaptation to the kind of migration data available." Practical considerations are: "conventional usage, popular understanding, simplicity, and ease of computation." His conclusion is that the midpoint population is the best compromise.

The present writer tends to favor the survived population as the most useful denominator for population projection analytical purposes. The reason is that the data from the census question regarding previous residence relate only to survivors who respond to the query. These data form the basis for the study of directional flows and they also are largely compatible with the standard five year projection interval. Ten year net migration values derived from the forward census survival method and from the life table survival method also refer to a survived migratory population. The logical consistency of these data series more than outweighs the factor of compatibility with fertility and mortality rates, at least where age-specific projection data are concerned. Midpoint data would be the logical choice if age and sex detail were lacking and if net migration rates were to be annualized.

Conversion from Ten Year to Five Year Rates

Age-specific net migration rates obtained from indirect measures typically report the experience of five year age groups over ten year periods. Age-specific population projections usually deal with five year periods for five year age groups. If, for example, the ten year period rates were directly used in standard population projection models, there would be a distortion of the age-specific net migration patterns from the empirical local experience, particularly for those age groups between 15 and 35 that represent modal points in the pattern (see Chapter Eight for examples of net migration patterns).

It is virtually impossible to obtain exact five year net migration rates from ten year data. However, five year rates may be approximated if it is assumed that migration levels have been fairly consistent over the entire decade being measured. The formula for estimating a five year net migration rate, N, is

$$_{a,\,a+5}N = 1 - \sqrt{(_{a,\,a+10}R)(_{a-5,\,a+5}R)} \qquad (2.28)$$

or

$$_{a,\,a+5}N = 1 - \sqrt{_{(a-5)+a,\,(a+5)+(a+10)}R} \qquad (2.29)$$

where the net migration ratio

$$_{a,\,a+n}R = _{a+n}P_{t+n}/(_aP_t \cdot _{a,\,a+n}S_{t,\,t+n}) \qquad (2.30)$$

and a is a five year age group.

The logic behind this technique is that all surviving members of a five year age group at one point in time must pass over a transition point to the next five year age category during a five year interval. That is, a cohort starting in group $25-29$ and finishing in group $30-34$ must pass the age 30 transition point, which represents the mean age of the cohort during the interval. For a ten year interval, we need the experience of the group that had the same midpoint age during that interval. In this case, it would be the age group that was $20-29$ at the start of the period and $30-39$ at the end of the period. Its five year net migration rate would be a value that, when compounded, would yield the ten year rate. This is why square roots are taken. Formula (2.28) indicates the computation procedure where the ten year net migration ratios of two five year age groups are combined, and equation (2.29) is the procedure where ten year net migration ratios for ten year age groups are available. A technique yielding similar results may be found in Tarver and Black [11].

NOTES TO CHAPTER TWO

1. George W. Barclay, *Techniques of Population Analysis* (New York: John Wiley & Sons, 1958).

2. Henry S. Shryock, Jacob S. Siegel, and Associates, *The Methods and Materials of Demography*, U.S. Bureau of the Census (Washington, D.C.: Government Printing Office, 1971).

3. C. Horace Hamilton, "Practical and Mathematical Considerations in the Formulation and Selection of Migration Rates," *Demography* 2 (1965):429–43.

4. Shryock and Siegel, pp. 378–9.

5. United Nations, *The Concept of a Stable Population: Application to the Study of Populations of Countries with Incomplete Demographic Statistics,* Population Studies, no. 39 (New York, 1968).

6. Barclay, ch. 4: Shryock and Siegel, ch. 15.

7. Everett S. Lee et al., *Population Redistribution and Economic Growth in the United States,* vol. I, *Methodological Considerations and Reference Tables* (Philadelphia: The American Philosophical Society, 1957).

8. Jacob S. Siegel and Horace Hamilton, "Some Considerations in the Use of the Residual Method of Estimating Net Migration," *Journal of the American Statistical Association* 28 (1952):475–500.

9. Gladys K. Bowles and James D. Tarver, *Net Migration of the Population, 1950–60 by Age, Sex, and Color,* Economic Research Service, U.S. Department of Agriculture (Washington, D.C.: Government Printing Office, 1965).

10. Hamilton, p. 442.

11. James D. Tarver and Therel R. Black, *Making County Population Projections—A Detailed Explanation of a Three-Component Method, Illustrated by Reference to Utah Counties,* Bulletin (Technical) 459 (Logan, Utah: Utah Agricultural Experiment Station in cooperation with Oklahoma State University Research Foundation, 1966), pp. 64–70.

Chapter Three

Projecting Total Populations— Extrapolation Techniques

INTRODUCTION

The earliest population forecasts dealt only with the total number of inhabitants of an area. Such characteristics as age and sex were usually ignored, although some forecasts did take racial categories into consideration (see Whelpton [1] on Bonynge's 1852 forecasts). This situation persisted throughout the nineteenth century and, with few exceptions, until the second quarter of the present century when the cohort-component methodology became accepted as being analytically superior.

Even today, populations are projected without reference to such demographic niceties as rates of fertility, mortality, and migration or consideration of the population's age and sex structure. There are several reasons for this situation. Often the user of the projection is only interested in "the bottom line"—total population—and doesn't really care about all the other details. If the user is in a hurry, and if the analyst charged with preparing the forecast is relatively ignorant of projection techniques or lacks access to a computer program for making a cohort-component projection, a "quick and dirty" technique is used to produce the requested number. A lack of data on age and sex of a population also necessitates the use of projection techniques that deal only with population totals. Sometimes totals are used as a simplifying device when population size is a relatively minor outcome of a very complex model designed to yield other data of interest. Examples would be econometric and transportation models. An econometric model might need population data only as a denominator for the calculation of per capita income. A transportation model may deal with population insofar as users of proposed highway networks need be identified. This is not to say that all econometric or transportation models treat population in such a simplified fashion; some do and some don't.

Another use for projections of population totals by simplified means is to provide an outside check on projections arrived at by more complex means. This is not always a good policy. Most of the techniques we will discuss in this chapter make some assumptions about the dynamics of population change that are, in most cases, inferior to the more explicit assumptions required by the sophisticated methods. Often the implicit assumptions of the simple techniques are at variance with the reality the technique is attempting to model. The truth of this assertion will become clear as the reader acquires a knowledge of population projection techniques during the course of reading the remainder of this study.

The present chapter deals with the projection of total populations by various means of extrapolation—the extension into the future of past and present tendencies. Each population is treated alone—without context to other populations. This viewpoint will be changed in Chapter Four, when we deal with the projection of total populations in terms of their share of a larger total population—i.e., a state's share of the national population.

JUDGMENTAL EXTRAPOLATION OF TRENDS

The quickest and simplest means of forecasting the total population of an area is to graph the historical population size data and then extend that line to represent the future. Such graphing should not be done in ignorance of what the graphs imply, however. As we shall see in this section, the very form of the graph coordinates chosen to represent population change have certain implications about the nature of that change.

Examples of Historical Population Data

Figures 3–1 and 3–2 represent the populations of selected states and counties in the United States. The data are presented on a Cartesian, or rectangular, coordinate system where two categories of data are represented at right angles to one another, one horizontally, one vertically. The scale used in these figures is arithmetic, which means that units of equal numerical distance are placed equally distant on the chart. That is, the distance on the graph between the values ten and 11, say, is identical to the distance between values 11 and 12 or between 20 and 21. This rule applies only within each category scale.

Figure 3–1. Population of Selected States, 1790–1970:
Arithmetic Scale

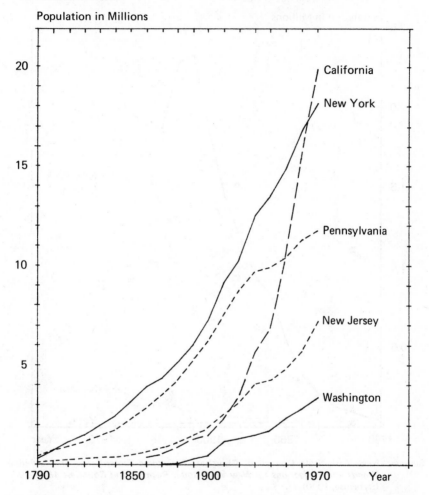

Population in Millions

Source: U.S. Bureau of the Census, *Census of Population: 1970 Number of Inhabitants,*
Final Report PC(1)–A1, United States Summary (Washington, D.C.: Government
Printing Office, 1971), Table 8.

The vertical and horizontal scales need not agree in the spacing of
values. Selection of scale values depends on the nature of the category being represented and the range of values assumed by the data.
Take Figure 3–1 for example. The horizontal scale represents time
by decades beginning with the year 1790, the date of the first U.S.
decennial census. The vertical scale represents size of total population in millions of persons. Note that the population size scale begins

Figure 3–2.   Population of Selected New York State Counties,
1790–1970: Arithmetic Scale

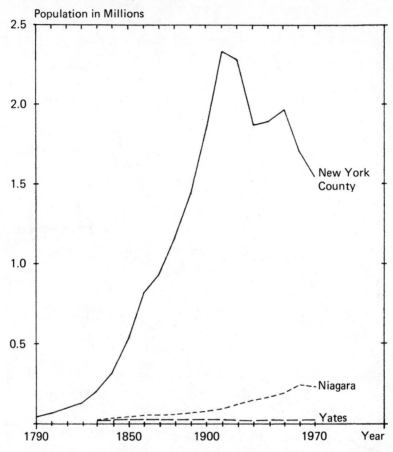

Sources: New York State Council of Churches, *A Graphic Presentation of Population Trends and Projections for New York State, Regions, and Counties: 1870–2000* (Syracuse, 1970).

U.S. Bureau of the Census, *Ninth Census of the United States: 1870,* vol. I, *The Statistics of the Population of the United States* (Washington, D.C.: Government Printing Office, 1872), Table II.

at zero population whereas the time scale does not begin at the year zero. The reason for this inconsistency is that we are dealing with many more persons than years and that to equate the two categories would result in a chart that would be unreadable.

Even though it is necessary to make somewhat arbitrary adjustments to the scales to make the charts readable, the selection of the scales may introduce psychological overtones to what one would like to think of as being cold, objective facts. Imagine that the time scale in Figure 3-1 was reduced by a half while the population scale remained unchanged. All the lines representing population would appear to rocket upwards. Now imagine that the time scale was tripled while the population scale again remained fixed. The population growth would now appear to be a rather slow process. Care should be taken to insure that the appearance of graphed data is as neutral as possible.

A convention in the graphic display of data is that the horizontal scale represents the independent, or "causal," variable and that the vertical scale measures the dependent variable. Our graphs indicate size of population to be dependent on time. In a narrow sense, this is not true. Population size may be *associated* with time, but in truth it is *caused* by a number of other factors which themselves are time-related. On the other hand, it would be absurd to take the position that time is caused by, or even associated with, population size. Hence, the convention of association of population size with changes in time—time being a simple index value summarizing a host of historical and other behavioral events.

Returning to Figures 3-1 and 3-2, we may observe the growth patterns of actual populations. Figure 3-1 presents data for selected states going back, in some cases, to the first United States census in 1790. The populations of the states of New York and Pennsylvania exhibited steady growth from 1790 until the 1930–1940 decade. There were some slight fluctuations from the general pattern, particularly for New York State—although Pennsylvania's growth appears to slacken somewhat during the period 1910–1930. New Jersey also had a steady growth pattern prior to 1930. It differed from its larger neighbors in that its numerical growth was slight until the 1840s. The states of Washington and California, which were not settled by Americans until the middle of the nineteenth century, present patterns that are more erratic than those of the three eastern states. This is especially true for Washington State. There was a spurt of growth in the 1880s, the decade when statehood was attained. Growth was less dramatic in the nineties, but then shot up between 1900 and 1910, partly as a result of the Alaskan gold rush. Then growth became moderate until the 1940s.

The growth for all five of the states we are examining fell off during the decade 1930–1940. This was largely because the nation as a whole experienced little growth. The great economic depression, in combination with restrictive immigration laws passed in the 1920s, reduced the flow of foreign migrants into the United States. At the same time, birth rates fell to levels that set historical records for the nation that were not broken until the 1970s.

Since 1940, the United States has experienced a run of prosperity punctuated only by relatively brief recessionary periods. Migration from abroad has been steady, although the composition of migrants by place of origin was altered by changes in the immigration laws in the 1960s. Between 1940 and 1970 the nation grew from 132 million to 203 million persons. Most of this growth was due to the famous "baby boom," which gathered momentum during World War II, surged to a peak in the latter half of the 1950s, and then declined throughout the sixties.

All five of the example states had more growth in the decades after the 1930s than they did during the thirties. However, many of the predepression patterns seem to have been broken. Washington and California appeared to grow more strongly than before, whereas New York and, especially, Pennsylvania had less growth. Only New Jersey reverted to its old pattern.

The data in Figure 3-2 are for selected counties in New York State and they illustrate some additional population growth patterns. New York County (Manhattan Borough of New York City) had spectacular population gains from 1790 until 1910. Except for a brief recovery between 1930 and 1950, the population has been declining since 1910. The decline from 1910 to 1930 coincides with the construction of New York City's comprehensive rapid transit system in the outer boroughs of Kings (Brooklyn), The Bronx, and Queens. The post-1950 loss is due to more complex events that include the flight of the white middle class to the suburbs and the relative decline of New York City as a corporate center. Niagara County is located just north of Buffalo and is most famous for containing the American side of Niagara Falls. With the exception of slow periods during the Civil War and the depression, the county experienced steady growth until the 1960-1970 decade when losses were reported. These losses coincide with the opening of the St. Lawrence Seaway and the slowdown in economic and population growth throughout the westernmost part of New York State. Yates County, southeast of Rochester and centered among the most westward of the Finger Lakes, has always been rural in character. Its population was relatively stationary between 1830 and 1900, with the greatest number being recorded in 1880. The population dropped to a stable, low stance between 1920 and 1940. Population gains have been reported since 1940, but some of this growth was due to the presence of a college. (Beginning with the 1950 census, college students have been reported as living at the place they attend classes if they lived in dormatories or apartments, and not in their parental household. This definitional change resulted in considerable "population growth" between 1940 and 1950 for counties, cities, and towns that contained colleges and universities. These areas also tended to report healthy population gains between 1960 and 1970 as a result of the higher education boom of that decade with its unprecedented growth in college unrollment.)

The findings from the data in Figures 3–1 and 3–2 may be summarized as follows: Not all populations grow. If they do grow, that growth is not necessarily steady. Likewise, declining populations need not decline steadily. Some populations neither grow much nor decline much; they may remain stationary for considerable periods of time. All of this suggests that population forecasting could be a tricky business.

Mathematics and Graphs—Alternative Data Perceptions

The graphed population data discussed in the previous section represents only one means of attempting to perceive reality. The graph is really a representation of certain mathematical statements. Alternative mathematical perspectives or statements may require different graphs.

Figure 3–3 represents an arithmetic, rectangular coordinate system such as was used in Figures 3–1 and 3–2. Each population reported for a given area is represented as a point located on the surface of the chart by two coordinates. One coordinate is located on the horizontal axis which, as was mentioned above, conventionally denotes the independent or causal variable. The horizontal axis is often referred to as the x axis and the data reading of the variable denoted by the x axis is called the *abscissa*. The vertical axis represents the dependent variable and it is usually called the y axis. A particular data observation for a variable associated with the y axis is called the *ordinate*. The coordinate number pair (x, y) denotes the location of a data point on the surface of the graph. In our example, we present a ficticious population with data for the census dates 1900 to 1960, inclusive. In addition to the numerical values for years and population sizes, letter designations for these values are indicated for four observations. The years 1910, 1920, 1930, and 1940 are respectively represented by letters a, b, c, and d. Respective populations for those years are noted as A, B, C, and D.

It follows that the locations of the various populations on the graph surface would be *(a, A)*, *(b, B)*, and so forth. We shall assume that $(b-a) = (c-b) = (d-c) = 10$ years for the purposes of our discus-

Figure 3–3.   Hypothetical Example of Population Growth: Arithmetic Scale

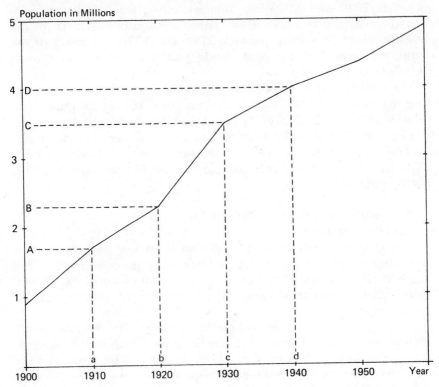

Source: Text

sion, even though this is not true. (All decennial censuses from 1930 to the present were taken as of April 1 of the census year. However, the 1920 census was taken as of January 1 and the 1910 census was taken as of April 15. All censuses inclusive of 1830 and 1900 had a June 1 date, and the four earliest censuses had dates varying between August 2 and 7). In the Figure 3–3 example, it happens that $(B-A) = (D-C) = 500,000$ persons. This is because of the property of the arithmetic scale that equal intervals represent equal amounts of the variable being measured. Even though the *numerical* growth was the same for the two decades, it is obvious that the *proportional* growth relative to the starting population was greater for the earlier decade than it was for the later decade. That is, $(B/A) > (D/C)$. Thus, if we are interested in the *relative* change in population size over time and wish to examine such information graphically, the arithmetically scaled grid system will not work. What is required is a scale system whereby equal proportional changes are equally spaced. Such a system exists, and it is called the *logarithmic scale.*

The logarithm of a number, N, is the exponent, n, of any given number, z, required to raise z to the value of N. The number z is called the *base* of the logarithm, and the function is called the logarithm to the base value, which may be abbreviated $\log_z$. Thus, $N = x^n$ and $n = \log_z N$. Although in principle any number may be used as the base for a system of logarithms, only two numbers are widely used for that purpose in practice. The numbers are the integer 10 and the irrational number e. The number e represents the limiting, instantaneous rate of compound or organic growth. That is, if we take the expression $(1 + 1/m)^m$ and let the value of m increase without limit, the result of the expression will approach, but never quite attain, the value represented by e. In practice, therefore, an approximation to the true value of e must be used. That approximation carried out to eight places after the decimal is 2.71828183.

In this study we shall make occasional use of the number e. However, most population projections are made for discrete time intervals, so the value of e is of less theoretical or practical interest than it might be in, say, stable population theory (for example, see Keyfitz [2] or Pollard [3]). For our present purposes, we shall deal with the conceptually and computationally simpler system of logarithms to the base 10. This system of logarithms is referred to as *common logarithms* and the common logarithm of a number is noted as log N or log x or log 56 or log whatever the number under consideration is. Logarithms to the base e are called *natural logarithms*, and are noted as ln N, ln x, ln 56, and so forth.

Logarithms to base 10 are computationally and conceptually simple due to the values of the number 10 when it is raised to integral powers. For example, $10^0 = 1$; $10^1 = 10$; $10^2 = 100$; $10^3 = 1,000$; $10^4 = 10,000$; log 10 = 1; log 100 = 2; log 1,000 = 3; and log 10,000 = 4. Each integral exponent of 10 is called an "order of magnitude"; each is also termed the *characteristic* of the logarithm. All decimal values of the exponent are called the *mantissa* of the logarithm. In the examples used above, the mantissa values are zero. To illustrate what happens when the exponent of 10 is not integral, consider the following examples: log 2 = 0.30103; log 3 = 0.47712; log 4 = 0.60206; log 20 = 1.30103; log 30 = 1.47712; log 40 = 1.60206; log 200 = 2.30103; log 300 = 2.47712; log 400 = 2.60206. Note that as size of the example numbers is increased by a factor of 10, the characteristic—or order of magnitude—increases by one, and that the mantissa does not change. Note also that equal numerical differences between the logarithms are equivalent to equal proportional differences in the original number, which was the result we were seeking. That is, 20 is ten times greater than 2, and 1.30103 minus 0.30103 is 1.0; 200 is ten times greater than 20 and 2.30103 minus 1.30103 is also 1.0.

These relationships are inherent in the *laws of logarithms* which may be expressed:

I. $\log_z (xy) = \log_z x + \log_z y$

II. $\log_z (x/y) = \log_z x - \log_z y$

III. $\log_z (x^n) = n \log_z x$

In words, the logarithm of the product of two numbers is equal to the sum of the logarithms of those numbers; the logarithm of the ratio of two numbers is equal to the logarithm of the numerator minus the logarithm of the denominator; and the logarithm of the value of a number raised to a power is equal to the power multiplied by the logarithm of the number. The practical result is that the mathematical operations of multiplication and division can be performed by the simpler processes of addition and subtraction once the transformation to logarithms has been made. Powers and roots are readily obtained by respectively multiplying and dividing logarithms of numbers—another computational simplification.

Let us return to the fact that equal proportional differences between numbers means equal numerical differences between the logarithms of those numbers. This means that it is possible to graph data so that equal spaces represent equal proportions. Thus, we might choose to graph population change using an ordinary arithmetic scale on the horizontal axis to represent time and with population represented on the vertical scale by logarithms. To make such a diagram more readable, the vertical scale need not be expressed in logarithms; instead, the scale values could be indicated by *antilogarithms*—the transformation of the logarithms into the "ordinary" numbering scheme. The grid system being described is called "semilogarithmic" because only one axis is scaled logarithmically, and graph paper for this system is readily available.

The state data in Figure 3–1 and the county data in Figure 3–2 that were graphed arithmetically are presented in semilogarithmic form in Figures 3–4 and 3–5. Note how the shapes of the curves have been changed by the transformation of the vertical scale. Some curves that appeared to sweep upwards in the arithmetic scheme become sluggish in the semilogarithmic system.

Figure 3–4. Population of Selected States, 1790–1970: Semilogarithmic Scale

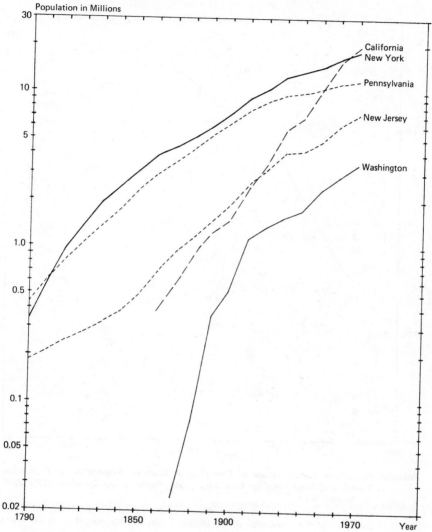

Source: U.S. Bureau of the Census, *Census of Population: 1970 Number of Inhabitants,* Final Report PC(1)–A1, United States Summary (Washington, D.C.: Government Printing Office, 1971), Table 8.

A useful property of semilogarithmic graph paper is that the slope of the line indicates the rate of growth. Steep slopes represent more rapid growth (or decline) than slopes that are more nearly horizontal. Equal slopes indicate equal growth rates; for example, the lines indi-

Figure 3–5. Population of Selected New York State Counties, 1790–1970: Semilogarithmic Scale

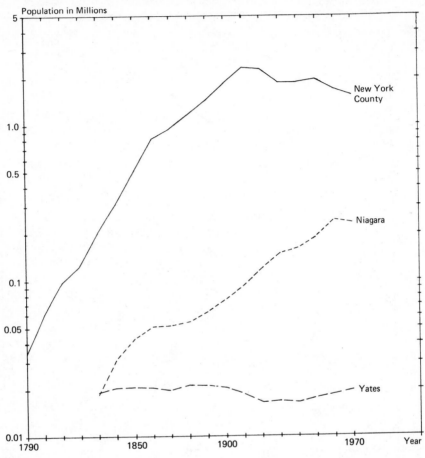

Sources: New York State Council of Churches, *A Graphic Presentation of Population Trends and Projections for New York State, Regions, and Counties: 1870–2000* (Syracuse, 1970).

U.S. Bureau of the Census, *Ninth Census of the United States: 1870,* vol. I, *The Statistics of the Population of the United States* (Washington, D.C.: Government Printing Office, 1872), Table II.

cate similar rates of growth for New Jersey and Washington for the period 1950–1970. This condition is obvious even though the population of New Jersey was more than twice that of Washington. The similarity in growth rates is not obvious from the arithmetic graphs in Figure 3–1.

If a population's rate of growth or decline persists over a period of time, then the graph of that population's size on semilogarithmic paper should maintain a constant slope over that duration. This may be observed in Figure 3—4 for New York County between 1820 and 1860 and, to a lesser extent, for the period 1870—1910. Although the line wavers somewhat, the long term growth rate for California from 1860 to 1970 appears to be basically constant.

The data in Figure 3—4 indicate that New York State and Pennsylvania have tended to increase at a decreasing rate because the slopes become increasingly horizontal as time passes. New Jersey, on the other hand, had a fairly constant growth rate from 1790 to 1840 followed by an increase from 1840 to 1860 and then a slight slackening from 1860 to 1930, where the above-mentioned effects of the depression were felt. Washington State's growth rates tend to fall into two patterns—very rapid from 1870 to 1910 and moderate from 1910 to 1970.

An Example of Judgmental Trending

If populations are plotted on graph paper as illustrated in this section, the analyst has gained some insights into the growth behavior of the populations being studied. He may then choose to project or forecast future population values making use of these insights either to judgmentally extend the lines in a freehand manner or to judgmentally posit future behavior of slopes or points in quantifiable terms. The former method is too subjective to illustrate here; the reader is invited to draw his own graphs and make judgmental sketches of future growth curves. The second procedure may be illustrated by the work of Bonynge and Gannett.

According to Whelpton [4], Bonynge used a "modified rate" method based on United States population data available in 1852, when his projections were made. He first assumed that the white population would continue its 35 percent per decade growth rate until 1860. Then it would fall to 30 percent for the 1860—1870 decade and stabilize at 25 percent per decade thereafter. Decade growth rates were 23 percent for black slaves and 15 percent for freed blacks. Bonynge's forecasts proved to be quite accurate for about half a century. Error for the total population did not exceed 2 percent until 1900 and 5 percent until 1910. However, the error was 14 percent in 1920 and increased thereafter. His forecast for 1980 was 452 million, which is double the current U.S. Census Bureau projection for that year. Turning to the component forecasts, we find that Bonynge's white number was only 3 percent off in 1910, while the black forecast was 7 percent high in 1890 and diverged even more in later years.

Henry Gannett [5] used a longer data series for his United States population forecasts, but the method was essentially the same. He observed that the national growth rate dropped from around 35 percent per decade between 1790 and 1810 to 21 percent for the decade 1890–1900. He then noted that the growth rates for densely populated Western European nations was about 10 percent per decade. Gannett then made the judgment that the U.S. population growth rate would fall to about that level by 1950–1960, maintain that rate for about 50 years (in two of these decades the rate was assumed to be 11 percent) and then fall off again, reaching 5 percent by the final decades of the twenty-first century. Gannett's accuracy was not as good as Bonynge's, but was still quite respectable. Between 1910 and 1950, his forecasts were never more than 3.5 percent off, and his 1950 figure of 150 million was the most accurate of all. His forecasts became increasingly low in later years—his 1980 forecast of 202 million was about the size of the population enumerated in 1970. On the other hand, his projection of 375 million for the year 2050 is not unreasonable should this country approach zero growth rates.

Let us now try judgmental trending of growth rates on a local population. Our example is Manhattan—or New York County. We observe that the decade growth rate was on the order of 60 percent for the 40 year period 1820–1860 and was around 25 percent for the 40 year period 1870–1910. Let us assume that we have no knowledge of the actual population of Manhattan after the year 1910 and that we are to make a forecast. Basing our judgment on historical growth, it is not difficult to reason as follows: Disregarding the decade 1860–1870, there are two 40 year periods of consistent growth. The growth rates during the second period were about 40 percent of that of the first period. If 40 years seems to be the length of a growth period, then growth rates should fall after 1910, and our best guess is that the new rate will be 40 percent of the old rate, or 10 percent per decade. We assume that the 10 percent rate will continue for 40 years, until 1950. Then we will assume a new cycle will start and that the growth rate will drop to 40 percent of the previous cycle's rate—that is, to 4 percent.

Projections using these judgmentally determined growth rates are presented in Table 3–1. They are wildly wrong. As it turned out, Manhattan's peak population to date was reached in 1910. But our forecast was for increasing population size, and it turns out that the forecast is more than 100 percent high by 1960.

So how could Bonynge and Gannett be so accurate and the present writer be so inaccurate using the same method? An easy answer is that this writer used bad judgment, but that isn't the whole

Table 3–1. Projections of New York County Using Judgmental Growth Trending Method, 1910–1990

	Projection	Actual	Difference	Percent Difference
1910 (Actual)	2,331,542	2,331,542	0	0
1920	2,564,696	2,284,103	280,593	12.3
1930	2,821,166	1,867,312	953,854	51.1
1940	3,103,283	1,889,924	1,213,359	64.2
1950	3,413,611	1,960,101	1,453,510	74.2
1960	3,550,155	1,698,281	1,851,874	109.0
1970	3,692,161	1,539,233	2,152,928	139.9
1980	3,839,847	—	—	—
1990	3,993,441	—	—	—

Assumptions: 1910–1950 decade growth ratio is 1.10
1950–1990 decade growth ratio is 1.04

Sources: Text and U.S. Bureau of the Census, *Census of Population: 1970, Number of Inhabitants*, Final Report PC(1)–A1, United States Summary (Washington, D.C.: Government Printing Office, 1971), Table 8.

story. Actually, Bonynge and Gannett had an easier job because they were dealing with a comparatively large nation which has a certain amount of "inertia" to its population growth. In addition, most nations are more likely to grow in a steady manner than are their component areas: the reason is that subareas do not have political restrictions on migration, so migration becomes an important element of population change. In the case of the U.S.A., national growth was slowed somewhat when foreign migration was restricted, but the impact was relatively small compared to the effect of net outmigration to the outer boroughs from Manhattan. This writer failed because he looked only at the past to divine the future. His judgment" extended only to the selection of the past trends to be continued into the future. A true judgmental forecast would include attempts to specify the extent to which outside events such as the extension of the subway and elevated system might affect the prospects for growth of the local area.

Advantages and Disadvantages
We will first mention some disadvantages to judgmental trending of historical population data to create forecasts. Perhaps the greatest danger, as we hinted in the previous section, is that judgment may be based on incomplete information. Underlying processes may be ignored or misunderstood. Undue emphasis may be placed on the wrong data. It is possible that an unclear picture of the situation will result in vague assumptions. Or perhaps the data might be good, but the analyst uses faulty reasoning. All of these possibilities and more

can be lumped into the category "bad judgment," whether we are referring to forecasting populations, betting on a horserace, or choosing a spouse.

On the other hand, there is such a thing a "good judgment," where the intellect examines all the information that appears relevant and then accepts or discards assumptions on the basis of that information. The advantage of judgment in specifying assumptions about the future is that the analyst is not locked into one model of population change that might be grossly simple or even inaccurate. Indeed, the various mathematical models outlined in the next section of this chapter rely on very simple descriptions to predict future population size. The use of such models of growth greatly constricts the realm of judgment in ways that, as we shall see, may result in faulty forecasts.

MATHEMATICAL TRENDING

We have seen that historical population data for political units such as states and counties can be plotted on graphs. It was also indicated that these points may be interpreted mathematically. This is because geometry and algebra are alternative ways of describing the same reality. In this section of the chapter we shall treat the more common mathematical formulas that have been used to describe historical population growth and to extrapolate that past growth into the future. All of these formulas presuppose that the historical behavior of the population in question exhibited some degree of regularity. That is, plotted data should not be scattered about so that a connective line would be a zigzag from very high to very low values from one point in time to the next. Fortunately, most plots of population size over time form fairly regular curves.

Arithmetic Change

Occasionally, a population will grow by the same number of persons each decade for several decades. (Of course, it may also decline in size. For the purposes of our discussion, the concept "growth" should be thought of as being either positive or negative in character. We will also use the word "change" in the context of increases or decreases in a population count.) Earlier in this chapter we noted that conditions of equal numerical change over equal time periods would plot linearly on a grid coordinate system that was scaled arithmetically. Let us examine this proposition more closely.

Consider Figure 3–6. There is an arithmetically scaled grid coordinate system with independent variable x on the horizontal axis and dependent variable y on the vertical axis. Assume that x represents

Figure 3–6. Graphic Explanation of Linear Growth Equation

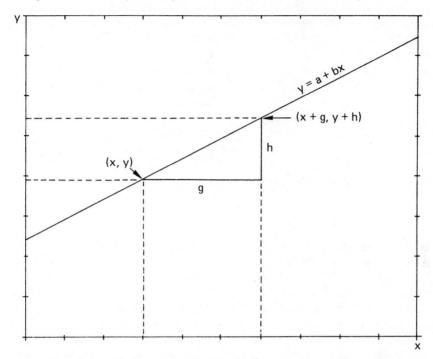

time and that y denotes population. Let g be a given time interval—the exact amount does not matter. Let h be a given change in population—the exact amount does not matter here either. Two points are plotted on the graph. One point has the coordinates (x, y). The other point represents the same population after g amount of time has passed. During the period $x + g$, the population grew by the amount h, so population is thus $y + h$, and the coordinates of the second point are $(x+g, y+h)$. These points and distances are all indicated in the graph.

Now, the important thing to consider is the relationship between change in x and change in y. This relationship may be expressed $b = h/g$, and we shall call the ratio b the *slope* of the linear curve in the diagram. Once the value of b is established, the amount of change in y for *any* change in x can be determined by multiplying that change in x by b.

One more detail is needed in order to describe the growth behavior of a population that changes arithmetically. That detail is an anchoring point for the growth relationship in terms of the actual population. We shall call the anchoring point the *origin*, which is the value assumed by y when the value of x is zero. We denote the origin by the letter a. In practical terms, this means that some point in time is arbitrarily set at zero and that all other points in time are provided values relative to their distance from the zero point. This operation is called a *transform*. For example, the year 1830 may be chosen as the zero point. The year 1840 would then be transformed as follows: $1840 - 1830 = 10$; $0 + 10 = 10$. The year 1900 would be $1900 - 1830 = 70$; $0 + 70 = 70$. The year 1790 would be $1790 - 1830 = -40$; $0 + (-40) = -40$. And so forth.

Given the reference value or origin a and the value of the slope b, it is possible to obtain any value of y if one knows the year, x, and if the growth of the population is arithmetic. To obtain the value of y, the following formula is used:

$$y = a + bx \tag{3.1}$$

It should be explained that a and b are what are called *parameters*. That is, they are values that remain fixed for any given application of the equation, but may vary from application to application. The numbers denoted by x and y, on the other hand, vary within applications as well as between applications of the formula, and therefore are called *variables*. In other words, we expect time and population size to vary in all of our work. But for a given population under study, we must fix parameter values. If we study another population, the values of the parameters must be altered to suit that population.

The values assumed by a and b may be estimated from empirical population data using the *least squares method*. The least squares method is a procedure that permits the analyst to select the parameter values which result in a line that passes among the actual (x, y) points in such a way that the sum of the squared deviations (or distances) of the points from that line is less than it would be if any other line were drawn and the difference calculation repeated. More specifically, the line represents the value of y for each indicated value of x, given the constraints imposed by the value of parameters a and b. The line is therefore an expectation of y for each given x, and the actual value of y for that value of x may be the same as the expected y or, as is likely to be the case, it will differ. The differences indicate "error"—or "lack of fit"—for the line. The overall error must be minimized, and the criterion used is that the sum of the squared differences of actual y values from calculated y values must be the smallest obtained from all possible combinations of the parameter values. It follows that there is only one line that fulfills this criterion. The reason for using squared deviations is that some deviations are positive and some are negative, and adding positive and negative numbers will result in cancellation, which hides the extent of the deviations. Squaring the deviations eliminates negative values and allows the examination of absolute deviations.

The parameters may be estimated by solving the following set of simultaneous equations:

$$\Sigma(y) = Na + b\Sigma(x) \tag{3.2}$$

$$\Sigma(xy) = a\Sigma(x) + b\Sigma(x^2) \tag{3.3}$$

where N is the number of data observations for either variable. The reader interested in the derivation of these equations should consult a statistical text such as Arkin and Colton [6]. Unfortunately, we are unable to illustrate the solving of these equations using arithmetic data because we could find no examples of populations that had experienced constant numerical growth for several decades. Such population growth behavior evidently is very rare, so the reader need not worry about having to use this model of growth extensively as a projection tool. However, the equations used in this growth model are used when the population data are transformed in a certain way. This will be discussed in the next section. Also, the notions of least squares, slopes, intercepts, and parameters are basic to many of the discussions in the remainder of this chapter.

In this writer's opinion, the only time when continuation of arithmetic population change is even remotely justified as a means of population projection is when data are so scarce that the analyst knows nothing but the population size at two points in time. In this case, he may choose to subtract the earlier value from the later value to obtain the numerical change and then add the amount of change (be it a positive or negative quantity) to the later population count. But given even this degree of ignorance about the history of the population, there is still a preferable estimation technique. That technique is to assume that growth will be *proportionally* the same in the next period of time as it was in the last period. The reason for this preference is that populations, in the absence of shifts in rates in the basic demographic processes, tend to approach a fixed, or intrinsic, *rate* of growth.

Geometric—or Exponential—Change
Since it is mathematically true that populations tend to grow at a fixed rate if the basic demographic change rates are left unperturbed for many decades, we cannot ignore models of growth that incorporate this property.

The continuous time model is the *exponential* model of growth, and it may be written:

$$y = ae^{rt} \; ; \; t = x_n - x_0 \tag{3.4}$$

or, alternatively:

$$y = a \cdot exp \, (rt) \tag{3.5}$$

where *"exp"* means "exponent of *e*" and the numbers in the parentheses denote the value of the exponent: *t* is time, and *r* is the rate of growth. The number *a*, as in equation (3.1), represents the value of *y* at the point where *x* equals zero.

It is sometimes more convenient to use the *geometric* model of growth when the data series is arranged in equal time intervals, as is the case for most U.S. census data. The conceptual difference between the exponential and geometric models of growth is that the former is, as we stated above, in continuous time, and the later is for discrete intervals of time. The geometric growth model may be expressed:

$$y = ar^t \; ; \; t = x_n - x_0 \quad . \tag{3.6}$$

It should be noted that even though the numerical values of *y*, *t*, and *a* might be the same for both models, the value of *r* will differ because one model measures growth rates "instantaneously" whereas the other measures rates of growth between points in time that are equally spaced.

Equation (3.6) may be rewritten in the following manner if the variables are transformed into common logarithms:

$$\log y = \log a + t (\log r) \quad . \tag{3.7}$$

Observe that the form of equation (3.7) is identical to the linear model expressed in equation (3.1). This means that we now can make use of the least squares method of parameter estimation using the simultaneous equations (3.2) and (3.3) outlined in the previous section.

We shall use Pennsylvania population data for our example. Observe in Figure 3-4 that the plot representing the population of Pennsylvania is roughly linear between the years 1860 and 1910 on a semilogarithmic scale. We will fit the line to these values under the assumption that the most recent available population data for Pennsylvania are for the year 1910 and that it is our task to project that population forward to the year 1970. The slope of the line in Figure 3–4 tells us that growth rates tended to be higher before 1860 than they were after that date. This means that the use of a constant growth rate model forces us to ignore the complete record of the history of the size of the population. In other words, we are *judgmentally* treating the data. We are in effect postulating that future growth of Pennsylvania will be like the past 50 years' growth, and that it will not be like the growth of the entire 120 year period for which we have data. This kind of hypothesizing makes a good deal of sense in the absence of any other information. The implicit reasoning is that events shape population growth and that the events shaping growth in the near future are likely to be more similar to events that shaped the growth of the recent past than they are to events that influenced growth in the distant past. This line of thought is common in many forecasting enterprises and will be encountered elsewhere in this study.

The calculation procedure is laid out in Exhibit 3–1. Six data points is a rather small number for curve fitting by the least squares method, but the infrequency of censuses often forces the population analyst to make do with fewer data observations than are recommended. Even so, the fitted population values for the years 1860 to 1910, inclusive, do not differ from the census data by more than 1 percent.

Unfortunately, everything goes wrong from the standpoint of accuracy when population values before 1860 and after 1910 are concerned (See Table 3–2). We already knew that the pre-1860 numbers would be off because the growth during that period was observed to differ from that of 1860–1910, and it was ignored on purpose. The post-1910 data are a different story. These are the projected values and they diverge from the census data year after year until, at some point in the 1960–1970 decade, the projected population was double the true population.

Why were the projections so high? Because conditions changed. For one reason or another, the basic demographic rates of fertility, mortality, and migration happened to balance each other so that the overall rate of population change was fairly regular for five decades. It is quite likely that this balance shifted somewhat among these basic components from decade to decade, but the end result was the same. But after 1910, certain things happened to change this balance. One was World War I, which had the effect of reducing immigration to the United States, including Pennsylvania. By the 1920s foreign migration was restricted by law. Meanwhile, birth rates were falling faster than death rates, so rates of natural increase dropped. Given

☆ ☆

Exhibit 3–1

Projection of Geometric Growth

The population of Pennsylvania is to be projected under the assumption of geometric growth using data from the 1860 census through the 1910 census. The computation equation is the logarithmic version of (3.6) which has been written:

$$\log y = \log a + t (\log r) \tag{3.7}$$

The basic data may be arranged:

Year	t	$\log y$	$t(\log y)$	t^2
1860	-2	6.463328	-12.926656	4
1870	-1	6.546783	$- 6.546783$	1
1880	0	6.631737	0	0
1890	1	6.720830	6.720830	1
1900	2	6.799486	13.598972	4
1910	3	6.884518	20.653554	9
Sum:	3	40.046682	21.499917	19

and entered into equations

$$\text{(I)} \quad \Sigma(y) = aN + r\Sigma(t)$$
$$\text{(II)} \quad \Sigma(t \cdot \log y) = a\Sigma(t) + r\Sigma(t^2)$$

so that

$$\text{(I)} \quad 40.046682 = a(6) + r(3)$$
$$\text{(II)} \quad 21.499917 = a(3) + r(19).$$

We then solve as follows:

(A): 3/6 = 0.5
$(III) = (I) \cdot (A)$: 20.023341 = $a(3) + r(1.5)$
$(II) - (III)$: 1.476676 = $r(17.5)$
$r = 1.476676/17.5 = 0.084381$
$(II)'$: 21.499917 = $a(3) + (0.084381)(19) = a(3) + 1.603239$
$a = (21.499917 - 1.603239)/3 = 6.632226$

where a is understood to represent the common logarithm of a and r the logarithm of r. The estimated values of a and r are entered into equation (3.7), and the results of solutions to the equation are summarized below.

Year	t	t(log r)	log y	y
1790	−9	−0.759429	5.872797	746,100
1800	−8	−0.675048	5.957178	906,104
1810	−7	−0.590667	6.041559	1,100,421
1820	−6	−0.506286	6.125940	1,336,411
1830	−5	−0.421905	6.210321	1,623,009
1840	−4	−0.337524	6.294702	1,971,070
1850	−3	−0.253143	6.379083	2,393,773
1860	−2	−0.168762	6.463464	2,907,127
1870	−1	−0.084381	6.547845	3,530,571
1880	0	0	6.632226	4,287,716
1890	1	0.084381	6.716607	5,207,233
1900	2	0.168762	6.800988	6,232,944
1910	3	0.253143	6.885369	7,680,138
1920	4	0.337524	6.969750	9,327,172
1930	5	0.421905	7.054131	11,327,420
1940	6	0.506286	7.138512	13,756,628
1950	7	0.590667	7.222893	16,706,789
1960	8	0.675048	7.307274	20,289,624
1970	9	0.759429	7.391655	24,640,811

☆ ☆

the decline in rates of foreign immigration and of natural increase, a constant rate of population growth could only be maintained by increasing rates of domestic net inmigration which, in turn, requires a booming economy. The fact is that Pennsylvania's economy did not boom. The reasons behind the failure to boom are for economists to explain.

A more fundamental reason why the projections were wrong lies in the model itself. The model is exceedingly simple. It merely says that population growth over a decade is proportional to the size of the population at the beginning of the decade. Nothing more, nothing less. In no way are underlying causal forces identified or measured. That historical population data could be fitted at all by the model implies nothing more than that model could accurately summarize the net effect of many forces acting in the real world for a period of several decades. To examine the model tells the analyst nothing about what actually molded the population growth; an empirical regularity is described, but no insights are provided.

The use of the exponential or geometric model of growth in the absence of any other data is really an admission of ignorance on the part of the analyst. He can describe past growth by the model, although he can't explain that growth. He can assume that future

Table 3–2.   Enumerated, Fitted, and Projected Pennsylvania Population Values, 1790–1970 (populations in thousands)

Year	Census	Geometric	2° Polynomial	3° Polynomial	Gompertz	Logistic	Modified Exponential
1790	434	746	516	444	471	449	
1800	602	906	586	592	628	596	
1810	810	1,100	746	791	827	788	
1820	1,049	1,336	995	1,049	1,079	1,037	
1830	1,348	1,623	1,334	1,375	1,391	1,357	
1840	1,724	1,971	1,763	1,778	1,776	1,760	
1850	2,312	2,394	2,282	2,266	2,246	2,263	
1860	2,906	2,907	2,890	2,849	2,813	2,873	
1870	3,522	3,531	3,589	3,534	3,493	3,598	
1880	4,283	4,288	4,378	4,331	4,227	4,429	
1890	5,258	5,207	5,255	5,248	5,245	5,351	
1900	6,302	6,324	6,223	6,294	6,350	6,333	6,210
1910	7,665	7,680	7,280	7,478	7,630	7,337	7,757
1920	8,720	9,327	8,428	8,809	9,100	8,320	8,814
1930	9,631	11,327	9,665	10,294	10,778	9,243	9,537
1940	9,900	13,757	10,992	11,943	12,679	10,076	10,030
1950	10,498	16,707	12,409	13,765	14,818	10,802	10,368
1960	11,319	20,290	13,916	15,768	17,211	11,415	10,598
1970	11,794	24,641	15,512	17,961	19,870	11,919	10,756

Note: Data below lines represent projections.

Sources: Text and U.S. Bureau of the Census, *Census of Population: 1970 Number of Inhabitants*, Final Report PC(1)–A1, United States Summary (Washington, D.C.: Government Printing Office, 1971), Table 8.

growth will be the same as it was in the past that he can't explain. It is not good to be placed in such a position, but sometimes total population data are the only data available and the analyst has no choice but to work in ignorance.

Fitting Polynomial Curves

One disadvantage of the geometric growth model is that it is limited in its possibilities for application. The data graphed on a semilogarithmic scale in Figures 3—5 and 3—5 are seldom linear for two decades, let alone five or more. As a consequence, the analyst must look to a model that can describe more complicated curves. One very common such model is the polynomial, which may be expressed:

$$y = a + bx + cx^2 + dx^3 + \ldots + mx^n ,\qquad (3.8)$$

The highest exponent in a given polynomial equation is the *degree* of the polynomial. The linear model (3.1), for example, happens to be a first degree polynomial. A second degree polynomial would describe a curve rather than a straight line when plotted arithmetically. Higher degree polynomials describe more complicated curves, particularly when the signs of the coefficients (or constants, or parameters) are minus as well as plus. Each sign change indicates a bend in the curve. Obviously, fairly complicated curves can be approximated by such a model.

The main drawback of polynomials as projection models is similar to that of the geometric growth model—namely, the model is atheoretical. No matter how well past growth can be fitted to a polynomial curve, there is no guarantee that an extension of the curve will even closely approximate future growth. A polynomial does virtually nothing to explain the past meaningfully, so it consequently cannot say anything meaningful about the future. The use of polynomial curves to project future population is an admission of ignorance caused by lack of demographically detailed data. Polynomials should be used as a last resort.

Once again we shall use Pennsylvania as our example, and once again we shall assume that our knowledge of historical population data is truncated a given point in the past; in the present case that point is the year 1900. Two polynomials will be calculated—a second degree polynomial and a third degree polynomial. The computation procedures for polynomials of higher degree are basically the same, although they can be rather tedious work if a computer is not handy.

The first polynomial example is a second degree polynomial which may be written:

$$y = a + bx + cx^2 \qquad\qquad (3.9)$$

Three simultaneous equations are required for least squares parameter estimation and they can be expressed:

$$\Sigma(y) = Na + b\Sigma(x) + c\Sigma(x^2) \qquad\qquad (3.10)$$

$$\Sigma(xy) = a\Sigma(x) + b\Sigma(x^2) + c\Sigma(x^3) \qquad\qquad (3.11)$$

$$\Sigma(x^2 y) = a\Sigma(x^2) + b\Sigma(x^3) + c\Sigma(x^4) \qquad\qquad (3.12)$$

Computation details are presented in Exhibit 3–2. Note that data for the year 1790 are indexed at $x = 0$. Actually, this is not necessarily the best placement of the origin, because relatively large values of x, when raised to higher powers, become numbers that are cumbersome to handle. The origin, where $x = 0$, could have been placed in the middle of the data array to make computation easier. Another computational aid is the expression of population in ratios to one million. This trick serves to cut down the size of numbers to be manipulated; without it, the products of certain population values and values of x raised to the fourth power would have exceeded the display capacities of many desk or pocket calculators. Of course, these data manipulation convenience considerations do not loom large if computers are used.

The third degree polynomial equation is as follows:

$$y = a + bx + cx^2 + dx^3 \qquad\qquad (3.13)$$

The least squares estimation procedure requires the solution of the following four simultaneous equations:

$$\Sigma(y) = Na + b\Sigma(x) + c\Sigma(x^2) + d\Sigma(x^3) \qquad\qquad (3.14)$$

$$\Sigma(xy) = a\Sigma(x) + b\Sigma(x^2) + c\Sigma(x^3) + d\Sigma(x^4) \qquad\qquad (3.15)$$

$$\Sigma(x^2 y) = a\Sigma(x^2) + b\Sigma(x^3) + c\Sigma(x^4) + d\Sigma(x^5) \qquad\qquad (3.16)$$

$$\Sigma(x^3 y) = a\Sigma(x^3) + b\Sigma(x^4) + c\Sigma(x^5) + d\Sigma(x^6) \qquad\qquad (3.17)$$

For higher degree polynomials the format of the equations is continued.

All of the estimated parameter values in each polynomial fitted

☆ ☆

Exhibit 3–2

Projection Using Second Degree Polynomial

Pennsylvania population data from the 1790 census through the 1900 census are used to fit a second degree polynomial for projection purposes. The data are entered in equations

$$\text{I. } \Sigma(y) = Na + b\Sigma(x) + c\Sigma(x^2)$$
$$\text{II. } \Sigma(xy) = a\Sigma(x) + b\Sigma(x^2) + c\Sigma(x^3)$$
$$\text{III. } \Sigma(x^2 y) = a\Sigma(x^2) + b\Sigma(x^3) + c\Sigma(x^4)$$

which are respectively equations (3.10), (3.11), and (3.12) in the text. The data for the equations are calculated as follows:

Year	x	$y = population$ (millions)	xy	x^2	$x^2 y$	x^3	x^4
1790	0	0.434374	0	0	0	0	0
1800	1	0.602365	0.602365	1	0.602365	1	1
1810	2	0.810019	1.620038	4	3.240076	8	16
1820	3	1.049458	3.148374	9	9.445122	27	81
1830	4	1.348233	5.392932	16	21.571728	64	256
1840	5	1.724033	8.620165	25	43.100825	125	625
1850	6	2.311786	13.870716	36	83.224296	216	1,296
1860	7	2.906215	20.343505	49	142.404535	343	2,401
1870	8	3.421951	28.175608	64	225.404864	512	4,096
1880	9	4.282891	38.546019	81	346.914171	729	6,561
1890	10	5.258113	52.581130	100	525.811300	1,000	10,000
1900	11	6.302115	69.323265	121	762.555915	1,331	14,641
Sum:	66	30.551553	242.224117	506	2,164.275197	4,356	39,974

and are entered into the equations:

I. $30.551553 = a(12) + b(66) + c(506)$

II. $242.224117 = a(66) + b(506) + c(4{,}356)$

III. $2{,}164.275197 = 2(506) + b(4{,}356) + c(39{,}974)$

Solving:

$(A):\ = 66/12 = 5.5$
$(IV) = (I)\ (A):\ 168.036 = a(66) + b(363) + c(2{,}783)$
$(V) = (II) - (IV):\ 74.188 = b(143) + c(1{,}573)$
$(B):\ 506/12 = 42.16667$

(VI) = (I) *(B)*: $1{,}288.276 = a(506) + b(2{,}783) + c(21{,}366.335)$
(VII) = (III) − (VI): $875.999 = b(1{,}573) + c(18{,}637.665)$
(C): $1{,}573/143 = 11.0$
(VIII) = (V) *(C)*: $816.068 = b(1{,}573) + c(17{,}303)$
(IX) = (VII) − (VIII): $59.931 = c(1{,}334.665)$
$c = (59.931)/(1{,}334.665) = 0.0449034$
(VII)′: $875.999 = b(1{,}573) + (0.0449034)(18{,}637.665)$
(VII)″: $39.104 = b(1{,}573)$
$b = (39.104)/(1{,}573) = 0.0248595$
(II)′: $242.224 = a66 + (0.0248595)(506) + (0.0449034)(4{,}356)$
(II)″: $34.046 = a66$
$a = (34.036)/66 = 0.515848$

Substituting the estimated parameter values into equation (3.9), we obtain

Year	x	bx	cx^2	calculated y
1790	0	0	0	0.515848
1800	1	0.024860	0.044903	0.585603
1810	2	0.049719	0.179614	0.745181
1820	3	0.074578	0.404131	0.994557
1830	4	0.099348	0.718454	1.333650
1840	5	0.124298	1.122585	1.762731
1850	6	0.149157	1.616522	2.281527
1860	7	0.174016	1.200267	2.890131
1870	8	0.198876	2.873818	3.588542
1880	9	0.223736	3.637175	4.376759
1890	10	0.248595	4.490340	5.254783
1900	11	0.273454	5.433311	6.222613
1910	12	0.298314	6.466090	7.280252
1920	13	0.323174	7.588675	8.427697
1930	14	0.348033	8.801066	9.664947
1940	15	0.372892	10.103265	10.992005
1950	16	0.397752	11.495270	12.408870
1960	17	0.422612	12.977083	13.915542
1970	18	0.447471	14.548702	15.512021

☆ ☆

here had positive signs. This implies that the projected population
values should increase indefinitely. As might have been expected, the
third degree polynomial fit the observed data better than did the
second degree polynomial (see Table 3−2). This was particularly true
for the earliest years. Ironically, the second degree polynomial
proved to provide the better forecast of the actual population of
Pennsylvania for the 1910−1970 projection period. The third degree

projection begins to diverge from the census count between 1920 and 1930; by 1970 the projection is more than half again as large as the observed population. The second degree polynomial projection does not seriously diverge until after 1930, and the 1970 forecast is less than a third higher than the census count.

It should be acknowledged that both equations yielded good results for the first few decades. This is no sign of infallibility for polynomial projections. All that the results indicate is that many populations—such as those of states or nations—possess a considerable growth inertia and that the polynomials, by doing a pretty good job of describing the whole range of the historical experience, can often do a decent job of forecasting the near future.

An example of the actual use of a third degree polynomial for population projection purposes is Pritchett's 1891 forecast of the population of the United States [8]. In his discussion, Pritchett noted that polynomial models have certain defects such as the lack of asymptotes which can lead to such odd results as negative population values. His main justification for the equations is that "it may be possible to represent the observation [of the interactions of complex phenomena] fairly well by a comparatively simple equation." As it happened, his parameters had positive signs, meaning future values for the U.S. population must become quite large; his projection for the year 2900 is a population of more than 40 billion persons. His 1900 projection was about 77.5 million compared to an actual 76.2 million. For 1910, he obtained 94.7, while the census tally was 92.2. The 1920 projection was 114.4, which compares to an actual 106.0. Pritchett's 1970 projection was 257.7 million, which proved to be more than 20 percent higher than the reported 203.2 million.

The Gompertz Curve

Another mathematical curve that is sometimes fitted to past population size in order to extrapolate future population size is the Gompertz curve. The formula for the Gompertz curve may be written:

$$y = ka^{b^x} \tag{3.18}$$

where parameter k is an asymptote—a value curve approaches but never quite attains. In the case of projection data, the asymptote is useful because it represents a "ceiling" on population growth. It is also useful on theoretical grounds because if a population continues to follow the growth "law" implied by the Gompertz curve, the fitted value of k is the maximum size that population can attain. The catch lies in the fact that the Gompertz curve, like the other curves we have been discussing, summarizes a potentially complex interplay of categories of demographic behavior. As a result, its analytical usefulness is limited.

Simply stated, the Gompertz curve describes a data series wherein the logarithms of the observations grow by increments that decline by a constant percentage [9]. This may be more readily apparent if equation (3.18) is rewritten

$$\log y = \log k + (\log a) b^x \qquad\qquad (3.19)$$

If a population is growing under conditions described by the Gompertz function, it increases in size by increasing arithmetic amounts during the early growth phase. All the while, the proportional growth is decreasing, but this effect is hidden by the rapid arithmetic gains. At a certain point, the declining proportional gains become declining arithmetic gains also. Eventually, proportional and arithmetic gains both become exceedingly small. The arithmetic growth increments thus start small, increase to a peak, and then become small again. If these increments were graphed, they would form a distribution skewed to the right. That is, it would look like a "bell-shaped" curve that was pulled or stretched to the right. The point of greatest numerical growth corresponds to the inflection point of the Gompertz curve which appears S-shaped when graphed to an arithmetic scale. A. L. Titus, in an appendix to an article by Murphy and Nagnur, demonstrates that the inflection point is reached when $y/k = e^{-1}$, which is about 37 percent of the maximum population size [10].

Croxton and Cowden indicate two tests that can be made on data to see if Gompertz growth is occurring. One is the plotting of growth increments, or first differences; a skewed frequency curve suggests the use of a Gompertz curve. The other is to calculate first differences of the logarithms of population size; the Gompertz curve is indicated if these differences decline by a constant percentage. These indexes for Pennsylvania for the years 1790 to 1900 are presented in Table 3–3. Although the growth increments of the logarithms of population are smaller in the later part of the series than they are in the early years, the ratios of these increments are not constant. The first differences of the population values also do not provide conclusive evidence. They monotonically increase without reaching an obvious inflection value.

Despite the fact that our indexes do not clearly support the use of a Gompertz curve to graduate and project the Pennsylvania data, we shall use it for illustrative purposes. The method used in Exhibit 3–3

Table 3–3. Test for Gompertz Growth Pattern, Pennsylvania, 1790–1900

Year	Population	Log Population	Change in Log Population	Ratio Change in Log Population	Population Difference
1790	434,373	5.637863	—	—	—
1800	602,365	5.779860	0.141997	—	167,992
1810	810,091	5.908534	0.128674	0.9062	207,726
1820	1,049,458	6.020965	0.112431	0.8738	239,367
1830	1,348,233	6.129765	0.108800	0.9677	298,775
1840	1,724,033	6.236546	0.106781	0.9814	375,800
1850	2,311,786	6.363948	0.127402	1.1931	587,752
1860	2,906,215	6.463328	0.099380	0.7801	594,429
1870	3,521,951	6.546783	0.083455	0.8398	615,736
1880	4,282,891	6.631737	0.084954	1.0180	760,940
1890	5,258,113	6.720830	0.089093	1.0487	975,222
1900	6,302,115	6.799486	0.078656	0.8829	1,044,002

Sources: Text and U.S. Bureau of the Census, *Census of Population: 1970 Number of Inhabitants*, Final Report PC(1)–A1, United States Summary (Washington, D.C.: Government Printing Office, 1971), Table 8.

☆ ☆

Exhibit 3–3

Projection Using the Gompertz Function

These projections of Pennsylvania's population use equation (3.19) fitted to three equal groups of census data; there are 12 census data points inclusive of 1790 and 1900 placed in groups of four observations each. The population values were transformed into logarithms (not shown) and these transformed values were summed for each group as indicated:

$$\Sigma_1 \log y \ (1790-1820) = 23.421237$$
$$\Sigma_2 \log y \ (1830-1860) = 25.193587$$
$$\Sigma_3 \log y \ (1870-1900) = 26.698836$$

The next step is substitution into the equations below and solving:

$$b^n = \frac{\Sigma_3 \log y - \Sigma_2 \log y}{\Sigma_2 \log y - \Sigma_1 \log y} = \frac{26.698836 - 25.193587}{25.193587 - 23.421237}$$

$$= \frac{1.505249}{1.772350} = 0.849296$$

$\log b^n = -0.070941$; $n = 4$,

$\log b = (\log b^n)/n = -0.017735$

$b = 0.959986$

$$\log a = (\Sigma_2 \log y - \Sigma_1 \log y)\frac{b-1}{(b^n-1)^2} = 1.772350\frac{-0.040014}{-0.150704^2}$$

$$= \frac{-0.070919}{0.022712} = -3.122534$$

$$\log k = \frac{1}{n} \ [\Sigma_1 \log y - \frac{b^n-1}{b-1} \ \log a]$$

$$= \frac{1}{4} \ [23.421237 - \frac{-0.150704}{-0.040014} \ \cdot \ (-3.122534)]$$

$$= \frac{1}{4} \ [23.421237 - (3.766282)(-3.122534)]$$

$$= \frac{1}{4} \ [23.421237 - (-11.760344)] = \frac{1}{4} \ (35.181581$$

$$= 8.795395$$

$k = 624{,}302{,}394$

Hence:

$$\log y = \log k + (\log a)\ b^x = 8.795395 - 3.122534\ (0.849296)^x.$$

Results of the computation are presented in Table 3–2.

☆ ☆

is a selected points technique from Croxton and Cowden. Its main advantage is that it is simple enough to be worked out using desk or pocket calculators. Its weakness lies in the possibility of error being introduced by the arbitrariness of the point selection. The article by Murphy and Nagnur referred to above presents a more precise method of curve fitting. This "descent" technique involves the estimation of parameter values through successive iterations of a computational procedure and this requires a computer. The interested reader should consult the Murphy-Nagnur article or Keyfitz [11] for details on the descent method of parameter estimation.

When working through the exhibit, the reader will notice that the sign of a parameter a is negative. The reason for this is that the part of equation (3.19) to the right of $\log k$ represents the distance of the dependent variable from the asymptote. As x becomes large, the value of the expression b^x becomes small because b is less than unity. The result is that very large x values become translated into very small values being subtracted from the asymptotic value.

As might have been expected, given the lack of an inflection point in the first difference data series, the asymptotic value for Pennsylvania's population is rather high—624 million, or more than three times the population of the United States in 1970. Given this high asymptotic value, it is not surprising that the Gompertz curve soon began to overproject Pennsylvania's population. The values for 1910 and 1920 are not too far off, but by 1920 the error was nearly 12 percent and the 1970 differential was 68 percent.

To summarize, the Gompertz curve shares the defects of the other simple mathematical functions in that it provides no insight into structural effects that can lead to changes in population growth patterns. Its form is more rigid than that of a high degree polynomial, so it is not likely to graduate historical data so well. On the other hand, its asymptotic property means that impossible results such as negative population values are not obtained. It also means that unlikely projection outcomes such as infinite growth cannot occur.

The Logistic Curve

Perhaps the most popular single function model of population growth is the logistic curve. It was originally discovered by the Belgian, Verhulst, who used it as a population model in 1838. It was subsequently forgotten and then rediscovered in 1920 by Raymond Pearl and L. J. Reed [12]. As a consequence, it is sometimes called the Pearl-Reed curve. The basic form of the function is

$$1/y = k + ab^x \tag{3.20}$$

where k, as in the Gompertz curve, is the upper asymptote. For purposes of fitting the curve by the selected points method, the logistic curve may be expressed:

$$y = \frac{k}{1 + e^{a+bx}} \tag{3.21}$$

The logistic curve also plots as an S-shape on arithmetically scaled paper. Its inflection point is located at $y = k/2$, which means that the arithmetic first differences are distributed symmetrically in a bell-shaped curve.

A major appeal of the logistic curve is that it implies a "law of growth" that both describes actual behavior and seems intuitively reasonable. Croxton and Cowden [13] and Lotka [14] briefly indicate some of the early studies using the logistic curve. Among the more successful uses were those of growth of populations of yeast cells and fruit flies in confined areas. The growth pattern was one of slow initial increase followed by rapid numerical growth which was followed in turn by a slowing of the growth and an eventual halt imposed by limitations in space or the food supply. It is not unreasonable to expect human growth to conform to this model if the conditions were comparable. In industrialized societies, however, the factor of science-based technology in the form of increases in the food supply tends to distort the pattern. The impact of migration into or out of an area may also modify the growth curve.

The logistic curve proved to be a popular means of projecting populations during the 1920s despite the fact that these applications were not for areas with sealed boundaries. Perhaps the best known application was the United States projection made by Pearl and Reed just before the results of the 1920 census became known [15]. The curve was fitted using population data from all censuses from 1790 through 1910 and the projections were not far from actual census counts through 1950. The 1920 figure was less than 2 percent high.

The best result was for 1930, when the curve read 122.4 million and the census tally was 122.8 million—an error of less than 0.4 percent. In 1940, the curve was 3.5 percent high because it did not pick up the low birth and foreign migration rates of the depression years. The 1950 projection was 148.7 million compared to the census' 150.7— less than 2 percent low. But the 1960 projection was 159.2 million, while the actual population—counting the new states of Alaska and Hawaii—was 179.3 million. The upper asymptote to the U.S. population calculated by Pearl and Reed was 197.3 million, which is less than the 1970 census count of 203.2 million.

One test to see if a population might be fitted acceptably by the logistic curve is to plot the first differences and observe whether or not they distribute symmetrically. If the curve is symmetrical, the logistic curve may be used. Another test is to calculate the first differences of the reciprocals $(1/y)$ of the population. The logistic curve may be used if these first differences decline by a constant ratio. Appropriate Pennsylvania data for the years 1790–1910 are presented in Table 3–4. The population first difference series presents the same picture as it did for the Gompertz trial—no evidence of a peak or inflection point and, hence, no clue as to whether the distribution is symmetrical or skewed. The first differences of the reciprocals of the population decline monotonically, but their ratios fluctuate in the range 0.6 to 0.912. In sum, the test is not conclusive, but once again we shall fit the curve for demonstration purposes.

The fitting technique is one suited for calculation on desk or pocket calculators and it involves the use of averages around selected points [16]. (For other methods of fitting the logistic curve, see Pearl [17], Cowden [18], and Keyfitz [19].) The details are laid out in Exhibit 3–4.

A few points about the computations should be noted here in the main text. First, populations are expressed in ratios to one million in order to keep the calculated values from overloading the display capabilities of small calculators. Secondly, the reader should observe the general operation of equation (3.21): Population is ultimately expressed as a ratio with the asymptote, k, as the numerator. As the denominator becomes small, approaching unity, the ratio value increases toward the value of k. This happens because the parameter b has a negative sign, and as the value of x increases, the value of the product bx also increases. The increasingly large product is subtracted from the constant value a, which means that the exponent of the number e becomes small, as does the value of unity added to the value of e raised to the exponent.

Table 3–4. Test for Logistic Growth Pattern, Pennsylvania, 1790–1910

Year	Population	Reciprocal of Population	Difference	Ratio Difference	Population Difference
1790	434,373	0.0000023021	—	—	—
1800	602,365	0.0000016601	0.0000006420	—	167,992
1810	810,091	0.0000012344	0.0000004257	0.663	207,726
1820	1,049,458	0.0000009528	0.0000002816	0.661	239,367
1830	1,348,233	0.0000007417	0.0000002111	0.750	298,775
1840	1,724,033	0.0000005800	0.0000001617	0.766	375,800
1850	2,311,786	0.0000004325	0.0000001475	0.912	587,752
1860	2,906,215	0.0000003440	0.0000000885	0.600	594,429
1870	3,521,951	0.0000002839	0.0000000601	0.679	615,736
1880	4,282,891	0.0000002334	0.0000000505	0.840	760,940
1890	5,258,113	0.0000001901	0.0000000433	0.857	975,222
1900	6,302,115	0.0000001586	0.0000000315	0.727	1,044,002
1910	7,665,111	0.0000001304	0.0000000284	0.902	1,362,996

Sources: Text and U.S. Bureau of the Census, *Census of Population: 1970 Number of Inhabitants*, Final Report PC(1)–A1, United States Summary (Washington, D.C.: Government Printing Office, 1971), Table 8.

☆ ☆

Exhibit 3–4

Projection Using the Logistic Curve

The logistic curve is fitted to Pennsylvania population data for the period 1790–1910 by using the arithmetic means of the populations enumerated in each of the three censuses nearest the years 1800, 1850, and 1900. For example, the census counts for 1840, 1850, and 1860 are averaged to obtain a 1850 point value to be entered into the fitting equations. These point data are indicated:

$$y_0 = 0.596237$$
$$y_1 = 2.262596$$
$$y_2 = 6.333022$$

where the population values are in millions. Entering the point data into the fitting equations, we obtain:

$$k = \frac{2y_0 y_1 y_2 - y_1^2 (y_0 + y_2)}{y_0 y_2 - y_1^2}$$

$$= \frac{17.087044 - (5.119341 \cdot 6.929259)}{3.775982 - 5.119341} = \frac{17.087044 - 35.473240}{-1.343359}$$

$$= \frac{-18.386196}{-1.343359} = 13.686733$$

$$a = \log_e \frac{k - y_0}{y_0} = \log_e \frac{13.090496}{0.596237} = \log_e 21.955189$$

$$= (2.302585) \log_{10} 21.955189 = (2.302585)(1.341537)$$

$$= 3.089003 \text{ , since } \log_e X = 2.302585 \log_{10} X.$$

$$b = \frac{1}{n} \log_e \frac{y_0 (k - y_1)}{y_1 (k - y_0)} \quad ; n = 5; \quad = \frac{1}{5} \log_e \frac{0.596237 (11.424137)}{2.262536 (13.090496)}$$

$$= \frac{1}{5} \log_e \frac{6.811493}{29.618504} = \frac{1}{5} \log_e 0.229974$$

$$= \frac{1}{5} (2.302585) \log_{10} 0.229974 = \frac{(2.302585)(-0.638321)}{5} \quad ;$$

since $\log_{10} 0.229974 = -0.638321; \quad = \frac{-1.469788}{5}$

$$= -0.293958$$

Thus,

$$y = k/(1 + e^{a+bx}) = k/(1 + m); \quad m = e^{a+bx}$$

and substituting:

$$m = e^{3.089003 - 0.293958x}$$

$$\log_{10} m = (3.089003 - 0.293958x) \log_{10} e$$

$$= (3.089003 - 0.293958x)(0.43429)$$

$$= 1.341535 - 0.127664x.$$

Once m is obtained, the value for y readily follows. Results of the computations are in Table 3–2.

☆ ☆

As it turns out, the logistic curve proves to be the most accurate function for projecting Pennsylvania's population. The 1970 projection is only about 1 percent higher than the census count, which is very good indeed. At some points during the intervening years the error was upward of 5 percent, which is still not bad. The value of the asymptote was 13.687 million, which seems low enough to be exceeded someday. However, the low growth rates exhibited by Pennsylvania in recent years suggest that it may be many decades before the asymptotic value is surpassed.

The reader should be cautioned that the closeness of projected to actual census data does not imply that the logistic curve is in fact superior to alternative functions. Keep in mind that the U.S. curve fitted by Pearl and Reed, using the identical 1790–1910 baseline period, began to go awry by 1960. All that can be said is that Pennsylvania's growth behavior has tended to follow the logistic pattern for many decades and that the United States has not.

Pearl and Reed also proposed the use of variations of the logistic curve that resulted in growth by stages and by a skewed distribution of first differences [20]. Their hypothesis was that growth could occur in waves or cycles, according to variations in the food supply. The waves were spliced to one another as indicated:

$$y_{t+n} = k_1 + \frac{k_2}{1 + e^{a+bn}} \tag{3.22}$$

The skewed form is expressed

$$y_{t+n} = k_1 + \frac{k_2}{1 + e^{a+bn+cn^2}} \qquad (3.23)$$

In both equations, k_1 represents the lower limit of the second wave and the upper limit is denoted by $(k_1 + k_2)$.

Modified Exponential Curve

The final model we shall discuss that has an asymptotic control on population size is the modified exponential curve. In this particular model, growth increments decline by a constant ratio. It can be written

$$y = k + ab^x \qquad (3.24)$$

where a is the difference between the value of the asymptote, k, and the value of the dependent population variable at the origin, and b is the ratio of change. The asymptote becomes the upper limit of y when the sign of a is negative, because the equation computes y in terms of decreasing distances from k.

Once again, we will use Pennsylvania as an example. Table 3–5 contains data on population size and numerical differences between

Table 3–5.   Test for Modified Exponential Growth Pattern, Pennsylvania, 1790–1970

Year	Population	Difference	Ratio of Differences
1790	434,373	—	—
1800	602,365	167,992	—
1810	810,091	207,726	1.2365
1820	1,049,458	239,367	1.1523
1830	1,348,233	298,775	1.4383
1840	1,724,033	375,800	1.2578
1850	2,311,786	587,753	1.5640
1860	2,906,215	594,429	1.0114
1870	3,521,951	615,736	1.0358
1880	4,282,891	760,940	1.2358
1890	5,258,113	975,222	1.2816
1900	6,302,115	1,044,002	1.0705
1910	7,665,111	1,362,996	1.3055
1920	8,720,017	1,054,906	0.7740
1930	9,631,350	911,333	0.8639
1940	9,900,180	268,830	0.2950
1950	10,498,012	597,832	2.2238
1960	11,319,366	821,354	1.3739
1970	11,793,909	474,543	0.5778

Sources: Text and U.S. Bureau of the Census, *Census of Population: 1970 Number of Inhabitants*, Final Report PC(1)–A1, United States Summary (Washington, D.C.: Government Printing Office, 1971), Table 8.

census observations. Ratios of the differences are also indicated. The data suggest that the modified exponential model would not be suited for Pennsylvania for the period 1790–1910, because the growth increments become larger. From 1900–1910 to 1930–1940 numerical growth drops, but not at a uniform rate. After 1940 the pattern becomes erratic. The most workable approach would be to use the data from 1900 to 1950, which provides us with three observation periods with two growth increments each for fitting by a partial totals method that can be worked out without benefit of a computer [21]. Computational details are presented in Exhibit 3–5.

Since the model used data for a period when Pennsylvania's growth was falling off rapidly, it is not surprising that the value of the asymptote is low. To judge from the census data, the population of the state passed the asymptotic value of 11,095,310 sometime around 1957. Obviously, the modified exponential model was not well suited for any observed period of Pennsylvania's history. This is not to say that the model would be inappropriate for other populations. However, the analyst should continue to keep in mind the limitations common to all single function models used to project human populations.

REGRESSION TECHNIQUES

This section will be rather brief, as no attempt will be made to work out computational examples. The reason for not working out examples is that the computation procedure for simple regression is the same as that required for the estimation of polynomial parameters described in the preceding section. The computation procedure for estimating the parameter values in multiple regression equations is analogous to the simple regression solution but is much more complicated to carry out. Most standard statistical program packages for computers have easily handled regression programs and the reader interested in the theory and derivations involved in regression analysis should consult a statistics text. Our treatment will be geared toward an "understanding" of the technique.

Simple Regression

The basic equation for the simple, linear regression projection model can be expressed:

$$y_{t+n} = a + bX_{t+n} \tag{3.25}$$

where X represents an independent variable that is not necessarily

☆ ☆

Exhibit 3–5

Projection Using the Modified Exponential Curve

The modified exponential curve is fitted using the method of partial totals. These partial totals are obtained as follows:

Year	x	Y	Y
1900	0	6.302115	
1910	1	7.665111	$13.967226 = \Sigma_1 Y$
1920	2	8.720017	
1930	3	9.631350	$18.351367 = \Sigma_2 Y$
1940	4	9.900180	
1950	5	10.498012	$20.398192 = \Sigma_3 Y$

where the Y values are Pennsylvania census counts in millions. These partial totals are entered into the fitting equations as indicated:

$$b^n = \frac{\Sigma_3 Y - \Sigma_2 Y}{\Sigma_2 Y - \Sigma_1 Y} \; ; \text{ where } n = 2, \text{ the number of elements comprising the partial total;}$$

$$= \frac{2.046825}{4.384141} = 0.466870$$

$$b = \sqrt{0.466870} = 0.683279$$

$$a = (\Sigma_2 Y - \Sigma_1 Y) \frac{b-1}{(b^n-1)^2} = 4.384141 \frac{-0.316721}{(-0.533130)^2}$$

$$= \frac{-1.388550}{0.284228} = -1.885339$$

$$k = \frac{1}{n} \left[\Sigma_1 Y - \frac{b^n-1}{b-1} a \right] = \frac{1}{2} \left[13.967226 - \frac{-0.533130}{-0.316721} (-4.885339) \right]$$

$$= \frac{1}{2} \left[13.967226 - (1.683280)(-4.885339) \right]$$

$$= \frac{1}{2} \left[13.967226 - (-8.223393) \right] = \frac{1}{2} (22.190619)]$$

$$= 11.095310$$

These parameter values were entered into equation (3.24) and the results are presented in Table 3–2.

☆ ☆

time (which was the independent variable used in the models described in the preceding section); *a* and *b* are respectively parameters of origin and slope; *y*, as before, is the dependent variable, population; and $(t + n)$ represents a counter for time, with *t* being a given year or transformed value representing a date, and *n* being specified unit of time such as one year. The form of equation (3.1) and the parameters values may be estimated by the simultaneous solving of equations (3.2) and (3.3).

In this model, the relationship between change in the value of the independent variable and change in the value of the dependent variable is linear when graphed on an arithmetically scaled coordinate system. As we have noted in the discussion above, population size change seldom is linear given constant change in time. Accordingly, the analyst should take care to graph the relationship between population size and the proposed independent variable's values to check for linearity.

A word should be said about "independent" and "dependent" variables in regression analysis. In theory, these labels are statements of truth regarding the relationship between the variables. If we were relating age and height of schoolchildren, for example, we should use age as the independent variable and height as the dependent variable. This is because height is well known to be a consequence of the maturation process which itself is related to age. If the contrary relationship were true, we would have age being causally determined by the height of the child, a relationship that is patently untrue. But a regression equation works the same no matter which variable is treated as being dependent, so caution in interpretation of results is urged.

Quite often in going about his research, the analyst encounters situations where the relationship between variables is not well defined in terms of the data at hand or in terms of a body of empirically grounded theory. For example, the analyst may assemble a series of data that indicate population size varies with the size of the labor force (labor force is defined as the population either working or seeking work). Obviously the two variables are associated, but it is not clear which is the independent variable and which is the dependent variable. In reality, the two variables are difficult to untangle because the labor force is a subset of the total population, and a large population is very likely to be associated with a large labor force, and vice versa. Even if change in population and in the labor force were considered, there would still be conceptual problems. It could be argued that economic growth means more jobs, which is likely to result in a larger labor force and, hence, more population. On the other hand, one could say that as a population increases in size due to past rates of fertility and mortality there will be more persons of labor force age, which in turn may attract jobs to an area or may actually result in the creation of jobs required for the sustinance of the larger population.

Where variables are as interrelated as population and labor force, the analyst is faced with the unpleasant choice of either abandoning the analysis or accepting the fact that there is an association between the variables that can be used if the analyst chooses to make assumptions about causality. Therefore, let us say that the analyst does find a strong association between population size and the size of the labor force, and that he wishes to make use of the association. Let us further assume that the analyst has a means of forecasting the labor force, but not the population. Thus, in the future, the labor force is "known," but the population is not known. In such a situation, the labor force might be usefully treated as being the independent variable and the population as the dependent variable.

The main problem regarding the use of regression analysis as a model for projecting populations is that, once again, the future is an extrapolation of relationships between variables that held in the past—a relationship that is expressed in a very simplistic manner. Worse yet, the population projection is related in this manner to yet another projection—the projection of whatever the independent variable might be. Therefore, we have the double uncertainty as to the value of the independent projection and of the continuing validity of the past relationship.

It is not necessary for the time of the observation of the independent variable to agree with that of the dependent variable. The relationship can be *lagged* as follows:

$$y_{t+n} = a + bX_t \tag{3.26}$$

That is, research may indicate that population change at one point in time is associated with a change in another variable at an earlier point in time and that this lagged relationship seems to hold over a number of such observations.

Of course, it is desirable that lagged relationships be explainable on theoretical grounds. To take a hypothetical example, say that the analyst observes that population growth varies directly with the area's ratio of per capita income to national per capita income and that the change in growth occurs two years after the change in the per capita income ratio. This situation might be explained by assuming that high wages could be indicative of a job shortage—that is, employers must bid up wages in order to attract workers. The high wages being offered would eventually attract migrants from areas where lesser wage rates prevail and the final result would be a population increase due to net inmigration.

Multiple Regression

There are many reasons for changing rates of population growth in the real world and it can be argued that a population projection model should take as many factors into account as is reasonably possible. The main technique used by population analysts for modeling the effects of several independent variables is multiple regression analysis. The linear formula for multiple regression may be written

$$y_{t+n} = a + b_1 X_1 + b_2 X_2 + \ldots + b_m X_m \tag{3.27}$$

where the subscripts on the right side of the equation are numbers indicating the variable and its associated weighting coefficient. Subscripts indicating time were not included in order to leave the equation as uncluttered as possible. The timing of the independent variables may be concurrent with that of the dependent variable, or it may be lagged, or it could be a mixture of the two, depending on theoretical considerations and empirical results.

Some of the pioneering work in the use of multiple regression as a population projection technique was done by Robert C. Schmitt [22]. We shall use his work as an illustration of the technique. His 1953 paper was concerned with the projection of city populations' intercensal growth rates. Two independent variables were used—population density in thousands of persons per square mile at the time of the first census; and the expected percentage increase during the intercensal period for the population of the state in which the city in question is located. His equation was

$$y = 23.54 - 1.355 X_2 + 0.3309 X_3$$

where X_2 was density and X_3 was the projected state growth rate. Note that the sign of density is negative. This means that very densely settled areas are expected to have little growth. In fact, an extremely densely populated city in a slowly growing state could have a declining population—an outcome that is not unreasonable. Schmitt asserted that his equation "should be relatively accurate for any city with a 1950 population over 250,000."

Schmitt used the city of Seattle as his computational example. Its density in 1950, according to Schmitt, was 7.083 thousand persons per square mile. The latest available state population projection indicated that Washington would grow by 20.9 percent between 1950 and 1960. Hence,

$$y = 23.54 - 1.355 \ (7.083) + 0.3309 \ (20.9) = 20.86$$

This works out to a 1960 population of 565,130, which compares to the 1960 census count of 557,087. The actual decade growth rate for Washington was 19.94 percent, which was close to the Census Bureau forecast used by Schmitt. However, it should be pointed out that most of Seattle's 1950–1960 growth was due to annexation—the 1960 population of the area within the 1950 corporate limits of the city was 471,008, a gain of only 3,417 over the 1950 population [23].

The lesson to be learned from this example is not that the method is bad, but that it has its limitations. As Schmitt himself indicates, the equation "assumes the same interrelationships as existed during the decade of the 1940s, despite the atypical nature of that period." And, "[i]t depends to a large measure on the accuracy of the recent Bureau of the Census state forecasts" which "are far from infallible," even though they were the best that were available [24]. He also cautioned that his method, like most others, is not very accurate for rapidly growing cities.

Nonlinear Regression

The regression models discussed in the last two sections were linear—that is, numerical change in the dependent variable was proportional to numerical change in the independent variable(s). It is possible to generalize these relationships to situations of nonlinearity. This may entail a logarithmic transform to any or all variables, which means that the linear equations can still be used; otherwise, it would mean the use of polynomial expressions to the right side of the equation. Isard notes that nonlinear expressions require much more computation for parameter estimation than do linear equations. Thus, this type of analysis "is not pursued unless its superiority to a linear regression is indicated by empirical and theoretical materials" [25].

Autoregression

Recently, yet another type of regression model has been considered for use in projecting populations. This is the autoregressive model [26].

The autoregressive model has seldom been applied to population projections because it ideally requires upwards of 50 observations of historical data. Excluding the use of population estimates in the data series, it is unlikely that there is a population in North America for which even 20 equally spaced observations exist.

Saboia has used data for Sweden to demonstrate autoregressive and moving average time series models based on the work of Box and Jenkins [27]. His results were more accurate in projecting the Swedish population for the years 1965 and 1970 than were a logistic curve projection and a projection using fixed rates of mortality and fertility, with no migration component. Saboia claims that the usefulness of the time series models has to do with the fact that the forecasts "can be given by normal distributions, and confidence intervals can be easily obtained. Thus, following the recommendation of Keyfitz we have a forecast given by a probability distribution and not simply by a number" [28].

The reader should refer to Saboia's article for details on the autoregressive model. Its basic principle can be summarized as follows: Observed values in a series can be related to one another by correlation and multiple regression. This relationship can be for adjoining observations or for observations separated by equal numbers of other observations. Once the relationships are established, future observations can be projected from existing observations.

Keyfitz observes that

> The most useful part of the theory is concerned with stationary time series, in which the extrapolation from one point in the curve to another depends only on the time interval between them. Unfortunately for the application to demography, each decade seems to see historic and more or less unprecedented population changes, especially in births, that are seriously inconsistent with the stationarity assumption. Nonetheless the treatment of sections of the population or birth curve as stationary could at least provide lower bounds to the error of prediction, even if it cannot greatly improve the prediction itself [29].

CONCLUSIONS

The present chapter has been devoted to techniques for projecting total population values into the future using only past total population size and, on occasion, other historical data to establish certain relationships that are assumed to hold in the future. The variables common to most of the models discussed here are population and time. The logic of virtually all of the models is that population is some kind of function of time.

Time is considered to be a very general variable that encompasses all possible events that can influence change in population size. The models examine population size at various times in the past and attempt to describe the form of the relationship between past size and the passage of time in equal intervals. These relationships are mathematical, either implicitly or explicitly. The form of the mathematical relationship between time and size is a summary description of the effects of all the forces that had shaped the size of the population in the past. Presumably, the closer the fit of the mathematical function to historical data, the better is the summary description of the molding forces. It follows that a mathematical function that describes the past well should also describe the future well. It can also be asserted that the compactness of the mathematical functions is an analytical virtue, given the impossibility of directly modeling every possible influencing factor.

As we saw when examples were worked out, functions that seemed to describe past population size adequately did not always produce accurate projections of future population size. The reason we usually gave for this inaccuracy was that "conditions changed." Past population size was the result of a balance of rates of fertility, mortality, and net migration. This balance was usually a shifting one that sometimes was manifest in a "law of growth" implied by a closely fitting mathematical function. But eventually, these balances shifted too much, and the growth "laws" failed to apply.

Apparently, the simple functions may be too simple, and the complexity of influencing factors may not be so complex. Note that we have continually been referring to the differing effects of the three basic components of demographic change—fertility, mortality, and migration. Each component may be influenced by outside forces, but each also has its own dynamics. It follows that population projection accuracy—as well as analytical rigor—could be improved by specifying the assumptions behind change in each component separately, rather than by making one assumption about the whole population. The projection models in the chapters that follow will, in one way or another, attempt to account for factors in population change other than past behavior of total size. Some of these attempts will be indirect, as will be the case in the next chapter. Other projection models will go into great detail with regard to the basic change components. Most population projection systems in use today rely on component assumptions; the main exception is in the field of small area projections, where data availability limitations sometimes force the analyst to use models such as were discussed in this chapter.

This is not to say that simple models are undesirable. Even though they have analytical limitations, they may prove to be very accurate—the logistic curve projection of Pennsylvania is a case in point. They may also be of theoretical interest. This is especially true for the models that imply growth limits. Even the great demographer Lotka, who did much of the pioneering work in stable population theory, found the implications of the logistic curve of interest [30].

NOTES TO CHAPTER THREE

1. P. K. Whelpton, "Population of the United States, 1925 to 1975," *American Journal of Sociology* 34, 2 (1928):253–70.

2. Nathan Keyfitz, *Introduction to the Mathematics of Population* (Reading, Mass.: Addison-Wesley, 1968).

3. J. H. Pollard, *Mathematical Models for the Growth of Human Populations* (Cambridge: Cambridge University Press, 1973).

4. Whelpton, p. 254.

5. Henry Gannett, "Estimates of Future Population," In *Report of the National Conservation Commission*, vol. II (Washington, D.C.: Government Printing Office, 1909), pp. 7–9.

6. Herbert Arkin and Raymond R. Colton, *Statistical Methods* (New York: Barnes & Noble, 1970).

7. Keyfitz, ch. 7.

8. H. S. Pritchett, "A Formula for Predicting the Population of the United States," *Publications of the American Statistical Association*, N.S. no. 14 (1891), pp. 278–86.

9. Frederick E. Croxton and Dudley J. Cowden, *Applied General Statistics* (New York: Prentice-Hall, 1945), ch. 16.

10. Edmund M. Murphy and Dhruva N. Nagnur, "A Gompertz Fit that Fits: Applications to Canadian Fertility Patterns," *Demography* 9, 1 (1972):35–50.

11. Keyfitz, ch. 9.

12. Harold F. Dorn, "Pitfalls in Population Forecasts and Projections," *Journal of the American Statistical Association* 45, 251 (1950):311–34.

13. Croxton and Cowden, p. 456.

14. Alfred J. Lotka, *Elements of Mathematical Biology* (New York: Dover, 1956), ch. 7.

15. Dorn, pp. 317–19.

16. Croxton and Cowden, ch. 16.

17. Raymond Pearl, *Introduction to Medical Biometry and Statistics*, 3rd ed. (Philadelphia: W. B. Saunders, 1940), ch. 27.

18. Dudley J. Cowden, "Simplified Methods of Fitting Certain Types of Growth Curves," *Journal of the American Statistical Association* 42, 240 1947:585–90.

19. Keyfitz, ch. 9.

20. Walter Isard, *Methods of Regional Analysis: an Introduction to Regional Science* (Cambridge, Mass.: The M.I.T. Press, 1960), p. 14.

21. Croxton and Cowden, ch. 16.

22. Robert C. Schmitt, "A New Method of Forecasting City Population," *Journal of the American Institute of Planners* 19, 1 (1953):40–42; and Robert C. Schmitt, "A Method of Projecting the Population of Census Tracts," *Journal of the American Institute of Planners* 20, 2 (1954):102.

23. Calvin F. Schmid and Stanton E. Schmid, *Growth of Cities and Towns: State of Washington* (Olympia: Washington State Planning and Community Affairs Agency, 1969).

24. Schmitt (1954) p. 102.

25. Isard, p. 21.

26. Nathan Keyfitz, "On Future Population," *Journal of the American Statistical Association* 67, 338 (1972):355; and Joao L. M. Saboia, "Modeling and Forecasting Populations by Time Series: The Swedish Case," *Demography* 11, 3 (1974):483–92.

27. Saboia, p. 485.

28. Ibid., p. 489.

29. Keyfitz, "On Future Population," p. 355.

30. Dorn, pp. 327–28.

Chapter Four

Projecting Total Populations:
Ratio, Share, Density, and
Other Noncomponent Techniques

INTRODUCTION

Whereas the preceding chapter dealt with direct methods of projecting total populations, the present chapter will present techniques for
projecting populations by relating the population under study to
other variables that are assumed to be meaningful in terms of measuring forces that can influence population size.

In many cases, this represents a means of avoiding at least some of
the rigidity imposed by the use of simple mathematical formulas.
The reader will recall that while such formulas could sometimes describe past population growth well, they fail to account for underlying shifts in rates of the fundamental demographic processes of
fertility, mortality, and migration. In the next chapter we shall begin
to directly consider the modeling of these processes.

One very common variable to which a population is related for
purposes of projection is the population of a larger geographic unit.
The larger unit may, in turn, be related to a still larger unit. Or the
larger unit may be projected independently using a technique that
makes use of component data. The relational measure is the share—or
ratio—of the subunit to the larger unit.

The logic of using this share or ratio approach generally runs as
follows: Larger populations are easier to project than are small populations because of a number of reasons: The population may have
more "inertia." The data necessary for making sophisticated projections—particularly in the area of cohort fertility—are often not available for smaller units. Such data as are available are statistically more
reliable for larger units than are data for smaller units—that is, year-
to-year proportional fluctuations in reported births and deaths are
less extreme for larger units than for smaller units.

In any event, the projection of the larger unit should account for anticipated shifts in rates of change in the fundamental demographic components. Subunits presumably will share the secular component effects with the larger unit in the future as they have in the past. If the subunit mirrored the behavior of the larger unit in all respects, its share would remain constant. If the share varied in the past, it was because of local variations in the component rates. It is assumed that the effects of local variations relative to larger unit variations have less impact on the accuracy of projections than would be the case of the effect of local component rate changes on the trajectory of local population size itself. In other words, the mathematical function projections of Pennsylvania in the previous chapter often worked well until nationwide demographic events such as dropping birth rates accompanied by near-zero net foreign migration gave way to baby booms and baby busts and thereby invalidated the projections. By placing the burden of accounting for such shifting component effects on the larger unit, the projection model for the smaller units has only to summarize drifts in socioeconomic conditions impinging on population size in terms of the ratio of the part to the whole.

Another indirect approach is to consider population in terms of the number of persons per square unit of land area—or floor space, in some cases. That is, population is converted into population density. Density is a concept that is particularly useful when projections are required for small subunits of cities and their suburban fringes. This is because zoning ordinances and other factors act to restrict the number of persons who can occupy a given area. Places that are suburbanizing often exhibit high rates of growth that, if allowed to continue without modification, would result in extremely large populations. But due to the density constraints that exist in the real world, empirical data show that suburbanizing areas that grow very rapidly also cease that growth suddenly once the land has been built up to its capacity. Later on, these areas often experience population decline as the children of the once-young suburbanites leave home to seek work, go to college, or establish their own households. Models that trend population size cannot easily capture this reality, hence the utility of the density approach.

Yet another indirect approach is to relate population change to "quasi-population" variables such as the number of jobs in an area or the present or anticipated housing stock. Techniques such as these require at least two ancillary projections. One is a projection of the variable being related to population. In the case of jobs, the data could be generated as a by-product of an econometric model of a region. The other needed projection is that for the translation ratio relating the quasi-population variable to population size. In addition, the translation of a job forecast to a population forecast requires that assumptions be made regarding a number of factors; each such assumption itself can be considered as a forecast. For example, the analyst could assume that the ratio of people to jobs that was obtained in 1970 will continue to hold. But that assumption implies a drastic shifting among the components that make up the people-jobs ratio, a shifting that would go against component trends. These trends include the huge number of persons born during the postwar baby boom reaching the job market from the mid-1960s into the early 1980s. They include the smaller number of young dependents of jobholders, a result of the low birth rates in recent years. They include higher labor force participation rates for females. In light of these component trends, the *only* way for the 1970 ratio to hold in the future would be for one additional component rate to change—the unemployment level would have to increase.

All of these models, and others, will be treated in this chapter. The first subject to be discussed will be shares of larger units.

SUBUNIT SHARES OF THE LARGER POPULATION

It was noted in the introduction to this chapter that a justification for projecting shares of a larger population rather than population size itself was that short term events such as fluctuations in birth rates or economic conditions could largely be ignored in favor of modeling long term drifts in the relation of the part to the whole. We shall begin the discussion of modeling shares by examining some graphed empirical data so that the reader can acquire a "feel" for data forms he is likely to encounter.

Graphic Data

Figure 4–1 presents data for large subareas of the United States in the form of ratios of subarea population to national population. The areal units are those used by the U.S. Census Bureau for statistical presentation purposes. There are four large units that the Census Bureau calls "regions." These regions are in turn divided into "divisions." The next smaller unit below the division is the state. Hence, regions and divisions are defined by state boundaries; no state is divided between two or more regions or divisions. It may be argued that the use of state boundaries, while useful in that they provide relatively unchanging analytical areas, may be artificial in social or economic terms. This is a valid criticism, so the Census Bureau has

Figure 4–1.   Shares of United States Population by Regions and
Selected Divisions, 1790–1970: Arithmetic Scale

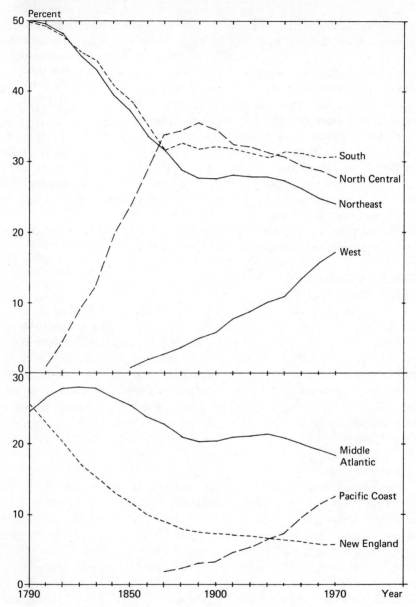

Source: U.S. Bureau of the Census, *Census of Population: 1970 Number of Inhabitants,*
       Final Report PC(1)–A1, United States Summary (Washington, D.C.: Government
       Printing Office, 1971), Table 8.

established other statistical areas that are intended to make more sense from a economic standpoint. These alternative units are state economic areas, economic subregions, and economic regions. State economic areas (SEAs) are based on county boundaries. An SEA may be a single county or may be comprised of a number of counties. In no case does a SEA cross a state line. Economic subregion boundaries can and do cross state lines. Consequently, the analyst has several alternatives if he chooses to project the share of a county population to a larger population: He may work through the region-division-state-county hierarchy, or he might go region-division-state-SEA-county, or perhaps economic subregion-SEA-county. Other, ad hoc, areal units could be used as well. The present treatment shall begin with regions and divisions.

The data in the figure are from all the national censuses starting from the first one in 1790. In that year, almost the entire population was concentrated in the Census Bureau's present-day South and Northeast regions. The Northeast was the larger of the two regions by a very slight margin. The 1800 census data begin to pick up persons in what is now the North Central region which is comprised of the Great Lakes and upper Plains states. The North Central region grew rapidly so that by the time the Civil War ended it was the largest single region. Population data for the West first appear in 1850, following the annexation of California, Oregon Territory, and of what is now the southwestern states. The Northeast ceased its initial share decline by 1890 and maintained a relatively stable ratio to the national population until the depression of the 1930s caused foreign immigration to decline to low levels. Since 1930, the Northeast has once again experienced a falling share of the national population. The early, rapid decline in the South's share ceased by 1870. Since then, there has been a slight drift downward with brief periods of recovery. The North Central region's proportional growth slowed after 1870 and ceased by 1890. Since then the region's share has been declining. The West has been increasing its share of the national population since the first data recordings in 1850.

In addition to regional data, Figure 4–1 also contains data for selected divisions. The Pacific Coast division is comprised of the states of Washington, Oregon, California, Alaska, and Hawaii. It contains the lion's share of the population of the West, and its share curve is similar to that of the region. The remaining divisions shown are New England and Middle Atlantic, which together comprise the Northeast region. The Middle Atlantic states are New York, New Jersey, and Pennsylvania. New England is made up of Maine, New Hampshire, Vermont, Massachusetts, Rhode Island, and Connecticut. The lines indicate that first New England and later the Middle Atlantic division played the dominant role in molding the Northeast region's population share history. The Middle Atlantic states actually increased their share of the national population from 1790 until the period 1810–1830. These gains were offset by the steady decline in the share held by New England—a decline that continued until the 1960s. The Middle Atlantic states also experienced declining shares from 1830 until 1890, when a recovery occurred. This recovery, coupled with a slackening in the decline of New England, resulted in the more or less stable regional share noted above. Since 1930, the Middle Atlantic share has again become steadily smaller.

The frame of reference is changed in Figure 4–2. Here, the shares are of the population of the Northeast. Shares held by the two divisions and their component states are graphed. We see that New England was larger than the Middle Atlantic division in 1790 and that its share of the regional population fell off steadily until 1930, when it comprised less than a quarter of the region. New England maintained this share from 1930 until the 1960–1970 decade, when it increased its share at the expense of the Middle Atlantic division.

Examination of state shares of the regional population provides insights regarding the internal dynamics of regional and divisional growth. New York, Pennsylvania, and Maine aggrandized their shares during the early decades, although their individual patterns varied. Maine peaked early and has had generally declining shares since 1840. Pennsylvania's share increased steadily until it reached a maximum in 1890. Its share declined thereafter. Connecticut's share decreased during the early decades, remained fairly constant from 1830 until 1910, and has tended to increase ever since. New Hampshire had a similar pattern, except that the period of decline was from 1790 to 1930 and the recovery began after 1960. Massachusetts experienced two declining periods and two recovery periods, if we can count its slight share increase from 1960 to 1970 as a recovery period.

It is noteworthy that no pattern of share change is really consistent over the period 1790–1970. Some patterns are more regular than others, but the fact remains that no state failed to change direction in its share pattern. A few states changed direction several times, hinting of cyclic or periodic fluctuations in regional influence.

Mathematical Functions

All of the mathematical models presented in the previous chapter may be used to describe shares of a population as well as to describe the size of any population or subpopulation. In this instance, the

Figure 4–2. Shares of Northeast Region Population, by Component States, 1790–1970: Arithmetic Scale

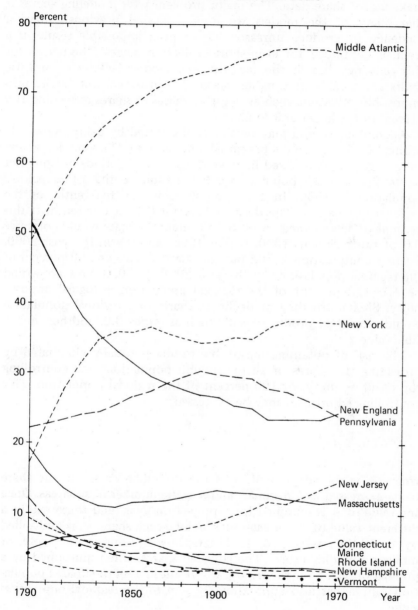

Source: U.S. Bureau of the Census, *Census of Population: 1970 Number of Inhabitants,* Final Report PC(1)–A1, United States Summary (Washington, D.C.: Government Printing Office, 1971), Table 8.

dependent variable that was symbolized by the letter y is a share, and the historical data series used to fit the desired equation must also make use of share data. The major problem with modeling shares is that many of the models we have discussed previously have a tendency to produce unreasonable or even impossible results if a trend is continued for even short projection ranges. The reason for this tendency lies in the fact that the models lacking asymptotic limits are capable of trending reasonable historical data series into impossible situations such as negative shares or shares exceeding 100 percent of the larger unit of analysis.

Anomolous results may be simply illustrated by using the simple arithmetic change model presented in equation (3.1), a model whereby change occurs in fixed increments over fixed periods of time. Let us say that a state's population is 0.4—or four-tenths—of its region's population in 1960. In 1970 the share is 0.5—five-tenths of the regional population. The decade change is 0.1, or one-tenth. If this amount of share change were to continue, the state would comprise 0.6 of the region in 1980, 0.7 in 1990, and 0.8 in the year 2000. Further continuation would put the share at 1.0—or 100 percent of the regional population—by the year 2020. In 2030 the share would be 1.1—110 percent of the regional population—a logical impossibility. Similar trending of declining shares of a regional population would ultimately produce results such as *minus* 0.2, another impossible value.

The risk of obtaining impossible results is usually eliminated by projecting the shares of all the subunit populations and controlling the result to unity, or 100 percent of the regional population. This controlling adjustment may be expressed

$$A = 1.0 / \sum_{i=1}^{n} s_i \qquad (4.1)$$

where A is the adjustment, s_i is the ith subarea's share—the share being expressed as a decimal—and n is the number of subareas. Once the value of A is obtained for a projection year (and there will be a different value of A for each such point), each share, s_i, is multiplied by A, and the resulting adjusted shares now will sum to unity, plus or minus a rounding effect. The adjusted shares, when multiplied by a population value for the region, will result in a set of subarea population values that also approximately sum to the regional population value.

The graphed data in Figures 4–1 and 4–2 on arithmetic coordinates and the same data plotted to semilogarithmic scale in Figures

Figure 4–3. Shares of United States Population, by Regions and Selected Divisions, 1790–1970: Semilogarithmic Scale

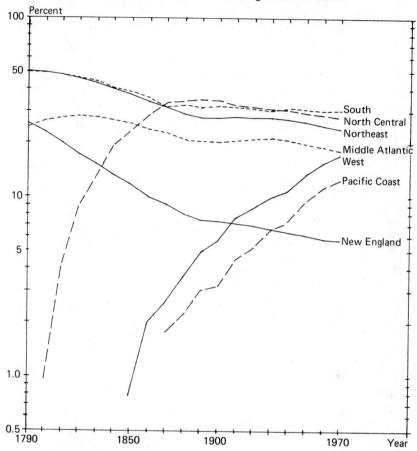

Source: U.S. Bureau of the Census, *Census of Population: 1970 Number of Inhabitants,* Final Report PC(1)–A1, United States Summary (Washington, D.C.: Government Printing Office, 1971), Table 8.

4–3 and 4–4 suggest another reason why great caution should be exercised, especially where long range projections are concerned. The graphed data indicate that share trends may be fairly regular for many decades and then suddenly reverse direction. Simple models that use time as the independent variable run afoul of the problem of parameter interpretation that clouded the task of modeling population size itself. True, nationwide events impinging on population size—such as wars, depressions, baby booms, and so forth—are to some degree controlled. But other factors—such as changing eco-

Figure 4–4.   Shares of Northeast Region Population, by Component States, 1790–1970: Semilogarithmic Scale

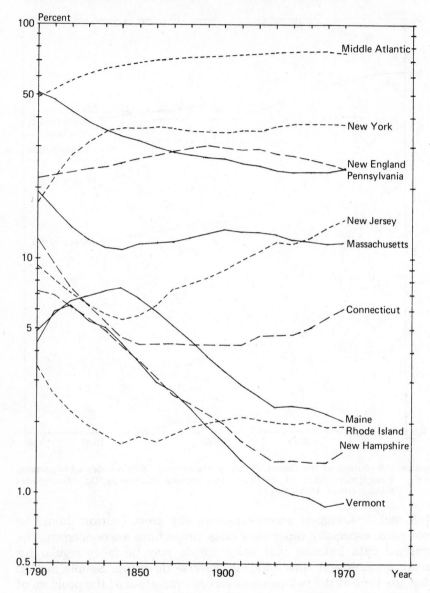

nomic dominance or the effect of "urban sprawl" crossing state lines, such as in southwestern Connecticut, and to a lesser extent in southeastern New Hampshire—are not made explicit in the model parameters, so trend reversals are very difficult to project.

We shall drop our discussion of simple mathematical models of share trends at this point. The reader interested in applying such models should refer to the previous chapter for computation details and discussions regarding the logic underlying the various functions. In the sections that follow, we shall consider some techniques that have been developed specifically for share type data.

The 1952 Census Bureau Ratio Method

The United States Bureau of the Census presently projects the populations of states using the cohort-component method. In 1952, the Census Bureau's projections of state populations made use of a ratio—or share—technique [1]. They were prepared by Helen L. White and Jacob S. Siegel and represent the Census Bureau's early efforts to produce "in-house" projections. Until the mid-1940s they relied on the Scripps Foundation, with its experienced staff, to provide national and state forecasts. The fact that the Census Bureau has abandoned this particular methodology does not mean that the technique lacks merit. It may still be of use for projecting populations of small areas where detailed age-specific fertility and migration rate data are lacking.

Before settling on their ratio method, Census Bureau analysts evaluated a number of alternative techniques giving due consideration to "validity and cost." The cost element was particularly important because electronic computers were not generally available in those days and the work had to be done by hand. Even methods that appear simple involved a good deal of repetitious calculation and its attendant risk of error. The present-day luxury of being able to manipulate parameter values one day and receive reams of printed results the following morning did not exist then. Trial and error work was very time-consuming. Results of some of the "validity" testing can be found in an article by White [2].

The Census Bureau summarized their method as follows:

Briefly, the ratio method consists of (1) extrapolating the ratio of (a) the population of the area for which a projection is desired to (b) the population of a larger area which includes the first area and for which acceptable population projections are already available; and (2) applying the extrapolated ratios to the population projections for the larger area to obtain projections for the smaller area. In preparing the projections for geographic divisions shown in this report, the ratio of the division total to the United States total was extrapolated and the extrapolated ratio was applied to projections of the United States total population; in preparing projections for States, the ratio of the State total to the appropriate division total was extrapolated and the extrapolated ratio was applied to the projections of the division total. Regional projections were obtained by combining the appropriate divisional figures [3].

The general method, then, is what can be called a "two step ratio technique." This approach should be used in preference to a one step method if it is known that identifiable clusters of the units to be projected behave differently from one another. We have already seen where U.S. regions and divisions vary in their share trends and it is reasonable to assume that the component elements of each division—in this case, states—tend to follow the general growth trend of the larger unit. That is to say, Pacific Coast states may be expected to grow more rapidly than New England states, if 1940–1970 growth patterns hold. Naturally, the better the definition of a cluster of elements as a homogeneous entity, the more effective will be the projection method.

Ratio data for three decades—1920–1930, 1930–1940, and 1940–1950—were assembled and evaluated. On the basis of the evaluation, the divisions and states were each placed into one of the three following groups: (1) areas with a constant direction of change over the entire three decade period; (2) areas with consistent change direction during the second two decades, but with a different direction in 1920–1930; and (3) areas where the direction of change differed in 1940–1950 from what it was in 1930–1940. Areas falling into the first group were assigned a rate of change in their ratio which was "the same as the average annual rate of change in the ratio for 1920–50, 1930–50, or 1940–50, whichever was the least in absolute value (closest to zero)" [4]. Second group areas were assigned the lesser of the annual rates for periods 1930–1950 or 1940–1950. Areas in the third group were given rates equal to one-half of the average annual rate for the decade 1940–1950. All rates were also trended under the assumption that their annual change would linearly decrease to zero in 50 years; values between initial and terminal rate values were therefore linearly interpolated. "Preliminary values of the ratios for July 1, 1955, and July 1, 1960, were then computed by multiplying the ratios for July 1, 1950, serially by one plus the projected annual rates of change for the appropriate years. The preliminary projected ratios for geographic divisions, and for the states within each division, for 1955 and for 1960, were then adjusted to sum to exactly 100 percent" [5].

The Census Bureau report points out that

The usual formula for the average annual rate of change in a series, say a series of proportions, is $t\sqrt{P_1/P_0} - 1$, where P_1 represents the proportion at the end of the period, P_0 the proportion at the beginning of the period, and t represents the number of years in the period. In order to simplify the procedure, the average annual rate of change was approximated by use of the formula $\dfrac{2(P_1 - P_0)}{t(P_1 + P_0)}$, which gives a satisfactory approximation when P_1/P_0 falls between 0.5 and 1.5 for the 10-, 20-, and 30-year time spans considered here [6].

It should be noted that the Census Bureau projections were only for a ten year period. This time limitation represents prudent thinking for two reasons. First, computation time and cost are minimized. Second, and more important, the risk of a share trend shifting its direction is small compared to the risk of such an event happening over a longer period of time.

An example of the 1952 Census Bureau ratio method is worked out in detail in Exhibit 4–1. Once again, the object is to project the population of Pennsylvania. The projection date is April 1, 1970, and the data base is the 30 year period 1930–1960. The main differences from the Census Bureau method are in the formula used to obtain annual change rates, in that the mid-decade projection point was not used, and in that no adjustment was made to change the projection date to July 1. The Census Bureau made the time adjustment by extrapolating the April 1, 1950, shares to July 1. The exact method of extrapolation is not indicated in the methodology statement; one plausible approach would be to use the 1940–1950 annual rate of change to provide an April 1, 1951, share and then to linearly interpolate one-quarter of the difference between the 1950 and 1951 shares, and adjust using formula (4.1).

Our rate change computation makes use of the formula containing the tth root of the ratio of shares observed where t is the number of years in the observation period—10, 20, or 30. We were able to use the more difficult formula because modern pocket calculators are often capable of obtaining the tth root of a number as a result of the operator pressing one button and we assume that most analysts have access to such devices.

The reader will observe that the technique projected the population of Pennsylvania in 1970 to be within 1.5 percent of the number

☆ ☆

Exhibit 4–1

Projection Using Census Bureau Ratio Method

The method is a two step (or more) ratio technique that operates on the divisional and state levels and which may be extended to smaller areas such as counties. The computation sequence indicated below can be carried out concurrently for all areas up to the point where the ratios are converted to population values; at that point, the national or control population must be stepped down or disaggregated by the various ratios sequentially from the least to the greatest geographic detail. The detailed computations below are for the three states in the Middle Atlantic division.

The first step is to examine state shares of the division to determine the migration group:

Shares of Middle Atlantic Division

Year	New York	New Jersey	Pennsylvania
1930	0.47935	0.15389	0.36676
1940	0.48945	0.15106	0.35949
1950	0.49166	0.16030	0.34804
1960	0.49116	0.17756	0.33128
Group	3	2	1

Group 1 is constant direction of share change, 1930–1960; group 2 is constant direction for 1940–1960; and group 3 is a residual category for places whose 1950–1960 growth direction differed from 1940–1950 growth.

Next, we obtain the ratios $(P_1/P_0) - 1$, where appropriate to the migration group.

Share Change Ratios

Period	New York	New Jersey	Pennsylvania
'60/30			−0.096739
'60/40		0.175427	−0.078472
'60/50	−0.001017	0.107673	−0.048155

These are annualized using the formula $|\sqrt[t]{(P_1/P_0)} - 1|$, where t is the number of years in the period P_0, P_1.

Annual Share Change Ratios

Period	New York	New Jersey	Pennsylvania
'60/30			0.0030828
'60/40		0.0081144	0.0037844
'60/50	0.0001016	0.0102786	0.0047142
Selection:	0.0000508	0.0081144	0.0030828

Note that, in accordance with procedure outlined in the text, the New York ratio is half of that reported as the annual value for 1950–1960. These selected annual ratios are trended toward zero for each year of a decade under the assumption of linear convergency to zero over a span of 50 years as follows:

Ten Year Convergence

Year	Multiplier	New York	New Jersey	Pennsylvania
	Basic Ratio:	0.000051	0.008114	0.003083
1	0.98	0.000050	0.007952	0.003021
2	0.96	0.000040	0.007789	0.002960
3	0.94	0.000048	0.007627	0.002898
4	0.92	0.000047	0.007465	0.002836
5	0.90	0.000046	0.007703	0.002775
6	0.88	0.000045	0.007140	0.002713
7	0.86	0.000044	0.006978	0.002651
8	0.84	0.000043	0.006816	0.002590
9	0.82	0.000042	0.006654	0.002528
10	0.80	0.000041	0.006491	0.002466

Adding 1.0 to each of the basic and trended ratios and cumulatively multiplying over all years, we obtain: New York, 1.000455; New Jersey, 1.074606; and Pennsylvania, 1.027779. The ratios for New York and Pennsylvania must be changed to values of less than unity to correct for the taking of absolute annual ratio, above. Hence: New York, 0.999545; and Pennsylvania, 0.972221. Multiplying these by the 1960 divisional shares and correcting the result so that the projected 1970 shares sum to unity, we obtain: New York, 0.48907; New Jersey, 0.19008; and Pennsylvania, 0.32085. The Middle Atlantic divisional share of the nation, obtained using the same methodology, was 0.18328. Since the 1970 United States population was 203,235,298, the projected divisional population is 37,248,965 (compared to an actual 37,199,040). The projected state populations and equivalent enumerated populations are: New York, 18,217,352 (18,241,266); New Jersey, 7,080,283 (7,168,164); and Pennsylvania, 11,951,330 (11,793,909).

☆ ☆

enumerated that year. The New York State projected value was 18,217,352 and the census count was 18,241,266—a difference of a little more than 0.1 percent. Although such precision is comforting, it should be kept in mind that Pennsylvania and New York are both large states possessed of considerable population "intertia." That is, short run departures from trends are not too likely, although it must be confessed that New York was a state that fell into the third group, having changed direction between 1940–1950 and 1950–1960. Pennsylvania, however, had its share moving in a consistent direction over the 30 year observation period.

Perhaps the main limitation of this technique and others like it lies in the fact that future outcomes are largely determined by past behavior, and little insight is to be gained with regard to events that might shape future population size. Judgment enters into this technique to the extent that a selection of the data base period is necessary and that rules are made regarding which aspects of the past behavior are to be selected as the model for future behavior. An additional assumption was made regarding dampening of rates of change, an assumption that posited that each state and divisional share will become fixed 50 years in the future. These assumptions could have been altered or ignored. On the other hand, the analyst is still limited to selecting among historical situations—no truly new share behavior patterns are possible using this technique.

The Ratio-Trend Method

A technique that is conceptually similar to the Census Bureau's 1952 ratio method is Jerome Pickard's "ratio-trend projection methodology" [7]. Pickard's method is also a step-down technique. The nation is divided into ten regions which, in turn, are broken down into either "urban region zones" or "free-standing metropolitan county areas." Then, the "urban region zones" are stepped down to their component elements, "metropolitan areas" and "urban region fringe areas." The reason behind the choice of these particular kinds of areas is that Pickard is interested in projecting metropolitan area populations, and if he is to use a ratio method, he must at each step project the area he is interested in as well as a residual area that is discarded before going on to the next step.

Pickard wishes to project farther into the future than did the Census Bureau analysts, and to do this, he decided to use a slightly different set of rules regarding the definition of the data base and its extrapolation into the future. Specifically, "the assumption is made that for a shorter term projection, a shorter historical trend is used and for a longer period of projection, a longer historical period is used" [8].

Rather than deal with shares directly, Pickard transformed shares (expressed as percentages) into logarithms. Rates of share change are thereby expressed as differences of the logarithms. Once the various manipulations required by the methodology are completed, the projected share must be transformed back into a percentage from its logarithmic form.

The most complicated part of Pickard's model is his weighting scheme for the historical data. His logic is that the more recent part of the historical trend should have more impact on future population shares than should share trends early in the observation period. To illustrate how this weighting is made operational, Pickard uses the following example: Say we wish to project the change in the population share from 1960 to 1970. We observe that the mid-point of that decade is the year 1965, a backward distance of ten years. The distance to the second most recent observation period, 1940 to 1950, is the 20 years to the year 1945. This second decade is twice as distant as is the first decade. Taking the reciprocals of 10 and 20 and multiplying the results by 100 we obtain: $1/10 = 0.1 \times 100 = 10$; $1/20 = 0.05 \times 100 = 5$. The ratio 10/5 conveniently reduces to 2/1, and the projection formula becomes

$$D1960-70 = \frac{2(D1950-60) + (D1940-50)}{3} \tag{4.2}$$

where D is the difference between the logarithms of the percent share values. In projecting the period 1970–1980, Pickard does not want to make use of the 1960–1970 projected share change, so the first observation is the 1950–1960 decade which is now 20 years removed in time. He also wishes to make use of change data going back 50 years—to the decade 1920–1930—so as to provide four successive time-distance values. Presumably, Pickard wants his observation period to be twice as long as his forecast period. He obtains reciprocal weights of 5, 3 1/3, 2 1/2, and 2. These are multipled by 6 to obtain whole numbers that, in turn, are divided by 5 to arrive at the weights: 6, 4, 3, and a number that is rounded down to 2. The resulting projection formula is

$$\tag{4.3}$$

$$D1970-80 = \frac{6(D1950-60) + 4(D1940-50) + 3(D1930-40) + 2(D1920-30)}{15}.$$

Note that in each formula, the sum of the weightings is divided by the sum of the weighting coefficients. Pickard next chooses to skip 1990 and to project the share in the year 2000. To do this, he uses a two decade jump that starts with the midpoint of the period 1960–1980. This midpoint is 1970, which is 20 years distant from the midpoint of the projection period 1990. In this instance, he is making use of the projected share in 1980 and its projected difference from the empirical 1960 share. Two 20 year empirical observation periods are used in addition to the projected 20 year base period. These provide observation distances of 20, 40, and 60 years from the forecast midpoint and, in turn, become weights of 5, 2 1/2, and 1 2/3 which are adjusted and become weighting coefficients in the formula

$$D1980-2000 = \frac{6(D1960-80) + 3(D1940-60) + 2(D1920-40)}{11}. \tag{4.4}$$

Pickard notes one drawback in his technique: The extrapolation of logarithmic change for rapidly growing areas may result in ratios that "run away"—become unreasonably large and require large adjustments so that the shares for all subareas sum to 100 percent. His solution is to transform the observed shares in such cases into their complements, obtain logarithms of the complements, and then take the differences of the logarithms, as before. That is, if a subarea's ratio to the larger area is 0.17 for one census and 0.26 at the next census, the ratios are respectively transformed to 0.83 and 0.74. Due to the property of logarithms, the differences between the logarithms of the transformed ratios are less than the differences between the logarithms of the untransformed ratios. His rule for making the transform is: If the ratio is larger in the more recent of two observation points (censuses), the transform is applied. Otherwise, it is not.

An example is worked out in Exhibit 4–2 using the three states in the Middle Atlantic division. It is assumed that the most recent available data are from the 1900 census and that we wish to project divisional shares for 1910, 1920, and 1940, which is analogous to Pickard's situation in the 1960s. In our example, the complement-transform rule was not applied in order to simplify the presentation. As it happens, the results of this exercise are not as impressive in terms of accuracy as were the results of the Census Bureau method, even if first decade's projection alone is considered. By 1940 the New York and Pennsylvania shares are around 10 percent off their census values, while the New Jersey error is nearly 5 percent.

These fragmentary results offer little proof as to which of the two ratio methods is superior. Pickard's method is conceptually attractive in that it does weight the recent past more than the distant past.

☆ ☆

Exhibit 4–2

Projection Using Ratio-Trend Method

In this example, it is assumed that 1900 census data are the most recent available for Pennsylvania and that it is our intention to project the state's population for various dates out to 1940. The control region is the Census Bureau's Middle Atlantic division. To simplify the presentation, only computations for Pennsylvania are shown.

The historical data for Pennsylvania are:

Year	Ratio, R to region	log (100R)	Δ log R
1860	0.38963	1.59065	—
1870	0.39973	1.60177	0.01112
1880	0.40802	1.61068	0.00891
1890	0.41382	1.61681	0.00603
1900	0.40778	1.61043	−0.00638

We then define the midpoint of the 1860–1870 decade (1865) as $D1$. $D2$ is 1875, $D3$ is 1885, $D4$ is 1895, $D5$ is 1905, $D6$ is 1915, $D7$ is 1925, and $D8$ is 1935. The historical data are used to solve the following three equations from Pickard:

$$D5 = \frac{2(D4) + (D3)}{3} = [2(-0.00638) + (0.00603)]/3$$

$$= [(-0.01276) + (0.00603)]/3 = (-0.00673)/3 = -0.00224$$

$$D6 = \frac{6(D4) + 4(D3) + 3(D2) + 2(D1)}{15}$$

$$= [6(-0.00638) + 4(0.00603) + 3(0.00891) + 2(0.01112)]/15$$

$$= [(-0.03828) + (0.02412) + (0.02673) + (0.02224)]/15$$

$$= 0.03481/15 = 0.00232$$

$$(D7 + D8) = \frac{6(D5 + D6) + 3(D3 + D4) + 2(D1 + D2)}{11}$$

$$= [6(0.0008) + 3(-0.00035) + 2(0.02003)]/11$$

$$= [(0.00048) + (-0.00105) + (0.04006)]/11$$

$$= 0.03949/11 = 0.00359$$

In logarithms, the projected percentage shares of the division are

    1910:   1.61043 − 0.00224 = 1.60819
    1920:   1.60819 + 0.00232 = 1.61051
    1940:   1.61051 + 0.00359 = 1.61410

and the respective percentages are 40.569, 40.786, and 41.124. Combining these shares with similarly calculated shares for New York and New Jersey and adjusting so that they sum to 100 percent, we obtain:

Year	New York	New Jersey	Pennsylvania
1910	46.475	12.986	40.539
1920	45.505	13.869	40.626
1940	43.528	15.815	40.656

The actual shares were:

Year	New York	New Jersey	Pennsylvania
1910	47.182	13.135	39.683
1920	46.652	14.177	39.171
1940	48.945	15.105	35.949

☆ ☆

It is also a consistent technique in that rules are simple and judgment is largely ruled out. The main intrusion of judgment is in the area of the length of the historical projection base. On the other hand, the Census Bureau method also has clear rules, and its judgmental element permits some flexibility. Careful choice of assumptions may yield better results than blind extrapolation of the past.

SHARES OF OTHER VARIABLES

The techniques presented in this section differ from the methods outlined in the previous discussion in that the concept of shares of parts to the whole is slightly modified. In one example, shares of *changes* in parts and wholes are measured and projected. The other example considers the relationship of shares of *attributes* of the populations of the parts and wholes and how the shares of the population values themselves may be seen to depend on them.

Apportionment Method
The apportionment method described here is the one used by Pickard [9] in one of his projections of metropolitan areas made

before he became convinced of the superiority of the ratio-trend method. Pickard does not project the future share of a subarea to a larger area. Rather, the apportionment method projects the subarea's share of the population *change* experienced by the larger area. This projection is based on the historical shares of the larger area's growth that were contributed by the subarea. Usually these techniques treat areas having population decline—or negative growth—as having a zero share of the larger area's growth.

Pickard operationalizes the method by stipulating that the distance into the future that is being projected must rely on an historical period of equal length as its model. That is, a projection from 1970 to the year 2000 involves a 30 year distance, which means that the historical base period must be the 30 year interval 1940—1970. A 1970—1980 projection would use a 1960—1970 base, and so forth. In each case, the subarea's ratio of past growth of the larger area is applied to the future growth of the larger area in order to determine the amount of numerical growth to be experienced by the subarea. The population of the larger area is projected separately, presumably using the best available technique.

An example is worked out in Exhibit 4—3. Once again we use Pennsylvania as the subject area and we assume that we have data for all censuses up through 1900 and must project ahead to the year 1970. The larger population is the United States; no effort was made to adjust for territorial annexations or admissions of states in the example, even though it is advisable to strive for geographical comparability in such exercises. For the projection of the U.S. population, the enumerated population from the censuses of 1910 through 1970 were used. In other words, we have set up the example so that projection error for the larger population has been eliminated.

Notice that the Pennsylvania–U.S.A. population growth ratios fluctuate so that the ratio for the period 1820—1900 is about the same as it is for the decade 1890—1900, even though the ratio reaches a low point at 20 years backward distance. This ratio equivalence is happenstance. However, we may expect a dampening in fluctuations as the ratio is taken for increasingly long base periods and the variability of data for any single decade becomes submerged in the aggregate.

The numerical results of the example come close to the actual population values for the years 1910, 1920, and 1930; the error is in the range of plus or minus 100 to 150 thousand. Thereafter, the projection diverges from the enumerated population through 1970, when the margin of error is on the order of 4.5 million. These results

☆ ☆

Exhibit 4-3

Projection Using Apportionment Method

Pennsylvania's population is projected from its 1900 population of 6,302,115 by taking the ratio of cumulated historical population growth for the state to cumulated national growth for periods of time equal to the length of the projection period. For instance, the 1900–1920 state growth uses the state-nation ratio for the period 1880–1900. In this example, the historical ratio is applied to known national numerical growth; under normal circumstances, projected national or regional values would be used.

The historical data are:

Population Change

Period	Pennsylvania	U.S.A.	Ratio
1890–1900	1,044,002	13,232,402	0.078897391
1880–1900	2,019,224	26,022,959	0.077593943
1870–1900	2,780,164	37,653,797	0.073834891
1860–1900	3,395,900	44,768,847	0.075854087
1850–1900	3,990,329	53,020,292	0.075260412
1840–1900	4,578,082	59,142,715	0.077407370
1830–1900	4,953,882	63,346,148	0.078203366

The projections are:

Period	U.S.A.	Ratio	Change	Pennsylvania Projected	Pennsylvania Actual
1900–1910	16,016,328	0.078897391	1,263,646	7,565,761	7,665,111
1900–1920	29,809,369	0.077593943	2,313,026	8,615,141	8,720,017
1900–1930	46,990,456	0.073834891	3,469,535	9,771,650	9,631,350
1900–1940	55,952,401	0.075854087	4,244,218	10,546,333	9,900,180
1900–1950	75,113,630	0.075260412	5,653,082	11,955,197	10,498,012
1900–1960	103,111,007	0.077407370	7,981,552	14,283,667	11,319,366
1900–1970	126,999,758	0.078203366	9,931,809	16,233,924	11,793,909

☆ ☆

are not particularly important in themselves but they do serve to highlight a disadvantage of the particular apportionment technique being illustrated. That disadvantage is that a contradictory trend can easily be built into the projections. For example, a subarea could have experienced a decade-by-decade decline in its share of the growth of the nation or of the larger analytical area. Yet as the historical aggregate time series of ratios of growth becomes increasingly long, the ratios will increasingly include data from the decades when the growth ratio was higher, thereby forcing the projected share of future national growth to become larger. The result would be the opposite for subareas experiencing increasing shares of growth—eventually, the projections would reflect to a certain extent a past era when the subarea's growth share was small. It can be argued that this is not a serious disadvantage because apportionment methods are seldom used to project more than a few decades into the future and such long term effects would be minimal. It can also be said that the inclusion of such countertrend effects is good because it serves to dampen trends, keeping trends from "running away." These objections have some merit, but they should not obscure the fact that apportionment methods can perpetuate the past into the future just as blindly as any mathematical trending technique.

Ratio-Correlation Method

The ratio-correlation method is primarily used as a means of estimating populations, but the technique might also be used for making projections. Structurally, it is a multiple regression model of the kind described in the last chapter. The only difference lies in the data used in the model. The dependent variable is the subarea share of the analytical area population. Independent variables are subarea shares of attributes of the populations. Possible attribute data series might be labor force, manufacturing industry employment, the rate of natural increase, housing starts, per capita expenditure on education—in short, almost any data series that the analyst suspects might be indicative of relative population change. The length of the base period used to calibrate the model and the particular variables to be used in the model will depend on the availability and quality of the historical data as well as the results of significance tests made during the calibration phase.

Perhaps the simplest approach to calibration would be to use a stepwise multiple regression program from one of the standard statistical packages for computers. The virtue of the stepwise routine is that it permits the analyst to see the amount of precision in the estimate of the dependent variable gained by the addition of each available independent variable beginning with the variable that "explains" the largest amount of variance in the prediction. The independent variables are inserted one step or iteration at a time in descending order of their explanatory ability. Typically, after only a few independent variables are inserted, the gains in additional explained variance become small, and the analyst then faces the decision as to when it is no longer worth while adding new independent variables. Once this cutoff has been determined, the analyst simply reads off the variable weighting coefficients from the step in the multiple regression computation that contains all of the desired independent variables and he is almost ready to begin making projections. Just one small matter needs attention.

The "small matter" standing between the analyst and his projections is the need to project the independent variables themselves. In the case of estimates, the coefficients in the equation are assigned values for a past period of time, and it is assumed that these relationships will hold into the near future; this assumption is the same for projections. The difference is that the estimates then make use of empirical data that are temporally coextensive with the estimate date, whereas no empirical data can exist in the present for future events. The one exception is where there is a lagged effect, when the independent variable preceeds the dependent variable in time, as in the case of machine tool orders being an index of future economic changes. In other words, the statistical association measurement tool—multiple regression—may provide a good "fit" or variance "explanation" of population share. But as good as this fit might be for the past, there is no guarantee that the relationships expressed by the coefficient values of the independent variables will hold in the future, even if the future independent variable data were known. But these future data are not known. They also must be projected, and therefore are themselves prone to error. Hence, the only reason to use a ratio-correlation or multiple regression type model is when the analyst is convinced that he can project the independent variable shares more accurately than he can population shares, and is further convinced that the relationship embodied in the coefficient values are likely to remain stable over time.

DENSITY MODELS

A commonly used proxy for population in population projection activities is population density—the number of persons per square unit of land area or floor space. The usual units of land area used in projection studies are miles and kilometers; occasionally acres and hectares are also used. The typical density model is similar to the other models discussed in the present chapter in that populations of subareas are tentatively calculated and then are forced to sum to an independently projected control total. The use of an independent control total is desirable because "projecting up" from the parts to the whole more often than not results in unreasonably large values for the whole. This is particularly important where the analytical area is a labor market region or metropolitan area where future population size is determined to a considerable degree by the number of jobs that exist at the future date. An area which is likely to have slow growth in the number of jobs cannot be expected to have a rapidly growing population, no matter what short term subarea density trends might indicate.

Density models are most often used to project subunits of cities or metropolitan areas. These subunits typically are census tracts or groups of census tracts. Minor civil divisions with relatively permanent boundaries such as towns or townships are also used in states where they exist. Such units usually contain relatively small populations—1,000 to 10,000 is the expected range. Small populations are difficult to project using complicated methods such as the cohort-component technique because of the degree of random variability in symptomatic data on fertility and net migration caused by the small size of their age-sex group data "cells." Some important historical data are not even available; fertility data are seldom recorded on the basis of census tracts. All of these difficulties, coupled with the large number of such units that are found within metropolitan areas, usually compel the analyst to attempt projections of total population only.

The problem with directly projecting total population for metropolitan subareas is that past trends are often an especially poor guide to future behavior. This is particularly true in the areas that are undergoing suburbanization or that are about to do so. A suburbanizing area is experiencing explosive population growth; population size can double or triple over a period of half a decade. If such short term trends were extrapolated using almost any of the mathematical function models described earlier, the analyst would obtain very small areas containing incredibly large populations. Likewise, areas that form the ring surrounding the suburbanizing belt, and which one would expect to grow in the future, would be projected as growing very slowly because they grew slowly in the past. Obviously, this set of circumstances is not satisfactory; the usual trend model will not work well.

It therefore seems necessary to place an upper limit on population size to prevent projected populations increasing to unreasonable levels. One possibility would be to assign an asymptotic limit to population size for each subarea and then employ a model such as a Gompertz or a logistic curve. The most reasonable way to do this has been to use a density value as the control. This is because the subunits are likely to vary in area, and whereas it might be difficult to decide that a larger area can hold 15,000 persons while a smaller area can only contain 9,000, it is relatively easy to stipulate that neither can contain more than 3,500 persons per square mile. The task of placing population constraints is further eased by the fact that most cities and many suburban areas are zoned so that they cannot contain more than a limited number of persons per unit area. However, one risk in using zoning ordinances as a control for population forecasts is the possibility that the zoning rules would be changed in the future.

A few words should be said about the problem of areas declining in population. It is well known that many of America's "central cities" are losing population. But population losses are also being experienced in older suburban areas. This is because suburbanizing areas are usually settled by young married couples who are about to have children or who are bringing very young children with them. After 15 or 20 years, the children become old enough to leave home to go to college, seek work, or marry—and they often do so, leaving the parents behind. Where there once were mile after mile of new houses, each containing an average of four or five people, we now find mile after mile of somewhat obsolescent houses containing perhaps two and a half or three persons on the average. Density models should take declining household size into account, but often do not do so.

An alternative approach to density modeling is to project the number of housing units in an area, preferably by type—that is, single family, duplex, multiple. By using the units themselves, there is less ambiguity as to whether an area is "filled up" with respect to the zoned number of structures per acre. Population could then be projected by multiplying the projected housing units by a projected mean persons per housing unit coefficient. Such household size measures would be modeled independently and could be based on the age structure, fertility rates, and mortality rates of areas with suburban characteristics. In addition, the model would have to take into account the spinoff of young adults from their parental family. Such a household size model would be similar in complexity to the cohort-component projection methods that will be discussed later. Perhaps that is why the two stage model suggested here is uncommon. At any rate, once population values were calculated for each subarea, the aggregate metropolitan area population would have to be determined and then compared to the independently projected control total and then the projected number of housing units in each area would have to be adjusted accordingly.

Two density models are presented in the sections that follow. They by no means exhaust the possible ways of using density as a means of arriving at future populations of comparatively small areas, but, in conjunction with the discussion in the present section, they should present the reader with a picture of approaches that have actually been attempted in recent years.

Genesse-Finger Lakes Region Dispersion Model

The model presented in this section was used by the Genesee-Finger Lakes Regional Planning Board in 1971 to project the populations of 111 minor civil divisions in eight western New York State counties surrounding the city of Rochester [10]. The primary analyst for the project was Bruce B. Herbert. As has been the case for all of the techniques discussed in this chapter, the model has two stages—in the present case, the regional population is projected by age and sex using a cohort-component method, and the resulting total population values served as controls for the minor civil division (MCD) model which projects only total populations for the region's subareas.

Underlying the model is the concept that urban centers expand into surrounding territory as their population grows. At any given time, it is possible, if data are available, to abstract the status of growth and its geographical dispersion by drawing a population density profile in terms of the mean persons per square land unit area at various distances from the center of the city. The shape of this profile may be expected to change over time as the center of the city declines in density as stores, offices, and warehouses crowd out residences, while outlying areas increase their population density as suburban residential tracts are built and occupied. This is an idealized concept. It provides a general description of the growth pattern of American and Canadian cities in the present century, but each urban region presents variations on the theme.

Topography, historical accident, the location and nature of satellite centers—all of these factors and more can alter the density pattern. In the case of the Rochester region, the perturbing elements tend to be minimal. The city has comparatively "clean" industries such as photographic products, optical equipment, and copying machines. This means that there is little concern about avoiding areas that are downwind of pollution sources. In fact, some of the nicer suburbs are downwind of the city. Topographically, there are few constraints other than Irondequoit Bay to the northeast, and Lake Ontario which is about eight miles north of the center of Rochester. Otherwise, the portion of the region near Rochester is either flat or rolling hills. Finally, there are comparatively few satellite centers in the entire region and those that exist are not large. All of these factors indicate that the Rochester region is suitable for density gradient projection.

One hundred and eleven subareas were defined for the region: 109 were towns, and the others were the city of Rochester and that portion of the Tonawanda Indian Reservation lying within the regional boundary. The three cities of Batavia, Canandaigua, and Geneva were each included with the surrounding towns. Geographic centers were determined for each MCD and grid coordinates were assigned for the purpose of establishing distances from the center of regional population. Population density per square mile was calculated and transformed into natural logarithms (logarithms to the base e) for each subarea for the years 1940, 1950, 1960, and 1970. Distances from each MCD to each of a number of selected points within Rochester were also calculated. The transformed density data were then fitted to distance using a least squares method on a polynomial of the form

$$ln Y_i = B + B_1 X_i + B_2 X_i^2 + B_3 X_i^3 + \ldots + B_n X_i^n + E_i \tag{4.5}$$

where i refers to the ith MCD, Y is population per square mile, X_i is the air distance in kilometers from the center of the ith MCD to the selected point in Rochester, E_i is the error term for the ith MCD, and B are coefficients selected by minimizing the sum of the squared error terms. The lowest value of the sums of squared errors was chosen as the regional center. As it happened, this point was the same for all four census years. The model finally selected was a polynomial of degree six that explained 91 percent of the variance for the 40 subareas within a 25 mile radius of the center and 63 percent of the variance for all MCDs.

It was decided that the model would be useful for projection work because the coefficients exhibited a nearly linear trend for 1950, 1960, and 1970. It was assumed that this trend would continue through the projection period. The projection equation may be written

$$ln Y_{i,\,t+10} = ln Y_{i,\,t} + \lambda (B_{1,\,t+10} - B_{1,\,t}) X_i + (B_{2,\,t+10} - B_{2,\,t}) X_i^2$$

$$+ \ldots + (B_{n,\,t+10} - B_{n,\,t}) X_i^n \tag{4.6}$$

where t is the starting year for the projections, 1970, and λ is an adjustment factor that forces the sum of the MCD populations to agree with the independent regional projection.

The model described above may be criticized on several grounds.

For one thing, it blindly projects past trends; only the independent regional population projection is subject to judgmental control. The report on the model concedes this point. We might add that trend line projections are not necessarily a bad thing, provided that the fact of trend continuation is stressed in any report on the results of the projection. If nothing else, such projections form a basis for comparisons with alternative projections. Unfortunately, alternative MCD projections were not made by the Rochester group. Another problem lies in the use of a six degree polynomial. Such a model is strictly empirical, giving no real insight into the dispersion process. Alternative models—perhaps probability density distributions with understandable parameters such as mean and modal values—might have been considered in preference to polynomial models if the loss of accuracy in fitting data had been slight.

Newling Model

A minor civil division projection technique involving density constraints that has been used in the state of New Jersey is the model developed by Bruce Newling [11]. The Newling model grew out of studies that indicated traditional growth models such as exponential and Gompertz curves were not well suited for projecting New Jersey minor civil division populations. New Jersey has a number of MCDs that have experienced suburbanization and its attendant high growth rates. Such rates are magnified by exponential models so that unreasonably large population values are projected. The high growth rates also tended to distort the Gompertz model, because the Gompertz curve and other related models having asymptotic limits are more accurately fitted when growth increments have begun to decline after having reached a maximum value.

The Newling model is based on the observation that New Jersey MCDs tended to have growth rates that were inversely related to population density at the start of the observation period 1950–1960. Following Greenberg [12] we may write the relationship

$$(1 + r_{d_t}) = A d_t^{-k} \tag{4.7}$$

where the expression to the left of the equality is the rate of growth in density for an area for a given density ceiling group; A is a constant for each such group, being the rate of growth where the density is one person per square unit; k is also a constant for each ceiling group, and it is the ratio of the growth rate to the rate of change in density; and d_t is density at time t. The density one time period in the future would be

$$d_{t+1} = (1 + r_{d_t})d_t = Ad_t^{-k} \, d_t = Ad_t^{1-k} \qquad .$$

Generalizing to m time intervals, we may obtain

$$d_{t+m} = \sqrt[k]{A} \, [d_t^{(1-k)^m} / \sqrt[k]{A} \, (1-k)^m] \qquad . \qquad (4.8)$$

The expression in the brackets approaches unity as m becomes large, so we may drop it to obtain

$$d_{t+m} = A^{1/k} \qquad (4.9)$$

or the kth root of A as the "critical density" or asymptotic density limit for the particular density ceiling group. This value can be either an upper or a lower asymptote, depending on whether or not the value of k exceeds unity.

Newling established parameter values in the following manner: County data for New Jersey were plotted on full log paper where the x axis was density in 1950, and the y axis was the ratio of population in 1960 to that in 1950. Three clusters seemed to emerge, and Newling indicated that each cluster was related to a fundamental type of settlement pattern in the state—urban, suburban, and rural. County data were used in preference to MCD data because Newling felt that the smaller number of observations, coupled with the reduction in random data variability concomitant with the larger populations involved, would make the clustering distinctions between the settlement patterns more distinct. Parameter values for each classification were obtained by linear least squares fits to logarithmically transformed data. MCDs were then assigned to one group or another depending on their position relative to lines drawn equidistant from the regression lines.

Newling's formulation of the model did not control projected population to independent projections of state or county populations, but this step was taken by Greenberg.

Greenberg, et al., also point out that great care must be taken when the county data are analyzed. This has to do with the problem of "outliers"—data plots that fall in odd parts of the plane, at some distance from the clustered data. He recommends two possible solutions to the problem [13]. One would be an analysis at the MCD scale, although the risk run here is that the picture might be even more obscured due to the more random character of the MCD data. The second alternative is to study other data on the outlier in an attempt to determine a cause for its behavior. They suggest that if the county, for reasons of topography and the artificality of its political boundaries, includes very densely populated areas along with areas that are uninhabitable or difficult to develop, then that county might well be excluded from the analyst's consideration. However, they point out that outliers could be harbingers of emerging land use patterns. In this case, the county should be included.

Examples of growth ratio and density data from New York State are presented in Figures 4—5 and 4—6. Figure 4—5 contains selected data for New York State counties with scale adjustments to reduce the flattening effect of the use of growth ratios. Figure 4—6 has plots of data for towns in the counties in the Western New York Planning Region—Erie County, which includes Buffalo; Niagara County, which lies to the north of Erie County; and Wyoming County, which is to the east of Erie County. Both sets of data are for the period 1950—1960—the same period used by Newling. The data clusters noted by Newling ran in an upper left to lower right direction, roughly parallel to one another at about a 45 degree angle from the horizontal. The present writer finds it difficult to observe such patterns in the New York data. The data appear to be random, and the use of imagination yields clusters that go in different directions; at one time the dots seem to run upper left to lower right, as Newling had it, and at another time, the "pattern" seems to go lower left to upper right, the opposite way.

This difficulty in replicating the model raises doubts as to the general usefulness of the technique. Perhaps some users will find the diagonal clusters emerging from their own data, and other analysts may choose to assume that Greenberg's or Newling's data are useful enough to be transferred without modification to their own region of interest. In any event, caution is urged for other reasons. For one thing, the Newling model does not seem to offer any means of transferring an MCD from one density ceiling group to another, short of intervention by the analyst. Another problem is that the use of one decade as a calibration period tends to introduce distortions peculiar to the historical circumstances that were obtained in that period of time. For instance, the use of the decade 1950—1960 builds into the growth ratio component of the model for more natural increase than occurred in the two preceding decades and in the subsequent decade and a half. The result of using that particular base period would be overstatement of growth in the future, unless the sum of the MCDs was controlled to an independently projected total.

OTHER TECHNIQUES

This final portion of the chapter contains reports on population projection techniques that are not readily classifiable under the section

Figure 4–5.   Newling Density Model Data, New York State
Counties with Positive Growth, 1950–1960

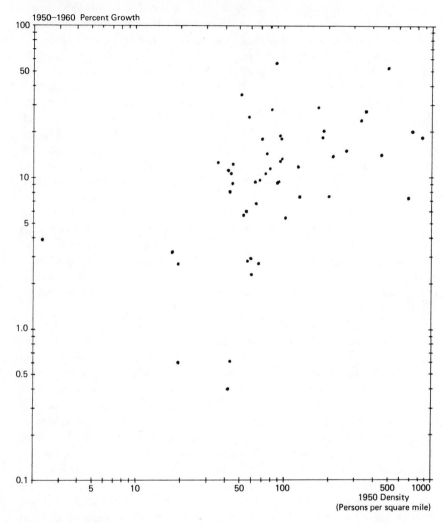

Source: U.S. Bureau of the Census, *U.S. Census of Population: 1960,* vol. I, *Characteristics of the Population,* Part 34, New York (Washington, D.C.: Government Printing Office, 1963), Table 6.

headings used above. All of the methods have found use at one time or another, although some have proved to be more popular than others. A technique that is seldom used is projecting population by applying ratios to projections of housing units; usually this method is used in the estimation of current population. Another method in-

Figure 4-6. Newling Density Model Data, Towns in Erie, Niagara, and Wyoming Counties, New York State, 1950–1960

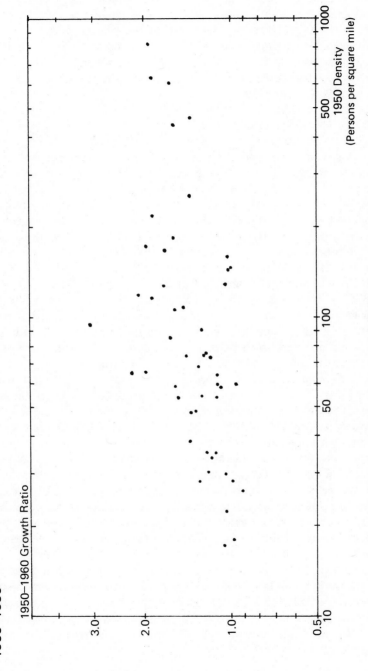

Source: New York State Office of Planning Services tabulation of U.S. Bureau of the Census data.

volves projecting population by applying a ratio to a projection of employment. This is a fairly common forecasting procedure, and there are variations on the method that range from fairly simple, such as the OBERS model discussed in the present chapter, to more complicated approaches that will be discussed in Chapter Eight. Yet another method is the covariance technique, which represents a relatively new development in forecasting. We shall begin by discussing the covariance technique.

Berry's Modified Covariance Method

The use of analysis of covariance as a means of projecting population was first proposed, to the best of the present writer's knowledge, by Isard and Carrothers in Isard's book on methods of regional analysis [14]. Since their chapter on population projection "draws heavily" on Carrothers' doctoral dissertation, the idea may have also appeared there. At any rate, they knew of no use of the technique in forecasting at that time. Since then, the only major application of the method known to this writer is the set of regional population projections developed by Brian Berry for the Commission on Population Growth and the American Future [15].

Before discussing Berry's projections, we shall first present an overview of covariance based on the treatment by Isard and Carrothers. In essense, covariance is a technique intended to enhance the statistical description of behavior by separating the independent variable into subgroupings based on nominal criteria.

Let us approach the concept step by step. A very simple way to describe the growth behavior of, say, a group of metropolitan areas, is to calculate the arithmetic mean of the growth ratios of the entire group of areas. Undoubtedly, there will be considerable dispersion of the growth ratios about the mean value. In order to improve our description, we must reduce the amount of dispersion of the data about a function (or plot on a scatter diagram) that represents our descriptive model. Now we shall postulate an independent variable that we think is related in some systematic way to population growth and plot the growth ratios against the independent variable (whatever it happens to be). Then we may calculate a regression line by fitting the data to a linear equation such as has been discussed in Chapter Three. The plot of the mean growth would be a horizontal line parallel to the x—or independent variable—axis and intersecting the y—or dependent variable—axis at the value of the mean. The regression line tends to follow the slope of the plotted data and the transition from the horizontal line representing the mean to the regression line may be visualized as a rotation of the line away from the horizontal until a point is reached where the sum of squared deviations of the data points from the line reaches a minimum.

Suppose we have reason to believe that regional location of the metropolitan areas is related to growth ratios. The concept "region" is nominal—a nonqualifiable category. If we separate the metropolitan areas by region and calculate mean growth ratios for each region (and if regional location is indeed associated with metropolitan growth), the plotted data from the previous example will tend to cluster in the vicinity of horizontal lines representing the regional means. If our hypothesis was correct, the sum of the squared variations about the regional means will be less than the sum of the variations about the overall mean and, possibly, even less than the sum of the variations about the regression line. What we have is an illustration of analysis of variance. Analysis of variance can be modified in a way analogous to what was done with the mean and the regression. Given that we have grouped the metropolitan areas by region and that we also have ordered their growth ratios by an independent variable, we can combine the two concepts and calculate regressions against the independent variable for those metropolitan areas within each region. It follows that the resulting regression lines may well differ in slope from one another. But if all goes well, the sum of the squared deviations from each regression line will be less than that of the analysis of variance and that of the overall regression. Isard and Carrothers caution that, in addition to the weaknesses inherent to regression analysis, analysis of covariance has some special problems. In particular, its "improvement in statistical explanation may be spurious and may lead the investigator to both fruitless paths and misleading conclusions. Stated in another way, covariance analysis may throw light on certain important relations; on the other hand, by attributing statistical significance to seemingly meaningful variables, it can obscure deep underlying causal bonds" [16].

Berry used a "modified" covariance methodology to project the populations of Daily Urban Systems (DUS). Berry states that the DUS term was coined by the planner C. A. Doxiadis in reference to commuting fields about large urban job markets. This concept was operationalized by Berry in the form of Bureau of Economic Analysis (BEA) economic areas. These are clusters of counties centered on metropolitan areas (where possible) which approximate job markets and which may cross state boundaries. One reason Berry gave for using the BEA areas was that considerable data were available—a consideration often ignored to the analyst's peril.

The first step in the analysis was to group the areas by size (the intervals were "roughly logarithmic": 100,000–225,000; 225,000–500,000: 500,000–1,000,000, and so forth) in 1960. Growth rates and interquartile ranges were calculated for the 1960–1970 decade. The following findings were noted:

1. The median growth rate increases progressively with size to a population of 1,000,000, where it stabilizes at about the national growth rate.
2. The interquartile range is stable for size classes of less than 1,000,000, and above that point also for the lower quartile. However, the upper quartile is markedly greater than elsewhere in the size class 1,000,000–2,225,000, indicating accelerated growth of many centers in this size range in particular.
3. The median growth rate is negative in the smallest size class, as is the lower quartile in the size range 225,000–500,000. This indicates that declining DUSs are disproportionately smaller.

    ... In brief, the argument is that the greater the size of the DUS, the more likely is growth to be determined by internal economies whose effects mirror the growth characteristics of the nation. The evidence for 1960–1970 clearly bears out this association, and we conclude that the size-growth-stability relationship should be built into any population forecasting procedure [17].

Berry then raises the question of deviations from the median for each size group. He suggests that this question may be answered by relating the 1960–1970 growth to the percent of total earnings in each economic area that were derived from agriculture, mining, manufacturing, federal government, and residentiary (nonbasic industry) activities. Again, to capture the flavor of the study, we quote Berry on his findings:

These comparisons show, for example, that the greater the earnings derived from agriculture the lower the maximum growth rate achieved. In particular, no DUS deriving more than 25 percent of its total earnings from agriculture grew between 1960 and 1970. Similarly (although few DUSs derive substantial income from mining), as the earnings from mining increased, the rate of population growth decreased; where mining earnings exceeded 12.5 percent, there was population decline. In the case of manufacturing, there is greater stability of the growth rate with increasing reliance upon a manufacturing base, but no systematic changes in the expected growth rate as manufacturing earnings increase. *The Federal Government, on the other hand, played a stimulative role in regional growth in the decade.* No DUS with more than 12.5 percent of its earnings derived from Federal sources lost population in the decade, *and the greater the Federal contribution to local earnings above this amount, the greater the*

decade growth rate. This finding is of particular importance, for it empha-
sizes that *among the consequences of the concentration of governmental
expenditures in particular places are systematic increases in the growth
rates of those places. . . .*

For the residentiary sector, the data are less clear. If the export-base
hypothesis is true, there should, of course, be no evident relationship between growth and the size of the residentiary sector; this is certainly true
for the majority of cases. On the other hand, it also has been argued that
residentiary activities can, at sufficient scale, give rise to sizable locally
generated growth; this, too, appears to be true where residentiary earnings
exceed 60 percent.

From the above, we can conclude that it will be important to differen-
tiate among types of economic bases as well as among size classes in any
population forecasting procedure. And to reiterate, a potential discretion-
ary ingredient is indicated; new and different spatial distributions of governmental expenditures seem capable of changing the location of growth
[18].

The findings discussed above form the basis for what Berry calls a
modified covariance projection methodology. This approach "is one
in which behavior of significant subgroups is related to behavior of
the whole in a manner analogous to the use of dummy variables in
regression" [19]. The unfortunate term "dummy variable" refers to
dichotomous nominal (or sometimes ordinal) variables such as
southern-nonsouthern, more than 20 percent agricultural labor
force–less than 20 percent agricultural labor force, and so forth.
These variables are entered in binary form, either as a 1 or as a 0.

A number of steps were taken to set up the data for the model.
First, eight approximately logarithmic size intervals from 100,000–
225,000 to 22,500,000–50,000,000 were established. DUSs within
each group were classed as either metropolitan or submetropolitan.
The resulting groups were further split on the basis of whether their
earnings were more or less than 25 percent agricultural. Then another
split was made on the basis of more or less than 12.5 percent earnings from mining, 12.5 percent federal, and 60 percent residentiary.
Those areas falling below all of the cutoff points were classed as
being "diversified." This subdivision process results in 256 possible
categories and it was found that only 33 actually had members.
Accordingly, 223 categories were discarded.

Second, mean and median growth rates were calculated for each
subgroup and, in turn, deviations of each subgroup from the national
averages were obtained. "Projected populations for each DUS were
then obtained by applying the relevant growth rates to the members
of each subgroup. Thus, the size, hierarchical status, and economic

base of each center played joint roles in determining their growth behavior. Individual centers could, of course, move from one subgroup to another in time as they grew" [20].

Finally, some adjustments were made for certain groups where 1960–1970 growth rates tended to be highly skewed upwards.

The projected national growth rates used were from the then current Census Bureau B and E series totals. Berry was prepared to force the sum of his projected DUSs to agree with the Census Bureau projection totals but he found that the agreement was so close that the exercise wasn't worth the effort.

In the way of criticism of Berry's model, let us first observe that the model appears to include many possible influences on growth behavior that are either implicit or ignored in the models discussed thus far. This is a virtue in that it permits a more critical evaluation of the assumptions behind the model. But Berry's modified covariance model falls victim to the curse of all other models that extrapolate the past in a blind manner—past conditions always change. Two years after the publication of Berry's article, the United States was plunging into an energy crisis that has served to stimulate the economies of areas that mine coal. A concurrent world food shortage has stimulated agriculture to the point where it is possible to speculate that populations in agricultural areas may cease their declines and stabilize, if not grow. There may be other conditions that will change and thereby undermine Berry's projections even further. The only answer is to include provisions for altering the future growth patterns of the subgroups—that is, to open the model to judgmental input.

Ratios to Employment—The OBERS Model

A number of projection models that relate future population to future jobs have been developed. In the present section, we shall present an important example of a comparatively simple link between future employment and future population—the OBERS model. The acronym OBERS comes from combining the initials of the Office of Business Economics and the Economic Research Service. The latter group is a branch of the U.S. Department of Agriculture and the former group was a part of the U.S. Department of Commerce, and has been renamed the Bureau of Economic Analysis (BEA) since the inception of the OBERS project in the mid-1960s. The work was initiated by the Water Resources Council in response to data needs of "public agencies engaged in comprehensive planning for the use, management and development of the nation's water and related resources" [21].

The projection of population is almost a by-product of the

OBERS system. The thrust of the model is economic, and population becomes a central concern to the model structure only where per capita income is considered. However, many users of OBERS data are primarily concerned about the population values emitted by the model, and the 1974 revision was prompted in part by certain criticisms raised by users of the population data.

Let it be emphasized here at the start of the discussion that any large scale modeling effort, such as OBERS, is a very difficult proposition. There are many constraining factors such as deadlines, budget, data availability, computer capabilities, and the human limitations that exist in any kind of undertaking. Given the state of the modeling art when the project was started, the staff had the choice of devoting their efforts to either producing a good economic model, working up a decent demographic model, or coming up with a so-so compromise model. Given that the orientation of the agencies concerned with the project was economic, the choice of an economic model was a wise one. Future versions of OBERS are likely to become more sophisticated demographically, particularly if the Commerce Department orders that the forecasting efforts of its subgroups, BEA and the Census Bureau, become better articulated.

The OBERS model operates on two levels—national, and economic area. There also are submodels that disaggregate economic area data into data for segments of the areas that are in different states; this is to permit the reaggregation of projection data on the state level. Additional procedures break out data for metropolitan areas (SMSAs). These procedures involve the trending of subarea shares of the economic areas. The present discussion shall ignore the projection of both national data and subregional data and stress the economic area or regional model which is the heart of the OBERS system.

Economic areas are projected using four models. One model projects basic industries, excluding agriculture and the armed forces. Another model deals with agriculture. A third model has to do with residentiary (nonbasic or nonexport) industries. A modification of this model projects property income, transfer payments, and personal contributions to social insurance. Finally, a fourth model derives population. Armed forces are treated separately, their domestic geographic distribution being held constant at 1971 levels.

Basic industries are projected by a "shift-share" model which

is designed to discern regional departures from national industrial growth rates. . . . In its simplest form, the shift-share technique distinguishes a proportional growth element and a differential growth element between a region and the Nation in each industry or income component.

$$E_{ij}^t = (E_{io}^t / E_{io}^x) E_{ij}^x + C_{ij}^{x-t}$$

The subscripts i, j refer to the ith industry and the jth region, the subscript o refers to a summation; when in the right hand position, it is the summation of regions (= the Nation); when in the left hand position, it is the summation of industry (= total employment or earnings). Subscripts t, x refer to the projected time point and the base point, respectively, C_{ij}^{x-t} equals the difference between the hypothetical level attained at the national growth rate of the industry over the period x to t and the regional level actually attained in the industry over the same period.

The first term on the right hand side of the equation assigns to industry i in region j a rate of change equal to that of industry i in the Nation (the proportional growth element). The second term on the right hand side is called the share, or regional share effect (C_{ij}) in shift-share analysis. It measures the difference between the proportional growth accounted for by the first term and the attained level of the left hand side. In basic, or export, industries, the share effect is presumed to be connected with some regional competitive advantage (or disadvantage if the term is negative) in the industry.

. . . That is, from the above equation the following relationship between changes in the regional share of the national industry (E_{ij}/E_{io}) and the regional share effect (C_{ij}) of the shift analysis holds:

$$E_{ij}^t / E_{io}^t = E_{ij}^x / E_{io}^x + C_{ij}^{x-t} / E_{io}^t$$

$$C_{ij}^{x-t} = E_{io}^t [E_{ij}^t / E_{io}^t - E_{ij}^x / E_{io}^x] = E_{io}^t (\Delta (E_{ij}/E_{io}) .$$

This technique yields a trend extension of a region's historic percent of the national total of earnings and employment in a given industry. It was accomplished by fitting a least squares regression line to the logarithm of the percentage shares and the logarithm of time. The use of the logarithm of percentages converted the data to a ratio scale so that the historical growth rate and the projected rate could be compared by observing the comparative slopes of the two portions of the trend line. The logarithm of time was used so as to dampen the slopes of rapidly rising or falling curves [22].

Judgmental modifications were made to the curves in cases where resource depletions were expected and where data were known to be weak or in error. Regional shares were forced to add to 100 percent and then were applied to the national industry projections.

Agricultural projections were based on state trends that were

stepped down to regions by use of substate trends. Using a 1947–
1970 historical base, trends were extended

> ... by the use of regression analysis in the following manner: (1) When the
> linear trend in the percentage contribution of a state to national output
> was increasing, the linear extension to 1990 was used as a constraint in a
> curvilinear "Spillman type" function. The contribution of a particular
> state to total national production in this case was projected to continue in-
> creasing through 2020 relative to the national total, but at a decreasing
> rate. The projected values can approach but never exceed the linear extra-
> polation for 1990. (2) Conversely, when the linear trend in the percent
> contribution of a state was decreasing, the value "zero" serves as a con-
> straint in the use of a "Cobb-Douglas type" function. In this case, the per-
> cent contribution of a given state will continue to decrease through 2020,
> but at a decreasing rate as it approaches zero. Thus the projection tech-
> nique provides for an extension of historical trends from 1970 through
> 2020 but at a decreasing rate of change [23].

The Spillman function has the form

$$Y = M - ab^X \tag{4.10}$$

where: Y is the dependent variable, state share of national produc-
tion; X is the independent variable, time; a and b are regression coefficients; and M is the linear trend extrapolation value for 1990.
Transforming the expression into logarithmic form, we obtain

$$M - Y = \text{antilog} (\log a + x \log b) \tag{4.11}$$

which is linear, and the parameter or coefficient values may be obtained by solving by the regular least squares method. The Cobb-
Douglas function may be written

$$Y = aX^b \tag{4.12}$$

where the meaning of the letters is the same as above. Its logarithmic
form is

$$\log Y = \log a + b \log X \tag{4.13}$$

and the coefficient values may be determined by the least squares
method also.

> Projected area earnings in each residentiary industry were derived from
> the following relationships: (1) the projected regional location quotient

(LQ) for the industry, i.e., the ratio of the industry's share of total area earnings to the industry's share of total national earnings; (2) the projected national ratio of earnings in the industry to total national earnings; and (3) projected earnings in total export industries in the area.

The area LQ's for each residentiary industry—item (1) above—were projected as follows: Analysis of changes in the area LQ's of individual residentiary industries from 1950 to 1971 showed that economic areas generally trend toward self-sufficiency in residentiary industries, i.e., LQ's trend toward 1.0. Analysis also showed that the slope of the trend depends upon the magnitude of the LQ. From this analysis, trend values for change in LQ's were set for several ranges of LQ value. These trend values were then applied to the LQ of each residentiary industry in 1969 and projected LQ's were determined for 1980, 1990, 2000, 2010 and 2020.

The projected national ratio of earnings in each residentiary industry to total national earnings (item 2 above) was calculated from the national industry earnings projections. . . .

Item 3 was derived by summing earnings of export industries already projected for each economic area.

Projected earnings for each residentiary industry in each area were derived as follows: First, the projected LQ for each residentiary industry (item 1) was multiplied by the projected national ratio of earnings in that residentiary industry to total national earnings (item 2). This computation gave the projected share of the residentiary industry in the area's total all-industry earnings. These shares were summed for all residentiary industries in the area. Subtracting the sum of all residentiary shares from unity gave the export industry share. Division of this share into the projected absolute value of total export industry earnings—already calculated—yielded projected total all-industry earnings for the area. To this total was applied the projected share of each residentiary industry in the area's total all-industry earnings (the product of items 1 and 2) to obtain the projected absolute value of earnings in each residentiary industry in each area. The sum of the area values for each residentiary industry was forced to equal the previously projected national total for the industry, thereby keeping the projected series within the framework of the national projections.

A comparable procedure was used to project residentiary employment by area. As in the case of the export industry projections, projected residentiary employment and earnings were reconciled [24].

In certain instances, adjustments were made in the definition of export and residentiary industries. Examples of residentiary industries that might be reclassified would be the hotel industry in Miami Beach and the printing industry in Albany, New York.

The sum of basic and residentiary industry earnings comprises about four-fifths of national personal income. Remaining major sources on income are property income, transfer payments, and contributions to social insurance (netted out of personal income).

These were projected in a manner similar to the method used for residentiary industries.

Now the stage is set for the population part of the projections. The reader might wonder why the prelude was so lengthy when this is a study of population projections, not economic projections. The answer is twofold: First, the OBERS projections are one of two major sets of population projections for subareas of the nation provided by the federal government. They are widely used for policy purposes and for purposes of comparison with locally produced projections. Accordingly, the reader who is even tangentially involved with population projections should be aware of the general design of the model. Second, the shift-share technique and the other ratio and trend methods described above may be borrowed for making population projections directly, and the reader should have knowledge of them.

The OBERS project staff operated on the hypothesis that regional variation in natural increase (from that of the nation) had less impact on population change than did net migration, and therefore migration of the labor pool age population and the dependent pre–labor pool age population is motivated by economic opportunity. These groups, aged 15–64 and 0–14, respectively, were projected as a function of area employment. The post–labor pool age population (65 and older) was treated separately, as its migration pattern is not determined by employment opportunities.

Labor pool population was projected with the use of the following formula:

$$\frac{P_j^t}{E_j^t} = \frac{P_o^t}{E_o^t} + \left(\frac{P_j^{1970}}{E_j^{1970}} - \frac{P_o^{1970}}{E_o^{1970}} \right) \cdot \left(1 - 0.15 \left(\frac{t - 1980}{10} \right) \right) \qquad (4.14)$$

where P is the population aged 15–64, E is employment, t is a projection year—each decennial year 1980–2020, inclusive—j is a region, and o represents the summation to the national total. The term to the left of the equality is the regional ratio of population to employment in a projection year. The first term to the right of the equality is the national ratio of population to employment in the projection year, the population aged 15–64 being taken from the U.S. Census Bureau "E" fertility series national projections, which serve as national control totals for the OBERS system. The central term to the right of the equality is the algebraic difference between the regional and national population-employment ratios at the initiation year, 1970. The final term on the right is a "closure factor" which trends the regional-national ratio difference in a convergent manner beginning with the 1990 projection. Note that the formula is structured so that closure is only 60 percent complete by the final projection year, 2020. Population ages 15–64 is obtained by multiplying the ratio described above by the regional employment projected by the economic model.

The pre-labor pool population was projected as a function of the total labor pool using the same approach as was used in projecting the labor pool with the same closure rate as used for the labor pool.

The post-labor pool population was projected independently of the employment data as this age group has little measurable relationship to levels of economic activity. Population aged 65 and over for each decade was projected in terms of the population aged 55 and over at the preceding decade using the formula:

$$\frac{P_t^{65+}}{P_{t-1}^{55+}} = \frac{P_{t-1}^{65+}}{P_{t-2}^{55+}}$$

The population 55–64 was broken out of the labor pool population at each point using regional percent shares trended to the national percent share in order to provide the necessary estimates of population aged 55 and over.

This formulation holds the relationship between the 55 and over age group at a given time and the 65 and over age group ten years later, constant. This is equivalent to assuming that the impact of migration for the 65 and over age group remains constant since the impact of mortality on the group aged 55 and over remains fairly constant throughout the projection period [25].

The OBERS population projection technique described above, while not being especially sophisticated from a demographic standpoint, does represent an advance over methods that simply used the ratio of the entire population to the work force. The use of three broad age groups takes into account the fact that there are indeed regional differences in age structure. In particular, by breaking out the population aged 0–14, historical differences in fertility are accounted for and are preserved, under the constraint of a convergence assumption, in the projections. The major demographic problem is the fact that all of the demographic processes that are operating at the regional level—fertility, mortality, and migration—are not made explicit. This makes OBERS projections difficult to compare to population projections that are demographically based—most modern demographic projections work off assumptions about rates of fertility, mortality, and migration.

Another potential problem of the OBERS method is that it per-
petuates trends from the past. The judgmental input appears to be
minimal at present; inconsistent data or impossible trends are corrected. Economic factors such as changes in competitive advantage
or energy source substitution appear to be ignored in the present
setup, although it may be possible to judgmentally alter these factors
as well.

Ratios to Projected Housing Stock

The writer of this study suggested in an earlier section that the
projection of populations in subunits of metropolitan areas might be
accomplished through the separate projection of housing units and
mean household size. It was also stipulated that the subarea populations be controlled to a separately projected metropolitan total. The
example presented in this section is a projection in which change in
housing stock is the generator of population change. This method of
projection is apparently rarely used; at any rate, it is the only example of its kind that this writer has encountered to date.

The housing stock projection method presented here was prepared
by the Erie and Niagara Counties Regional Planning Board's Goals
and Objectives Committee with the assistance of a consulting firm
[26]. In brief, the projected population of the planning region
(which comprises the Buffalo, New York, Standard Metropolitan
Statistical Area—SMSA) is the sum of the populations of the component subareas which, in turn, are obtained by adding group quarters populations to household populations that are the product of
projected mean household size and projected number of housing
units.

The report's methodology statement is not clear as to how housing
units are projected. Historical trend data were constructed from
building permit and demolition records that were reconciled against
change in housing stock reported in censuses. The number of units
for which building permits were issued during the period January 1,
1970, to June 30, 1972, was doubled to provide a projection for the
entire 1970–1975 period. As for the five remaining half-decade projection periods between 1975 and 2000, nothing is said about the
trending method. Some judgment was involved, because the report
notes that the continuation of building trends of the early 1970s
would result in unreasonably high populations for highly built-up
areas such as the cities of Lackawanna and Niagara Falls and that
adjustments were made accordingly.

The only departure from the building of population projections
from housing projections was for the city of Buffalo. Here, as was
the case for the other cities in the region, housing forecasts were ori-

ginally made separately for white and nonwhite populations. The results were not satisfactory in that the sum of the separate projections did not agree with projections made where race was ignored. The solution was to project the population of Buffalo directly, by racial group, using fixed rates of natural increase and net migration for each group.

Once housing units were projected, it was necessary to project mean household size. This was accomplished by obtaining the ratio of change in mean MCD household size to the amount of national change in household size and then applying these ratios to national household size projections. The resulting projected MCD household size was then multiplied by the projected number of occupied housing units (adjusted using the local occupancy rates from the 1970 census) to obtain a preliminary population projection. The final projection resulted from the addition of the projection of the local group quarters population (no details on how this was projected) to the preliminary projection.

A second major feature of the model was the projection of MCD populations by age and sex. This involved doing a cohort-component projection, comparing the result with the housing unit model control total, and letting the algebraic difference be the positive or negative MCD net migration control total. Five year net migration rates (derived from mid-decade special censuses and the 1970 census) provided patterns for age-specific migration. Migration based on the age-specific rates was forced to agree with the control total. When the reader familiarizes himself with the chapters on cohort-component projection techniques, he should be better able to grasp what was done here.

By way of evaluation of the method described above, it should be stressed that housing unit methods, while of some use for making local population estimates, are a hazardous means of projecting population. For one thing, the data base is often poor. Demolitions often go unreported: likewise conversions. Not all permitted construction is begun or ultimately completed. Then there is the likelihood that much of the construction since the mid-1960s has been in response to housing demand created by the exodus of members of the 1945–1965 baby boom birth cohort from their parental households as they reach maturity. This impetus to growth in the housing stock should cease by the mid-1980s, and any trends measured in the period 1965–1980 are likely to be unrealistically high if they are carried beyond 1985. The solution to this problem would be to attempt to sort out the proportion of recent housing growth attributable to changing age structure. Yet another problem is that a certain amount of construction is the result of pressure to replace obsolescent housing, so this too must be accounted for.

The truth of the matter is that, over the long haul, the housing stock changes in response to the demands created by population and not vice versa. Within subareas of a metropolitan region, it is likely that the availability of housing might attract population. However, the opening of a vast number of new housing units in Cleveland, say, is not going to motivate mass migration from Buffalo or Pittsburgh to Cleveland; only economic opportunities are likely to attract large numbers of people. Thus, the logical way to project housing is to forecast changes in the job market and then to translate this into positive or negative net migration. This will result in a control total for the population of a region. Then it is possible to project the number of households that are likely to exist in the region in the projection year. Finally, the difference between the projected number of households and the existing housing stock (with due allowance for vacancy rates) becomes the "demanded" new housing which then may be projected for subareas. To repeat: Subregional populations may be projected by using a housing unit method. But *only* after a regional population control total has been established first.

NOTES TO CHAPTER FOUR

1. U.S. Bureau of the Census, *Current Population Reports*, series P–25, no. 56 (1952).

2. Helen R. White, "Empirical Study of the Accuracy of Selected Methods of Projecting State Populations," *Journal of the American Statistical Association* 29, 267 (1954):480–98.

3. U.S. Bureau of the Census, p. 1.

4. Ibid., p. 2.

5. Ibid, p. 2.

6. Ibid., p. 2.

7. Jerome Pickard, *Dimensions of Metropolitanism*, Research Monograph 14A (Washington, D.C.: Urban Land Institute, 1967).

8. Ibid., p. 53.

9. Jerome Pickard, *Metropolitanization of the United States*, Research Monograph 2 (Washington, D.C.: Urban Land Institute, 1959).

10. Genesee–Finger Lakes Regional Planning Board, *Regional Population Distribution and Projections* (Rochester, N.Y.: 1971).

11. Bruce Newling, *Population Projections for New Jersey to 2000* (New York: Bruce Newling, 1968); Michael R. Greenberg, "A Test of Combinations of Models for Projecting the Populations of Minor Civil Divisions," *Economic Geography* 48, 2 (1972):179–188; Michael R. Greenberg et al., *Long-Range Population Projections for Minor Civil Divisions: Computer Programs and User's*

Manual (New Brunswick, N.J.: Center for Urban Policy Research, Rutgers University, 1973).

12. Greenberg, et al., pp. 16–17.

13. Ibid., p. 25.

14. Walter Isard, *Methods of Regional Analysis: an Introduction to Regional Science* (Cambridge, Mass.: The M.I.T. Press, 1960).

15. Brian J. L. Berry, "Population Growth in the Daily Urban Systems of the United States, 1980–2000," in U.S. Commission on Population Growth and the American Future, *Population Distribution and Policy*, Sara Mills Mazie, ed. vol. V of Commission Research Reports (Washington, D.C.: Government Printing Office, 1972).

16. Isard, p. 27.

17. Berry, pp. 235, 237.

18. Ibid., p. 237. Emphasis in original.

19. Ibid., pp. 237–38.

20. Ibid., p. 238.

21. U.S. Water Resources Council, *1972 OBERS Projections*, vol. 1, *Concepts, Methodology, and Summary Data* (Washington, D.C.: Government Printing Office, 1974).

22. Ibid., pp. 24–25.

23. Ibid., p. 29.

24. Ibid., pp. 26–27.

25. Ibid., p. 28.

26. Erie and Niagara Counties Regional Planning Board, "Regional Population Projections, Erie and Niagara Counties" (Grand Island, N.Y., 1972).

Chapter Five

Projecting Population by Components of Change: An Overview

INTRODUCTION

The previous chapters have treated techniques for the projection of population totals. Although many of the techniques yielded reasonably accurate results when we worked out computation examples, we pointed out again and again that the methods had a failing. That failing was analytical. The parameter values of the various equations tell us nothing directly about what demographic processes have shaped historical growth and, when trended into the future, will shape the projected growth. This same criticism may be applied to the share and ratio methods; almost without exception, the model parameters provided no demographic insights.

There is only one logical solution to the problem of lack of demographic meaning in projection parameters and that solution is to cast the projection methods directly in demographic terms. That means that the fundamental demographic processes—fertility, mortality, and migration—must be modeled or explicitly projected in some manner.

The conclusions drawn in the preceding paragraph began to seep into the consciousness of demographers interested in population projections during the 1920s, about the time that the logistic projection model was at the height of its prestige. The seminal work in the area of component projections, so far as impact on American demography is concerned, is that of Pascal K. Whelpton of the Scripps Foundation and his colleague Warren S. Thompson. For a period of nearly 20 years, their projections were preeminent in the United States. Most of the material in the remainder of this study represents variations on, or refinements of, the model described by Whelpton in 1928 [1].

Whelpton's projection method is generally referred to as the "cohort-component" method today. The term "cohort-survival" is also sometimes used, although it can be argued that the latter term should be applied strictly to cohort-component variations that lack an explicit migration element. At any rate, true cohort-component models share the following attributes: First, the fundamental demographic process components are analytically distinct, and are separately assigned parameters for projection purposes. Second, the populations and the projection rates are disaggregated by age and sex—this is the "cohort" aspect.

The reason for refining a population and its change processes into these elements is based on two empirical observations. The first observation is that the components of total population change have differed historically in their behavior. We have mentioned earlier how the Great Depression of the 1930s temporarily reduced the flow of foreign migration to the United States. We have also stated that birth rates have fluctuated considerably both upwards and downwards over the last 50 years. Mortality rates for white Americans fell steadily over much of the history of the nation until about 1950. Since then, mortality rates have declined very slowly for some age groups, and have actually increased for others. It becomes obvious from what is being described that, if it is known or even suspected that rates of component change have been moving in different directions in the past and are likely to do so in the future, then it would be a good idea to have this behavior made explicit in the projection model.

The second observation is that rates of change of the fundamental demographic components vary by age and, furthermore, the age structures of populations are likely to differ from one population to another and differ for the same population at different times in its history. The reason for this is that a population's age structure—the number or proportion of persons in each age group—reflects the combined effects of the historical behavior of each of the components of change during the lifetimes of the observed population. Given the facts that rates of change impact age groups differentially and that weightings of the age groups themselves vary from population to population as well as within populations over time, there are bound to be many subtle interactions of change rates and age structure that would be very difficult to model with relatively unrefined data and techniques. Therefore, it seems advisable to explicitly take age structure and age-related component change rates into account when making projections.

The points we have been making should become more clear after reading the following section, which deals with the projection of crude rates of change and why such projections are inadvisable.

PROJECTING CRUDE RATES OF COMPONENT CHANGE

The simplest measures of demographic change, as we have seen in Chapter Two, are crude rates of fertility, mortality, natural increase, and migration. In principle, it is possible to project populations by means of projecting the values of these rates. Indeed, if the basic data are so scarce that crude rates of component change represent the greatest possible refinement over crude rates of total population change, then the analyst has little choice but to use such rates.

Given the availability of sufficiently long historical data series, the analyst can project the crude rates of component change by using almost any of the techniques discussed in the previous chapters. Mathematical functions can be used. Ratios of local crude rates to regional or national crude rates can be used. Allocation models of regional or national births, deaths, and the migrant pool can be used. Since the general techniques are described elsewhere, we need not repeat them here. Instead, we shall focus our attention on the weakness of using crude component rates to project population.

We stated in the previous section that component change rates impacted age groups differentially and that age structures of populations are variable. These phenomena are illustrated in Exhibit 5–1. In the exhibit, we show the effect of three different age structures on fixed age-sex–specific schedules of rates of fertility, mortality, and mobility as they are manifest in crude component rates.

Population age structures can exhibit considerable variation, but we had to limit our selection of examples to a manageable number. Three populations were chosen. The 1966 census population of Algeria [2] was selected to represent the age structure of an area with comparatively high rates of fertility and mortality. Note that the size of the population in the age categories falls off monotonically from the 0–4 age group to the 75–79 age group. If graphed, this population would be roughly pyramidal in form.

At the other extreme is a population taken from an abridged United States life table for the year 1970 [3]. This is the "stationary" population, or the numbers in the $_nL_x$ column which represent the population in the given age interval during a period of time equal in years to the age interval. The term "stationary" refers to the fact that a life table can be viewed as a population that has experienced the same age-specific pattern of mortality since the birth of the very

☆ ☆

Exhibit 5–1

Effect of Age Structure on Crude Rates of Population Change

A. *Male Data (in thousands)*

| | Population | | | | Deaths* | | |
| | U.S.A. | Algeria | Life Table | Mortality Rates | U.S.A. | Algeria | Life Table |
Age							
0–4	10,330	1,187.4	488.1	0.00386	39.9	4.58	1.88
5–9	9,504	909.0	486.3	0.00226	21.5	2.05	1.10
10–14	8,524	821.1	485.1	0.00475	40.5	3.90	2.30
15–19	6,634	553.2	482.7	0.00891	59.1	4.93	4.30
20–24	5,272	400.9	478.0	0.00982	51.8	3.94	4.69
25–29	5,333	385.5	472.8	0.00999	53.3	3.85	4.72
30–34	5,846	351.0	467.9	0.01290	75.4	4.53	6.04
35–39	6,080	298.5	461.7	0.01903	115.7	5.68	8.79
40–44	5,676	231.7	452.7	0.02944	167.1	6.82	13.33
45–49	5,358	202.1	439.2	0.04700	251.8	9.50	20.64
50–54	4,735	178.7	418.6	0.07314	346.3	13.07	30.62
55–59	4,127	156.9	388.4	0.10933	451.2	17.15	42.46
60–64	3,409	132.9	346.3	0.15815	539.1	21.02	54.77
65–69	2,931	101.5	291.9	0.22479	658.9	22.82	65.62
70–74	2,185	64.3	227.8	0.30258	661.1	19.46	68.93
75–79	1,318	40.8	159.2	0.39539	521.1	16.13	62.95
80+	1,069	46.4	165.2	0.59974	641.1	27.83	99.08
Total	88,331	6,062.9	6,711.9		4,694.9	187.26	492.22

B. *Female Data (in thousands)*

| | Population | | | | Deaths* | | |
| | U.S.A. | Algeria | Life Table | Mortality Rates | U.S.A. | Algeria | Life Table |
Age							
0–4	9,991	1,155.8	490.6	0.00301	30.1	3.48	1.48
5–9	9,187	881.5	489.2	0.00150	13.8	1.32	0.73
10–14	8,249	748.4	488.5	0.00215	17.7	1.61	1.05
15–19	6,586	542.5	487.4	0.00328	21.6	1.78	1.60
20–24	5,528	421.7	485.8	0.00386	21.3	1.63	1.88
25–29	5,536	413.1	483.8	0.00506	28.0	2.09	2.45
30–34	6,103	378.9	481.3	0.00750	45.8	2.84	3.61
35–39	6,402	304.5	477.8	0.01126	72.1	3.43	5.38
40–44	5,924	237.9	472.4	0.01692	100.2	4.03	7.99
45–49	5,522	195.0	464.4	0.02531	139.8	4.94	11.75
50–54	4,871	178.8	452.5	0.03678	179.2	6.58	16.64
55–59	4,303	142.1	435.8	0.05383	231.6	7.65	23.46
60–64	3,733	135.0	412.5	0.08242	307.7	11.13	34.00
65–69	3,327	96.5	379.8	0.12782	425.3	12.33	48.55
70–74	2,554	76.9	333.7	0.19338	493.9	14.87	64.53
75–79	1,659	45.8	270.2	0.29716	493.0	13.61	80.29
80+	1,516	58.1	371.7	0.56248	852.7	32.68	209.07
Total	90,992	6,012.3	7,477.7		3,473.8	126.00	514.46

*For Five Year Intervals **Annual

	Movers*		
Mobility Rates	U.S.A.	Algeria	Life Table
0.5565	5,749	660.8	271.6
0.4368	4,151	397.1	212.4
0.4297	3,663	352.8	208.4
0.7319	4,855	404.9	353.3
0.8059	4,249	323.1	385.2
0.6760	3,605	260.6	319.6
0.5389	3,150	189.2	252.2
0.4290	2,608	128.1	198.1
0.3556	2,018	82.4	161.0
0.3107	1,665	62.8	136.5
0.2835	1,342	50.7	118.7
0.2681	1,106	42.1	104.1
0.2780	948	36.9	96.3
0.2578	756	26.2	75.3
0.2506	548	16.1	57.1
0.2739	361	11.2	43.6
0.3313	354	15.4	54.7
	41,128	3,060.4	3,048.1

	Movers*				Births**		
Mobility Rates	U.S.A.	Algeria	Life Table	Fertility Rates	U.S.A.	Algeria	Life Table
0.5562	5,557	642.9	272.9				
0.4384	4,028	386.4	214.5				
0.4603	3,797	344.5	224.9	0.0006	4.9	0.45	0.29
0.7752	5,105	420.5	377.8	0.0538	354.3	29.19	26.22
0.7634	4,220	321.9	370.9	0.1531	846.3	64.56	74.38
0.5978	3,309	247.0	289.2	0.1253	693.7	51.76	60.62
0.4708	2,873	178.4	226.6	0.0610	372.3	23.11	29.36
0.3778	2,419	115.0	180.5	0.0216	138.3	6.58	10.32
0.3280	1,943	78.0	154.9	0.0046	27.3	1.09	2.17
0.2992	1,652	58.3	138.9	0.0002	1.1	0.04	0.09
0.2829	1,378	50.6	128.0				
0.2772	1,193	39.4	120.8				
0.2781	1,038	37.5	114.7				
0.2692	896	26.0	102.2				
0.2786	712	21.4	93.0				
0.3162	525	14.5	85.4				
0.3688	559	21.4	137.1				
	41,204	3,003.7	3,232.3		2,438.2	176.78	203.45

C. *Crude Rates*

	Annual Crude Birth Rate (per 1,000)	*Annual Crude Death Rate (per 1,000)*	*Annual Rate of Natural Increase*	*Five Year Mobility Rate (per 1,000)*	*General Fertility Rate (per 1,000)*
U.S.A.	13.60	9.11	4.49	459.1	67.58
Algeria	14.64	5.19	9.45	502.2	76.91
Life Table	14.34	14.19	0.15	442.6	70.43

Sources: 1960 U.S. Population: U.S. Bureau of the Census, *Census of Population: 1960*, vol. I, *Characteristics of the Population*. pt. 1, United States Summary (Washington, D.C.: Government Printing Office, 1964), Tables 47, 156.

1966 Algeria: United Nations, *Demographic Year Book 1969* (New York, 1970), Table 6.

1970 U.S.A. Life Table: U.S. National Center for Health Statistics, *Vital Statistics of the United States, 1970*. vol. II-section 5, *Life Tables* (Washington, D.C.: Government Printing Office, n.d.).

1965–1970 Mobility: U.S. Bureau of the Census, *Census of Population: 1970 Detailed Characteristics*, Final Report PC(1)–D1, United States Summary (Washington, D.C.: Government Printing Office, 1973), Table 196.

1967 Mortality: Derived from U.S. Bureau of the Census, *Current Population Reports*, series P–25, no. 470 (1971), Table B–5.

Fertility; Projected Year 2005: U.S. Bureau of the Census. *Current Population Reports*, series P–25, no. 493 (1972), Table A–3.

☆ ☆

oldest group of people represented in the table, and that each year since that time a fixed number of persons was born. Under these conditions of fixed numbers of births and fixed mortality patterns the numbers of yearly births and deaths become equal and the population is thereby stabilized at a fixed size. Such a population is presently nothing more than a theoretical construct; it is unlikely that any actual human population has operated strictly by the rules indicated above. But these populations potentially can exist, so they are of great interest to many demographers. The United States life table populations are formed by mortality patterns that are typical of populations with relatively low death rates and long life expectancy at birth. The age structure, if graphed in conventional population pyramid form, would be bullet-shaped; the sides would be nearly vertical for some distance, and then there would be a sharp tapering at the highest age levels. The one unrealistic feature is the fact that the male and female populations represent two different life tables, each of which assumes a starting (or birth) population of 100,000. This does not jibe with the empirical fact that the ratio of male to female births is on the order of 1.05 to 1. Accordingly, our combining of the results of our rate manipulations to a population representing the sum of the separate stable populations from the male and female life tables represents a slight distortion of a "true" combined population. No attempt was made to correct for this.

The third population selected was the population of the United States reported in the 1960 census [4]. The age structure has an irregular form that reflects the fluctuating fertility patterns from 1930 to 1960. In particular, the pinched waist of the population pyramid that would appear if the data were graphed represents the effect of the low birth rates of the 1930s. This indentation is most pronounced for age groups 20–24 and 25–59, the groups that exhibit some of the highest rates of fertility and mobility.

The mortality rate schedules are the complements of five year survivorship rates based on the 1967 United States mortality experience and used in the 1971 Census Bureau national population projections [5]. These rates are typical of low mortality countries, where death rates remain less than 1 percent a year below age 50; high mortality populations exhibit high death rates for the very young as well as the very old.

The fertility rates applied to the female populations are taken from the 1972 U.S. population projections [6]. They are the "E" series age-specific birth rates for the year 2005 which result in a lifetime average of 2.1 births per female which, given anticipated American mortality levels, is just enough births to offset female mortality through the childbearing ages.

The migration component is represented by mobility rates experienced in the United States for the period 1965–1970 [7]. Each age-sex–specific rate represents the proportion of that age-sex group who reported themselves as not living in the same housing unit in 1970 as they did in 1965.

The age-sex–specific population values for each of the three populations were multiplied by the corresponding rates of fertility, mortality, and mobility, and numbers of births, deaths, and movers were obtained. These were then summed over all age groups. Crude rates were obtained by dividing total events by the total population. The crude death rates, based on five year survivorship, were divided by five in order to obtain annual rates comparable to the birth rates, which were originally computed using annual age-specific rates. Mobility rates were left unchanged as five year rates because of the manner in which the data were originally collected. (The census question as to residence five years previously obtains no information regarding intervening moves. Accordingly, any given single year is likely to have experienced more moves than would be indicated by dividing the five year net change through movement rate by five.)

The crude rates of fertility, mortality, natural increase, and mobility reveal the impact of variation in age structure. The younger Algerian population has the highest crude rates of mobility and fertility, and the lowest crude death rate. Consequently, it has the greatest rate of natural increase. The "old" life table population has the highest crude death rate and (by a slight margin) the lowest mobility rate. Although its crude birth rate is nearly the same as that calculated for the Algerian population, the rate of natural increase is practically nil due to the high death rate. The 1960 U.S. population had the lowest birth rate and nearly the lowest mobility rate because of its "Coke bottle" age structure. Its mortality rate was intermediate, which resulted in an intermediate position for the natural increase rate.

Calculations of the general fertility rate—births to females ages 15–44—are also included. The *GFR* is supposedly a refined rate because it makes use of age detail missing in the crude rates. Our illustration indicates that even a refined rate can be influenced by age structure. The relatively few females in the peak childbearing ages in the U.S.A. in 1960 result in the lowest *GFR*, whereas the concentration of Algerian females in the younger end of the childbearing age range produced the highest *GFR*.

The conclusion to be drawn from these illustrations is that crude rates of demographic change should be used with great caution because they are influenced by the age structure of the population. Age-specific rates should be used instead if they are available.

THE COHORT-COMPONENT PROJECTION METHOD

The original Whelpton technique will serve as an introduction to the cohort-component projection methodology. Fundamental differences between the cohort-component system and the then currently popular fitted-function techniques are described by Whelpton as follows:

> Other population estimates are based almost entirely on the size of the population in the past. These census enumerations are used for calculating absolute increases, rates of increase, or as a basis for computing growth curves. In the forecasts of the Scripps Foundation, however, the total population is used as a point from which to start. Future trends are estimated separately for such factors as birth-rates, death-rates, and immigration. The total population at future dates is therefore the calculated result of several predicted factors, rather than an original prediction in itself [8].

Cohort-component projections are *potentially* ahistorical in that the analyst may use the most current available data as rates of fertility, mortality, and migration for the projections. This is seldom done; even Whelpton did not do it. The usual procedure is to examine past trends in the component rates as a guide to making judgments about future values of these rates. On some occasions, the component rates are trended into the future by the very procedures Whelpton suggests can be avoided.

Whelpton's projections were for the entire United States for the period 1925–1975. Since there was no 1925 census, he had to estimate the 1925 population using the January 1, 1920, enumeration as the base and recorded natural increase and immigration as control values to bring the population into line with its probable January 1, 1925, value.

> Because of the large variations in the birth- and death-rates of different groups in the population, it has seemed desirable to keep native whites, foreign whites, and Negroes separate, and to subdivide each of these groups into urban and rural. Five-year age divisions have been used in every case. Children of foreign or mixed parentage within each five-year age divisions have been counted as part of the native-born population under five years of age at the end of the period, the foreign-born group

being kept up by immigration only. Internal migration from rural to urban communities has been estimated for each group. The sexes have not been kept separate for native whites and Negroes, the present sex ratio of each being assumed to continue in the future about as at present, since it depends so largely on the ratio at birth. With foreign whites, however, immigration under the new quota regulations may be sufficiently different from the unrestricted movement of earlier years so that the sex ratio may change considerably [9].

Several points need to be made regarding the passage just quoted. First is the use of five year age groups in a system of projecting ahead by five year intervals. Such a "square" age-time module is still the preferred practice because it is conceptually and computationally easy to handle. For projections going beyond ten years into the future, the contemporary analyst will choose, as did Whelpton, the five year module with the standard age groups, 0–4, 5–9, 10–14, . . . up to a convenient, final open-ended age category. Normally this open-ended age group will be either "75 and over" or "85 and over," and it will be determined by the format of age distribution data in the base year census report. Projections for points less than ten years in the future are usually done with a one year module if the basic age-detailed data are available and if there are not too many populations to be projected. (Modern computers can handle large amounts of data; the problem lies in the fact that the handwork needed to analyze and specify change rates is increased fivefold.)

Whelpton's practice of using combined sex data was soon abandoned. His statement that sex ratios were largely dependent on the initial sex ratio at birth is misleading. In nearly all nations, females have lower mortality rates than males at every age level. As a result, the initial male majority is immediately under erosion. If mortality rates by age and sex remained the same over time, Whelpton's use of existing age-specific sex ratios might be empirically acceptable. However, such a condition is not likely to exist, which means that the best way to project age cohorts is to turn them into age-sex cohorts.

Whelpton's further stratification by race, nativity, and urban-rural status made good analytical sense when the projections were created. Today, for example, the population of the United States is largely urban, and there are comparatively few persons who are of foreign birth, so these elements might well be ignored. States with large rural populations might require such special treatment as might certain Canadian provinces which have relatively large immigrant populations. Because of their higher fertility rates and higher mortality rates, it is usually wise to project black populations separately where their share of the total population is significant (exceeding 10 percent, or perhaps even 5 percent, of the total).

Whelpton found it necessary to adjust the population total upwards for age group 0–4 in 1920. This was because comparison of the census population with survivors of births reported during the five years prior to the census indicated that the expected survivors exceeded the number of persons aged 0–4 reported in the census. What happened was that this age group was undercounted. In fact, undercounts of the very young flaw nearly every census, so it is a good practice to make an adjustment to the base year data. Undercounts can best be checked on the national level, where the reported precensal births can be survived and then compared to the censused native population of the appropriate racial groups aged 0–4 and 5–9, and correction ratios obtained. To attempt such an adjustment using state or local data would be unwise because of the effects of migration on the population during the interval between birth registration and census enumeration.

Mortality rates for Whelpton's projections were based on the experience recorded in U.S. death registration areas for the periods 1900–1904, 1910–1914, and 1920–1924. Death data were not reported uniformly on a national level in those days, so the states having the best data were used to infer the national rates. Target mortality levels for native whites for 1975 were the New Zealand rates for ages under 75 in the year 1922, which Whelpton claims was "a particularly favorable year," and the 1920 registration area death rates for persons over 75, which were already lower than those in New Zealand and were trended even further downward. Rural-urban ratios to total mortality were taken from 1910 life tables and were trended into the future under an assumption of greater relative mortality decline for urban populations. The mortality rates for foreign born whites and for blacks were taken from their 1920–1924 death data for urban and rural areas and were assumed to show the same percentage decline in the future as would the native white rates. In all cases, the actual projection computations used *survival* rates, which are the complement of the death rates. This procedure is also commonly used today.

The fertility rates were five year age-specific rates for women in five year age groups, 15–19, 20–24, . . . , 45–49. Baseline data were from the periods 1905–1909 and 1915–1919. Reported births from 1920 to 1926 permitted an extension of the general trend with due allowance for the short postwar baby boomlet. The long range assumption was that birth rates would continue to decline, but at a decreasing rate of decline. It is interesting to note that Whelpton's fertility forecast for the period 1970–1974 works out to a total fertility rate of 1.769 births per native white woman, which is not far below the rates actually being attained during the first half of the seventies. Of course, Whelpton did not forecast World War II and the extended baby boom that followed, so his fertility rates from 1945 to 1972 were much too low.

Immigration was assumed to be one million persons every five years, and a fixed numerical schedule of migrants by age and sex was added to the population for each projection period. Internal rural-urban migration was trended so that the downward trend in percent rural would decrease at a decreasing rate. Using these predetermined shares, the net number of migrants from rural to urban areas was derived from the difference in percent rural population at the next projection date that would be expected on the basis of natural increase from the stipulated future rural percentage. In the case of blacks, the assumption was that the rural population would remain static at the 1925 level. Thus, the amount of net black rural-urban migration would be equal to the rural natural increase. In both cases, the age distribution of rural-urban migration was assumed to remain in fixed, predetermined proportions.

As it turned out, Whelpton's projections proved to be fairly similar to the 1920 Pearl-Reed logistic projections in spite of the vast difference in method. For the census years 1930, 1940, and 1950, Whelpton forecast the U.S. population to be 123.6, 138.2, and 151.6 million on January 1 of the respective years. Pearl and Reed projected 122.4, 136.3, and 148.7. The April 1 census counts were 122.8, 131.7, and 150.7. After 1950, both sets of projections go awry because the postwar baby boom was not built into the assumptions. The 1970 Pearl-Reed projection was 167.9 million and Whelpton's projection was 171.5, whereas the census reported 203.2, including Alaska and Hawaii, which attained statehood between 1950 and 1960.

We shall return to the consideration of complete cohort-component projection methodologies in Chapter Nine. This writer hopes the sketch of Whelpton's technique will serve as a reference point for the discussions that follow in Chapters Six through Eight which deal with details of the various components of demographic change and how they have been treated in projection models since Whelpton's early efforts. The following chapters are arranged in order of increasing difficulty in "projectibility" for smaller areas. We first deal with mortality which, assuming there is no catastrophy such as war or worldwide crop failure, is a relatively stable change element. Then we treat fertility, which is much less easy to forecast. Finally, we discuss migration, which is by far the most volatile component of local demographic change.

NOTES TO CHAPTER FIVE

1. P. K. Whelpton, "Population of the United States, 1925 to 1975," *American Journal of Sociology* 34, 2 (1928):253–70.

2. United Nations, *Demographic Yearbook: 1969* (New York, 1970).

3. U.S. National Center for Health Statistics, *Vital Statistics of the United States, 1970*, vol. II–section 5. *Life Tables* (Washington, D.C.: Government Printing Office, n.d.).

4. U.S. Bureau of the Census, *U.S. Census of Population: 1960*, vol. I. *Characteristics of the Population*, pt. 1, United States Summary, (Washington, D.C.: Government Printing Office, 1964).

5. U.S. Bureau of the Census, *Current Population Reports*, series P–25, no. 470, (1971).

6. U.S. Bureau of the Census, *Current Population Reports*, series P–25, no. 493, (1972).

7. U.S. Bureau of the Census, *Census of Population: 1970 Detailed Characteristics*, Final Report PC(1)–D1, United States Summary, (Washington, D.C.: Government Printing Office, 1973).

8. Whelpton, p. 255.

9. Ibid., p. 256.

Chapter Six

Projecting Populations by Age and Sex: The Mortality Component

INTRODUCTION

This chapter will necessarily be brief because mortality has proved to be the least volatile component of population change and therefore has been given the least attention of any component in small area projection methodologies. This would not be the case if the purpose of the projection was to assess the effects of a catastrophic event such as war or famine. But ordinarily most population projections are based on the explicit assumption that such catastrophies will not occur.

At the national level—particularly for nations that are experiencing a transition from high to low mortality levels—the mortality component becomes relatively important where projection techniques are concerned. This is partly because the impact of migration is usually comparatively small, due to the fact that international migration is subject to numerous restrictions that are absent where intranational population movement is concerned. Fertility is the most volatile national change component, so it receives the greatest amount of attention. However, enough attention has been paid to mortality for a number of projection techniques to have been devised. As we shall see, solutions to the problem of projecting national mortality are usually accepted as the basis for projecting local mortality. Accordingly, this chapter begins by outlining national methods and then turns to a short discussion of techniques that have been used locally.

Before moving on to discussions of specific techniques, it is necessary to make a few observations on the problems that underlie mortality projections of any kind. Basically, mortality rates are the result of a complex interaction of causal variables. Because of this interaction, it is very difficult to identify the "pure"effect of each.

A key variable is physiological aging, the precise nature of which is only partly understood. Most analysts would agree that ultimate length of life for humans has changed little during recorded history; very few individuals survive beyond age 110. It is also known that death rates are related to age. The risk of death is relatively high at birth and then falls off rapidly to reach a low point around age 10. Thereafter, the risk increases year after year until at some point it becomes a certainty. Once the individual reaches maturity, his body begins the degeneration process associated with aging, and as the body degenerates its susceptibility to disease increases. The amount or degree of susceptibility can be modified by the environment to which the body is exposed. This environment is social and economic as well as physical. Availability and quality of sanitary and medical facilities are factors. So are the attitude and behavior of the individual; some persons do not choose to eat a balanced diet even if the food is available. Occupational hazards, including stress, can affect the risk of death.

Some factors can be accounted for in approximate ways. The U.S. National Center for Health Statistics has prepared sets of life tables that indicate what death rates would be if one or another of the major causes of death were eliminated [1]. These studies are helpful in a general sense, but the analyst must come to a decision on when or whether any of these causes can actually be eliminated. There is also the question of whether a breakthrough is possible in the field of gerontology—whether the aging process itself can be slowed.

As will become evident in the sections that follow, virtually all of the methods of projecting mortality include no detailed assumptions regarding changes in the factors underlying age- and sex-specific death rates. However, we may assume that, eventually, research efforts will culminate in mortality models that are considerably in advance of the present crop in terms of the number and explicitness of their underlying assumptions.

PROJECTING NATIONAL MORTALITY

In this section, two general approaches to projecting mortality on the national level will be discussed. In a large sense, all the approaches may be considered as "models." However, we shall use the distinction observed in Shryock and Siegel [2] and treat analogue methods such as model life tables as "models," and all other techniques as falling under the rubric of "trending."

Model Life Tables

Shryock and Siegel state: "Mortality models, representing generalized schemes for projecting mortality applicable to a group of countries, are generally employed when satisfactory statistics are not available regarding the current level and trend of mortality for a country or group of countries" [3]. However, since they are sometimes used where data are plentiful—often as a low mortality level target to which current data are trended—they warrant a brief description. We shall consider the two most widely used sets of model life tables—the 1956 United Nations tables and the 1966 Princeton tables.

The United Nations model life tables were

based on the observed close correlations—in a wide selection of countries and at different periods of time—between life-table death rates (q_x) for pairs of adjacent age groups. For each such pair of q_x-values, this correlation was established in the form of a parabolic regression equation. For instance, given the value of q_{10-14}, the value of q_{15-19} which normally go [sic] with it can be estimated with the regression equation for this pair of values. From the values of q_{15-19} so obtained, the corresponding value of q_{20-24} can be found by using the regression function for that pair of values, and so forth. Thus, all the values of q_x consistent with any one q_x-value can be computed. By doing this for a sequence of forty different values of q_0, forty model life tables, ranging from very high to very low mortality, were established [4].

In their final form, the United Nations life tables were paired by sex and related to life expectancy at birth (e_0). There were 24 sets of tables with e_0 values ranging from 20 to 73.9 years. These were given labels as "mortality levels" ranging from 0 to 115 in increments of five. These increments represent a projection system whereby the value difference of five in the labeling stands for a five year improvement in the transition from high to low mortality by a population. The writer of the report cautions that "[t]his generalization requires a rather liberal interpretation. It is not asserted that mortality will always decline in this particular way. It may decline more slowly, more rapidly, or with different rapidity for different age groups. The model assumption is merely one of the more typical conditions to be found in the world today, and it can be modified as required" [5]. The assumption for the system is that expectation of life at birth increases by 2.5 years per five year period for all life expectation levels (at birth) under 55 years, and increases at a decreasing rate thereafter, in recognition of the fact that it becomes increasingly difficult to reduce mortality levels once the early, easy successes have been attained.

The model life tables represent "cross-sectional" or single point in time mortality pictures, or synthetic cohorts—exactly as is the case for national life tables published for a given date. The assumed mortality experience of a given birth cohort as it passes through time can be traced from year to year and age to age in the model system. This is illustrated in Figure 6–1, where death rates (q_x) by age for selected male life tables are plotted as solid lines, and a birth cohort that is born under conditions at level 15 and evolves through the system has its death rates plotted by a dashed line.

Given the fact the mortality levels in most developed countries are within the range of the top four or five levels of the U.N. system, it seems likely that the tables would be most useful for the selection of one or perhaps two target mortality levels for trending purposes. The reader who is interested in making use of the model life tables in their systemic form should consult the reference cited above for details.

The Princeton model life tables currently in use are a revision of a set created during World War II which, according to Coale and Demeny, was "the first attempt to construct a model life table summarizing age patterns of mortality in several countries in a form that could be associated with any arbitrarily specified value of a parameter indicating the level of mortality . . ." [6]. That arbitrary parameter was life expectancy at age 10, a feature that was continued in the newer system of life tables.

The 1966 Princeton model life tables were derived from a group of 326 life tables that were screened from a large initial collection. The screening criteria were: the tables had to be derived jointly from census and vital statistics data; the tables had to be for each sex and five year age detail for ages above age five; repetitive tables such as annual life tables for intercensal years were eliminated; wartime life tables were eliminated; and life tables for entire nations were used—the exceptions were certain nineteenth century German states; southern Italy, which had persistently different characteristics from the rest of the nation; and white life tables for the United States and New Zealand which were felt to be more accurate than tables containing nonwhite data.

Since an entire life table can be constructed from life table death rates ($_n q_x$), where subscript n is the length of the measurement period and subscript x is the exact age at the beginning of the measurement period, the model life tables were based on estimated values of $_1 q_0, _4 q_1, _5 q_5, _5 q_{10}, \ldots, _5 q_{75}$, and values for total years

Figure 6–1. United Nations Model Life Table Death Rates for Males, Selected Mortality Levels

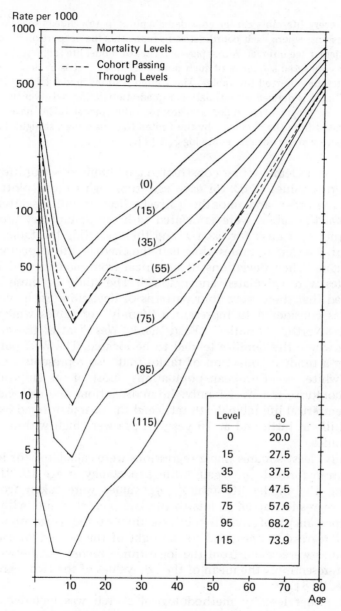

Rate per 1000

Level	e_0
0	20.0
15	27.5
35	37.5
55	47.5
75	57.6
95	68.2
115	73.9

Legend: Mortality Levels; Cohort Passing Through Levels

Source: United Nations, *Methods for Population Projections by Age and Sex,* Manuals on Methods of Estimating Population, Manual III, Population Studies, No. 25 (New York, 1956), Table II.

lived after age 80 were estimated by the ratio of survivors to starting population (l_x) at age 80.

Thus, every life table can be considered a point in a Euclidean space of 17
dimensions, where each coordinate axis represents the proportion dying in
a particular age interval. A one-parameter set of model life tables is, then, a
singly connected sequence of such points—a "line" that is as close as possible to the observed life tables. The United Nations model tables form a
"line" that is derived by estimating a quadratic relation between the $_nq_x$
values in progressively older age groups; other model tables have been
calculated from the data used by the United Nations using a straight line in
the space whose coordinates are log q_x's [7].

Coale and Demeny first constructed a preliminary set of life tables
by ordering values of q_x for each age from high to low, plotting q_x
against the order, and smoothing irregularities from the scattergram.
Empirical life tables were associated with the preliminary tables by
comparing q_x values for each x and then selecting the table in the
array of associated tables that had the median life expectancy at
birth value. Then deviations of empirical from median model table
q_x values were calculated and graphed. The study of these graphs
indicated that there were four patterns of deviation. Each such pattern was considered to represent a "family" of tables which were
labeled "North," "South," "East," and "West," after the areas of
Europe where the families tended to be located. The West pattern is
actually a residual collection of tables that also represents a number
of nonwhite, non-European populations; most of the empirical life
tables comprise the West family. Intercorrelations among logarithms
of the empirical life table death rates and the untransformed expectation of life at birth and at 10 years of age were high within each of
the families.

Finally, least squares linear regressions were calculated for log $_nq_x$
and untransformed $_nq_x$ against life expectancy at age 10. "In con-
structing the model life tables, $_nq_x$ values were taken from the
simple regression at all points to the left (i.e., at points with lower
life expectancy) of the first intersection of the [logarithmic and
simple] regression lines; and to the right of the second intersection,
$_nq_x$ values were taken from the logarithmic regression. Between the
two interesections, the mean of the $_nq_x$ values of the two regressions
was used" [8].

This rather lengthy methodological sketch was included in our
study for the purpose of indicating how model life table systems can
be developed. By knowing the general procedure involved, it should
be easier to decide whether a target mortality pattern should be

taken from a model life table, from an empirical life table, or by some other means.

Trending Observed Rates

The trending of observed time series of age-specific death rates is manifestly possible only for places that have several decades' worth of reliable data. The use of such data in preference to trending toward life table values is advantageous in that the "environment" of the population may be uniquely mirrored by peculiarities in the pattern of the death rates.

Shryock and Siegel observe that:

> Projected death rates for a given country may be derived on the basis of a number of general procedures or assumptions. These are: (1) Maintaining the latest observed death rates, (2) extrapolating past trends in the county's own death rates in some fashion, (3) applying standard percentage decreases in death rates depending on the level of the death rates at each successive date, and (4) establishing target rates for a distant future date and securing rates for intermediate rates by some form of interpolation.
>
> The first alternative would be applicable only where (a) mortality had reached a standstill and there were no signs of further progress or (b) the implications of other more realistic assumptions were being evaluated against this "base." The series of death rates may be extrapolated either graphically or by fitting an appropriate mathematical curve. The extrapolations under (2), (3), and (4) should all provide for improvement in mortality, with rare exceptions, and, if death rates are already low, the improvement should be at a decreasing rate. The extrapolations should be carried out independently for each age-sex group; and the same or different method of extrapolation may be used for different age-sex groups.
>
> The risk of arriving at unreasonably low levels of mortality in the projection period when direct extrapolation is employed suggests that a limit should be set to the improvement assumed to occur. Accordingly, after a given future date, the rates at every age may be assumed not to change any farther. The target rates set to avoid unreasonable levels of future mortality may be reached in different years for different age-sex groups. They may be derived in a number of different ways: (1) Use of the rates already attained in some advanced geographic subdivision of the country; (2) use of the rates already attained in another, more advanced country, somewhat similar to the given country in certain socioeconomic features but having better public health organization and lower death rates; (3) analysis of age-specific death rates in terms of components, such as principal causes of death, for which judgmental projections could be more confidently made; and (4) determination of the lower biological limit for mortality at each age on the basis of present knowledge, and of the date by which this limit will be attained [9].

An example of trending without target would be the survivorship rates used in the 1969 Canadian projections [10]. The reader should be reminded that survivorship rates are the rates actually used in projection models. They are the ratio of persons alive in a given age-sex group at the end of a projection period to the number of persons in that same birth cohort who were alive at the beginning of the projection period. This ratio is the complement of the age-sex-specific rate of deaths during the projection period to the population alive at the start of the period. Analysts often seem to find it more convenient to manipulate death rates than survival rates, so death rates are usually projected first, and then transformed into survivorship rates.

The Canadian analyst chose to work directly from life table survival values for sex and single years of age for the periods 1955–1957 and 1960–1962. Single years were used because the projections were to be for one year increments by single year of age and by sex. The periods indicated above represent the range of mortality data used in computing the life tables. Most life tables dealing with one year age groups are based on the mean number of deaths in a three year interval centered on a census date; this is to minimize the effect of year-to-year random data fluctuations. Canadian censuses are taken every five years on years ending in 1 and 6—that is, 1956, 1961, 1966, 1971, and so forth. United States unabridged (single year of age) life tables are similarly centered around censuses. Since American censuses are taken in years that end in zero, they are designated as life tables for 1959–1961, 1969–1971, and so on.

The survival ratios obtained from the two life tables were "projected graphically to 1969, 1974, 1979, and 1984 by taking into account the following observations: (a) the rate of increase in life expectancy at birth has been diminishing, (b) the excess of female life expectancy over male life expectancy continues to increase, (c) the ratio of male accidental deaths to female accidental deaths has varied between 2.4 and 2.9 since 1950, and (d) the ratios of male to female age-specific death rates have been increasing consistently since 1931" [11]. Once the projected values for the forecast dates had been established, survival ratios for the intervening years were "interpolated assuming a constant annual rate of change." Presumably, this entailed the calculation of the fifth root of the ratio of the survivorship rates, which is geometric interpolation. The general solution may be expressed:

$$r_1 = \sqrt[n]{(_nP_{x,\,t+n})/(_nP_{x,\,t})} \tag{6.1}$$

where r_1 is the annual change ratio which may vary on either side of unity; $_np_x$ is the probability of surviving from age x to age $(x + n)$; and t represents a given year such as 1974. The reason for taking the nth root, where n is the number of years in the interval, is that the n year change ratio is the one year change ratio compounded n times, that is,

$$r_1^n = (_np_{x,\ t+n})/(_np_{x,\ t}) \ .$$

We have already cited Whelpton's 1928 projections as an example of trending mortality from historical data to target values obtained from another population [12]. Therefore, we shall now discuss trending mortality by cause of death, the final alternative trending method that has been used for projections in North America. (To this writer's knowledge, the technique of trending toward a targeted biological lower limit of mortality has not been used in any official projections here. Experimental mortality projections of this kind may well have been attempted, however.)

Mortality rates derived from trending the effects of different causes of death form the basis for survivorship rates used by the U.S. Bureau of the Census in their national population projections. The survivorship rates—or survival ratios—were created by the Office of the Actuary, Social Security Administration, U.S. Department of Health, Education, and Welfare, for use in cost estimates for the social security program [13].

Target mortality rates for the year 2000 were established by age and sex for ten classes of cause of death by judgmental assignment of ratios to 1968 cause-specific sets of mortality rates. The year 2000 rates were then aggregated across all causal categories, presumably by using a weighting scheme based on the proportional contribution of each cause, so that sets of age-sex– specific target rates were obtained. Next, the grouped age-specific rates were transformed into single year of age rates by an undescribed, but apparently routine, procedure. These death rates and similar death rates for 1972 were then converted into life tables, and survival ratios were derived from the life table L_x (mean number of persons in the age interval) column by calculating the ratio L_{x+1}/L_x. Once these survivorship ratios had been established for 1972 and 2000, ratios for the intervening years were calculated using the geometric interpolation method outlined above.

It is worth noting that no increases in death rates by cause were stipulated in the OASDI projections; this may not be a valid assumption, and users of these survival ratios should bear the fact in mind. On the other hand, there is no reason why such rate increases cannot be built into mortality projections of this type. Consequently, cause of death based projections are an attractive technique. One possible drawback is the amount of work required to set up the method for local areas. Random data fluctuations in low mortality age groups in small areas such as counties may make "true" baseline rates difficult to obtain. It is entirely possible that this type of projection is practical only at the state or large metropolitan area level.

PROJECTING LOCAL MORTALITY

It was mentioned earlier that little attention has been paid to mortality by analysts making small area population projections. The present section includes discussions of the techniques this writer has come across in his survey of local population projection literature. State and local mortality projections may be accomplished in two basic ways: they may be related to national projections, or they may be projected independently. Both approaches will be treated in the sections that follow.

Relating to National Projections

The simplest—and most common—way mortality is treated in state and local population projections is for the analyst to use the survival ratios used in the U.S. Bureau of the Census projections [14]. Aside from their convenience, the use of the same rates as the Census Bureau facilitates comparison with other projections that use the same rates. That is, if it is known that rival projections of an area both use the same mortality assumption, then the differences in the outcome are the result only of differences in fertility and migration assumptions. (And, to get ahead to the following chapter's subject, it might be added that many state and local projections also make outright use of Census Bureau fertility and mortality rates. Thus the only possible differences, computation procedures aside, would be due to the treatment of migration.)

There seem to be two important potential disadvantages to hitching local projection models to national mortality rates. The first is that the national projections might be based on incorrect assumptions, and therefore would be inappropriate for use even at the nation level. The analyst should be on guard against this risk and is advised to keep an eye on the literature concerning trends in mortality by cause of death.

The second possible disadvantage is that there may be systematic differences between state or local mortality patterns and national patterns. This means that, even if the assumptions behind the national mortality projections are correct, future state or local survivorship would be systematically distorted. This may be illustrated by Figure 6–2, which contains five year survivorship ratios derived from 1959–1961 unabridged life tables. The populations involved in the comparison are white males in the United States, in New York State, and in Washington State. The Washington rates tend to be the highest for white males under age 40. Beyond age 40, the New York rates are highest. Unless these relationships changed since 1959–1961, the use of national survivorship ratios would tend to understate New York mortality in the high impact age groups and would tend to overstate the mortality of Washington.

(Actually, the preceding statement is a simplification, because the current national projection rates are for all racial groups combined and the patterns shown here are those of the presumably more accurate white data. But if the analyst is required to project populations of more than one racial group, and if he wishes to use national mortality projections, it might be necessary to calculate national race-specific rates, take age-specific ratios of these to the national rates, and then use state ratios to the nation within each sex-race group such as are implied in the figure in order to further adjust the already adjusted national values. In addition, most prudent analysts assume that there will be tendencies toward convergence of all subgroups to the national values. This means that the racial groups would be trended toward the national rates, and that the state race-specific rates would be trended toward the national rates for the appropriate racial group. Male and female rates would remain as specified in the national projections.)

If the ratios of state or local mortality by age, sex, and, possibly, race to equivalent national rates work out to percentage differences of as much as 1 percent for the older age groups, serious long term distortions in numbers of deaths or survivors are possible. This is because the error is compounded projection period after projection period. A 1 percent bias in one projection period means a better than 6 percent bias over a 30 year projection range if the projection interval is five years.

It is worth the analyst's while to compile comparisons for three or more decades in the past to determine whether state-national differences have been consistent over time and to determine if there has been any sign of convergence. These findings should be a useful guide for specification of state or local mortality assumptions.

A simple solution for linking state to national mortality projec-

Figure 6–2. Five Year White Male Life Table Death Rates, United States, New York State, and Washington State, 1959–1961

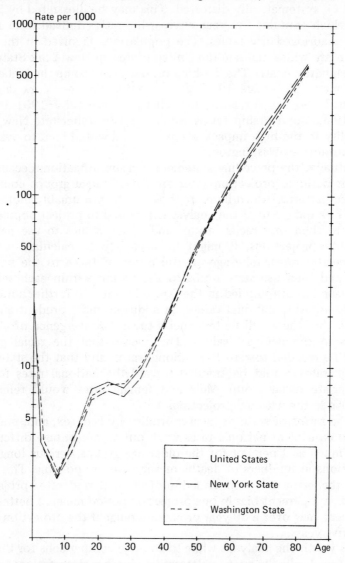

Sources: U.S. National Center for Health Statistics. Life Tables: 1959–61, *United States Life Tables: 1959–61,* vol. 1, no. 1 (Washington, D.C.: Government Printing Office, 1964).

_____ . Life Tables: 1959–61, vol. 2, no. 33, *New York State Life Tables: 1959–61* (Washington, D.C.: Government Printing Office, 1966).

_____ . Life Tables: 1959–61, vol. 2, no. 48, *Washington State Life Tables: 1959–61* (Washington, D.C.: Government Printing Office, 1966).

tion, which is recommended only if historical convergence is not observed, is to assume that observed ratios remain constant over time (this is proposed in Tarver and Black) [15].

Independent Projection

State and local projections need not have their survivorship ratios linked to national patterns. The main risk of independent projection is that, because of the intermingling of populations due to the constant migration of persons and because of the creation of a truly national economy since World War II, the American population is becoming more homogeneous. Such increasing homogeneity may be expected to affect future regional mortality differentials. This does not rule out the use of independent projections; it is only a cautionary note.

The most common type of local mortality component is derived from the most recent state life table; these survival rates are then assumed to remain constant over all projection periods. Examples of this technique are Michigan's 1960–1980 projections [16]; Wisconsin's projections for the same period [17]; and the 1975–2020 Kentucky projections [18]. This method has the virtue of preserving a valid mortality pattern for the area being projected. Should progress in the fight to decrease mortality cease, then this method will also have long term validity in terms of projection results. The analyst must decide whether to accept or reject this assumption.

A slight variation on the technique outlined in the preceding paragraph was used by Simon Kuznets and his associates for their projection of Philadelphia in 1950 [19]. They used an abridged 1939 life table for Northern cities with more than 100,000 inhabitants, assuming it would be applicable to Philadelphia until the 1950s.

Other techniques for projecting local mortality would be those described in the section of national mortality projection, above. The advantages of each method are similar for states and other small areas as they are for nations. The main differences are likely to be data quality (some states are better, some worse than the national average) and the fact that data tend to be more variable for smaller populations.

NOTES TO CHAPTER SIX

1. U.S. National Center for Health Statistics, *United States Life Tables by Cause of Death: 1959–61*, vol. I, no. 6, Public Health Service Publication no. 1252 (Washington, D.C.: Government Printing Office, 1968).

2. Henry S. Shryock, Jacob S. Siegel, and Associates, *The Methods and Materials of Demography*, U.S. Bureau of the Census (Washington, D.C.: Government Printing Office, 1971), pp. 778, 779.

3. Ibid., p. 779.

4. United Nations, *Methods for Population Projections by Age and Sex*, Manuals on Methods of Estimating Population, Manual III, Population Studies, no. 25 (New York, 1956), p. 70.

5. Ibid., p. 27.

6. Ansley J. Coale and Paul Demeny, *Regional Model Life Tables and Stable Populations* (Princeton: Princeton University Press, 1966), p. 8.

7. Ibid., p. 11.

8. Ibid., p. 20.

9. Shryock, Siegel, and Associates, p. 778.

10. Statistics Canada, *The Population Projections for Canada*, Analytical and Technical Memorandum no. 4 (Ottawa, 1970).

11. Ibid., p. 11.

12. P. K. Whelpton, "Population of the United States, 1925 to 1975," *American Journal of Sociology*, Vol. 34, No. 2 (1928).

13. Francisco Bayo and Steven F. McKay, *United States Population Projections for OASDHI Cost Estimates*, U.S. Department of Health, Education, and Welfare, Social Security Administration, Office of the Actuary, Actuarial Study no. 72 (Washington, D.C.: Government Printing Office, 1974).

14. U.S. Bureau of the Census, *Current Population Reports*, series P–25, no. 541 (1975), p. 4.

15. James D. Tarver and Therel R. Black, *Making County Population Projections—A Detailed Explanation of a Three-Component Method, Illustrated by Reference to Utah Counties*, Bulletin (Technical) 459 (Logan, Utah: Utah Agricultural Experiment Station in Cooperation with Oklahoma State University Research Foundation, 1966), p. 45.

16. Michigan Department of Commerce, State Resources Planning Program, "Michigan Population: 1960 to 1980." Working Paper no. 1 (Lansing, Michigan: 1966).

17. Wisconsin Bureau of State Planning, "Wisconsin Population Projections" (Madison, Wisconsin: 1969).

18. Kentucky Program Development Office, "Kentucky Population Projections: 1975–2000," vol. I (Frankfort, Kentucky: 1972).

19. Simon S. Kuznets with the Assistance of E. Douglas Burdick, Edward P. Hutchinson, and David T. Rowlands, *The Population of Philadelphia and Environs in 1950*, A Report to the Philadelphia City Planning Commission (Philadelphia: Institute of Local and State Government, University of Pennsylvania, 1946).

Chapter Seven

Projecting Population by Age and Sex: The Fertility Component

INTRODUCTION

Fertility is presently the most actively researched field of demographic study. This observation may be substantiated by the fact that the index to the first ten volumes of the Population Association of America's journal—*Demography*—contained 20 pages of article listings by subject and six of those pages were devoted to one aspect or another of fertility [1]. The reason for this activity lies in the concern about the prospect of world overpopulation. Some of this concern has been translated into research grants from the federal government and from privately endowed organizations such as the Population Council and the Ford Foundation. One result of this large amount of research is that demographers now have the theory and data available to construct very detailed computer models of human reproduction.

Most of the more sophisticated fertility models are intended to investigate statistically likely outcomes of the use of various contraceptive methods. For this reason, their basic data are as likely to come from clinical sources as they are from the more traditionally demographic vital statistics sources. In principle, such models based on stochastic processes or on Monte Carlo simulation techniques may be used to project fertility rates for use in cohort-component projection systems. But this has not happened in practice.

This writer does not know exactly why the models have not been used for population forecasting. One may speculate that demographers are inherently cautious souls and are waiting to see proof that such models are really worthwhile before committing themselves to their use. Or it might be suggested that demographers have been trained to feel more comfortable with deterministic models and therefore continue to use the more traditional methods out of habit. The most likely reason for failure to use the models for projection purposes lies in a gap between the data requirements of the models and the availability of fertility data for the population that is to be projected. One particular problem area is the blending or splicing of the often highly detailed model data with the less detailed empirical data at a benchmark date from which the model projects the future.

Such data tensions also exist for even the simpler, traditional, deterministic fertility projection methods that are treated in the present chapter. Generally speaking, highly detailed fertility data that have some claim to statistical reliability are available at the national level. Data similar in scope may be found at the state level, but their usefulness is lessened due to uncertainties as to the effect of "contamination" due to migration. That is, while it is an easy matter to create a set of age-specific fertility rates for a state for several points in the recent and more distant past, it is not possible to cleanly trace an age-specific history of fertility for a given birth cohort of females. This is because there are constant additions to the population and subtractions from the population due to migration. The net effect of such turnover will be greatest in places that are growing rapidly through net inmigration; over the course of a decade or two, the character of a population can change drastically. The classic case is that of a rapidly suburbanizing county. At one census, its population might be rural and its birth rates high. Twenty years later, its population could be largely white collar suburban and its birth rates would be low.

As a rule, the smaller the area (or size of population), the greater the possible migration contamination effect and, in addition, the greater the random variability of vital statistics and census data.

The task of the projection analyst is to make use of the maximum amount of information from his data, given two major constraints: (1) highly detailed data from small areas should be used with great caution; (2) highly complex models should be avoided if a simpler model will do just about as well. It should be noted that these desiderata are seldom attained in practice. The most usual failing has to do with making maximum use of available data; that is, most state and local projections err on the side of excessive simplicity.

The next section of this chapter will deal with some of the more common shortcut methods that have been found in state and local population projection methodologies. None of these methods can be strongly recommended except where a detailed study of local data indicates that there are no viable alternative means of projecting fertility by age of the female population. The final section of the chapter treats some relatively complex age-specific fertility projection techniques. Some are more practical for state and local use than others, as will be made evident in the discussion. Unless birth data by five year age group of mother are lacking or are considered unreliable, the analyst is urged to evaluate these techniques carefully for adoption or adaptation for his own projection system.

SIMPLE FERTILITY PROJECTION METHODS

The methods described in this section make few, if any, demands in the way of detailed fertility data. They also require little or no analysis of historical fertility trends and are equally undemanding with regard to assumptions about future fertility. The price paid for this simplicity of use is that the analyst runs a very real risk of making projections that are inappropriate for the population he is supposed to project. These shortcomings should become apparent in the discussion that follows.

Use of Census Bureau Fertility Rates

The most widely known and used fertility rates for projection purposes in the United States are the various series developed by the U.S. Bureau of the Census for use in their national population projections. Although there have been some detail changes, the basic methodology for the last decade has involved the setting of target total fertility rates *(TFRs)* and their component age-specific fertility rate *(ASFR)* values 30 years in the future. The cumulative fertility rates *(CFRs)* of birth cohorts at the projection baseline date are trended toward interstitial completed cohort fertility rates *(CCFRs)*, so that past and future *ASFRs* are realistically modeled as the fertility of the population moves from the baseline values to the target values.

The individual fertility scenarios can be called "fertility assumption series," each series being designated by a letter. The letters have run from *A* through *F*, and each time the Census Bureau produced a set of projections, four fertility series in alphabetical sequence were used. In the mid-1960s, the series were *A* through *D*; by 1972, they were *C* through *F*. The *TFR* and individual *ASFR* values would change slightly within each series from revision to revision, although the *TFRs* remained fairly consistent. For example, series *C* trended to a *TFR* value of 2,775 in the 1967 projections and to a value of 2,800 for the 1972 projections. The system was changed in 1975 so that only three fertility series were used for any one set of projections, and the labeling system was changed from letters to the numerals I, II, and III. Details of the Census Bureau methodology are presented later in this chapter.

Many state and local population projections incorporate one or another of the Census Bureau fertility rate series that are current at the time the projections are made. Examples are Illinois [2] and the multicounty planning region around Rochester, New York [3]. The main advantage in using the Census Bureau rates directly is that the rates are based on relatively sophisticated techniques that are not easy to duplicate locally without the aid of someone with demographic training. Therefore, in the absence of a staff demographer, using Census Bureau rates is the easy route to take.

Unfortunately, the appropriation of Census Bureau fertility rates for local projection purposes may result in short term fertility projection error. Consider the data in Figure 7–1. The upper panels chart *ASFR*s for the United States and three counties in New York State in 1960 and 1970; the U.S. data are for July 1 and the county data are centered on April 1, and in each case, births to females under age 15 and over age 44 are included in age groups 15–19 and 40–44, whichever is closer. The lower panels represent the same data in normalized form. (That is, the individual age-specific rates were summed and then each was divided by that sum.) The three counties were selected because they illustrate local areas with differing characteristics. Franklin County is in the far reaches of Upstate New York. The southern part of the county is in the Adirondack Mountains, and the northern edge lies along the Canadian border. The county has no cities or towns of great size. Monroe County may be classed as a metropolitan county, as it includes the city of Rochester and most of its suburbs. It grew rapidly during the 1960s. Nassau County is suburban. It is on Long Island, and lies immediately to the east of the New York City borough of Queens. Nassau experienced explosive population growth during the 1950s, but that growth slowed considerably during the 1960–1970 decade as most of the land available for housing became occupied.

The plots in the figure indicate that as the character of the county varies, so does its *ASFR* pattern. Franklin, the most rural county, has the highest fertility levels (*TFR* = 4,686 in 1960; 2,943 in 1970) as well as the "earliest" age-specific fertility pattern. Suburban Nassau County has the lowest fertility levels (*TFR* = 3,182 in 1960; 2,056 in 1970) and the "latest" age pattern. It is possible that part of the reason for Nassau's pattern is because much of its population consists of migrants from New York City, and that this migration may well take place after the birth of one or two children to married couples,

Figure 7–1. Observed and Normalized Age-Specific Fertility Rates, United States and Selected New York State Counties, 1960 and 1970

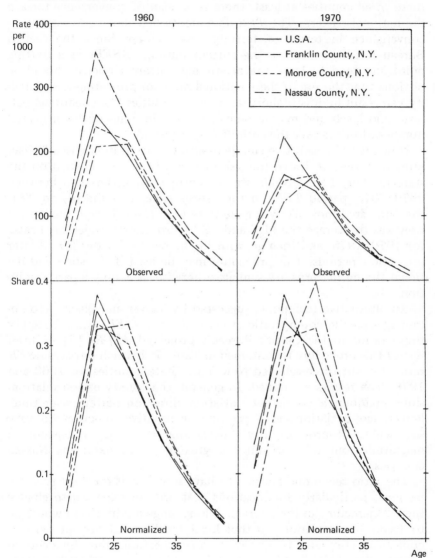

Source: Table 7–1.

thus reducing *ASFR* values for the younger, more migratory age groups. Monroe County falls between the extremes illustrated here (*TFR* = 3,598 in 1960; 2,491 in 1970) although its age pattern is still later than that of the entire nation (*TFR* = 3,655 in 1960; 2,428 in 1970 for the U.S.).

The graphs illustrating the normalized patterns indicate that, for these three counties at least, there is no sign of convergence toward the national pattern. The *TFR* data mentioned above also suggest no convergence in terms of fertility level, either. Since the Census Bureau fertility rates use the current national *ASFR*s as a starting point and tend to leave the age-timing pattern alone, it should be obvious that the use of these national rates for projecting local fertility can result in drastic short term discontinuities from historical patterns and levels and may also be unrealistic in terms of the projected number of births over the entire forecast period.

Now let us present two simple modifications to the Census Bureau rates that tend to lessen the risk of error. One method used on the state level by Pennsylvania was to correct for differences between 1970–1975 period *TFR*s in the census series and the period *TFR* that appeared most likely for the state [4]. The nature of the correction was to average the "D" and "E" (zero growth trajectory) rates for 1970–1975, and then go with the higher "D" series for all later projection periods. This procedure may be used if the state and national timing patterns are similar; otherwise, it is only a partial solution.

An alternative technique, suggested by Tarver and Black, is to obtain age-specific county ratios to the national *ASFR*s and then apply those ratios to the Census Bureau's projected *ASFR*s [5]. A brief test of this procedure is contained in Table 7–1 which displays *ASFR* ratios for our three selected New York State counties for 1960 and 1970. The results are mixed. In general, the county-nation relationships maintain a consistent deviation direction pattern over time. Percentage deviations in a positive or negative direction do vary somewhat: Monroe County's deviations are fairly consistent in magnitude, but the variability is greater for Franklin and Nassau counties.

The ratio technique appears to have some merit for short run projections, particularly for locations that are not expected to change their "character" in the interval. A long range modification would be to trend the deviations so that local fertility matches, or perhaps comes to a stipulated lesser deviation from national rates by a certain future year. This modification also assumes no drastic "character" changes. In any event, it is recommended that some kind of historical test of fertility pattern stability or change, such as is illustrated in the table, be made prior to stipulating operating assumptions. Where an

Table 7–1. Ratios of Selected New York County Age-Specific Fertility Rates to U.S. Rates, 1960 and 1970

		Age-Specific Fertility Rates			Ratio to U.S.A.		
Age	*U.S.A.*	*Franklin*	*Monroe*	*Nassau*	*Franklin*	*Monroe*	*Nassau*
1960							
15–19	91.9	76.0	53.8	26.5	0.827	0.585	0.288
20–24	257.0	354.0	238.4	207.5	1.377	0.928	0.807
25–29	196.8	252.9	218.4	211.8	1.285	1.110	1.076
30–34	112.3	146.7	131.2	119.5	1.306	1.168	1.064
35–39	56.6	77.1	61.7	56.0	1.362	1.090	0.989
40–44	16.4	30.5	16.0	15.1	1.860	0.975	0.921
1970							
15–19	70.5	64.0	54.5	17.2	0.908	0.773	0.244
20–24	163.4	222.8	154.2	112.7	1.364	0.944	0.690
25–29	138.3	147.6	163.2	163.6	1.067	1.180	1.183
30–34	71.6	96.5	82.5	80.4	1.348	1.152	1.123
35–39	32.8	42.5	35.1	30.3	1.296	1.070	0.924
40–44	9.0	15.2	8.7	7.1	1.689	0.967	0.789

Sources: U.S. Bureau of the Census, *Current Population Reports*, series P–25, no. 493, December 1972, Table A–3; New York State Department of Health birth tabulations for New York State Office of Planning Services.

historical evaluation is not possible, use of a convergence assumption is suggested.

The final variation on the use of Bureau of the Census fertility rates comes from the Bureau of the Census itself in its methodology for the projection of states. Their technique is as follows: *GFR* values are calculated for each state and the nation using data for a period surrounding a census year. Ratios of the state to the national *GFR* are then calculated and used to translate projected national *GFR* values to state *GFR* values for each projection period. These resulting state *GFR*s are next multiplied by the projected state female population aged 15—44 to obtain trial birth projections. The projected births are summed over all states and this total is divided into the independently projected national number of births. The ratio thus obtained is used to adjust each of the state birth values so that their sum agrees with the projected national total. In 1966 the *GFR* ratios were trended linearly to converge to a ratio of 1.0, or equality with the projected national *GFR* [6]. By 1972 the assumption had been changed to one of fixed ratios—no convergence—for the entire projection period [7].

The Census Bureau method does capture the transient character of state fertility in terms of its intensity relative to the nation as a whole. However, neither convergence assumption is supported by an accompanying historical analysis such as we recommended above. The use of the *GFR* also seems a little crude, although it might be justified on the questionable assumption that state age structures and *ASFR* values do not vary much from the national measures. In summary, this technique is best used at the small area level where basic fertility data detail is lacking, and not at the county or state level.

Continuation of Current Rates

Another approach to fertility projection that requires little expenditure of analytical effort is to assume the continuation of benchmark fertility rates into the future. This simple assumption is a very dubious one, given the drastic fluctuations in fertility rates since World War I.

Possibly the United States, Canada, and other industrialized nations are settling into a long term fertility pattern that ultimately will result in a halt to population growth. But the prudent model builder, recognizing that states and smaller areas have plenty of potential for variability through population "character" changes (caused, in part, by net change due to migration), should design some flexibility into his projection system. In other words, static fertility schedules are not recommended other than for analytical, baseline projections.

Having condemned this procedure at the outset, let us briefly present some examples from the population projection literature.

Utah population projections initially assumed continuation of 1959–1961 *ASFR*s into the future, but then were modified to use a ratio to Census Bureau rates [8]. Projections for Wisconsin counties continued county-specific fertility rates for the period 1964–1966 in the following manner: First, the mean annual number of births for each county over the three year period was obtained and the result multiplied by five to arrive at half-decade values. For each projection period, these values were multiplied by the ratio of the female population aged 20–34 in the projection year to the females of those same ages in the base year—1965 [9]. Thus, as the number of females in the peak childbearing ages increased or decreased, so would the number of births. Implicit in this method is a static ratio of births to females aged 20–34 in 1965. Kentucky projections for counties used general fertility rates calculated for the counties in 1970 or thereabouts for all projection periods [10].

Our final example is the technique used in an earlier set of Pennsylvania county projections [11]. Here, a variation of the child-woman ratio was used. Separate ratios of males ages 0–4 and females ages 0–4 to females aged 15–34 in 1960 were multiplied by the projected females aged 15–34 in 1970 to project the numbers of males and females under age five in 1970. Ratios of males ages 5–9 and females ages 5–9 to females 20–39 in 1960 were used similarly to obtain the 5–9 populations in 1970. The same 1960 ratios were used again to establish 1980 populations under age ten. In fairness, it should be noted that flexibility was built into the projection system to the extent that child-woman ratios from other historical periods such as 1940 and 1950 could also be used. No mention is made as to whether there was an adjustment for census undercount of the 0–4 population.

COMPARATIVELY COMPLEX FERTILITY PROJECTION METHODS

The word "comparatively" is used in the title of this section to indicate that we are dealing with a class of models that involve more complexity than the models discussed in the preceding section, yet are not as complicated as certain analytical models of fertility that were noted in the introductory section of this chapter. It should be added that the term refers more to conceptual or analytical complexity, meaning that the models are more difficult to understand and to operate than those treated above.

Three types of fertility projection techniques will be discussed in this section. One technique involves trending benchmark *ASFR*s to *ASFR* values that form a target *TFR* level. Another methodological approach is to fit *ASFR* or *CFR* values to mathematical curves. The third general method is to project the components of *ASFR*s.

Target Total Fertility

Two methods of trending benchmark fertility to target levels are discussed below. One is the cohort approach used by the U.S. Bureau of the Census. The other is a period technique used in the 1974 New York State projections.

Census Bureau Cohort Method. The U.S. Bureau of the Census has been using a cohort fertility technique as the basis for its fertility component of national population projections since the mid-1960s. Although the various fertility rate values have changed from time to time in the intervening years (see above), the basic concept, data, and developmental procedures have changed little.

Essentially, the Census Bureau procedure involves two elements. One element is a set of target fertility patterns consisting of *TFR*s and their component *ASFR*s, the latter being keyed to a predetermined mean age at childbearing. The assumption is that in 30 years, after there has been a complete replacement of women in the childbearing ages 15–44, all women will thereafter reproduce according to the target fertility schedule. Also, women entering the childbearing ages at any time during the projection period also reproduce according to the target schedule.

The second element is the projection of future fertility of women who are in childbearing age groups at the benchmark date. Each five year age subgroup has followed a unique empirical *ASFR* schedule that has left it at a given *CFR* level. National *CFR*s as of 1970 are presented in Table 7–2. The females are grouped by year of birth, and each cohort's *CFR*s are read horizontally, with the value in the column labeled "50 years" being *CCFR*s, the cohort analogue to the *TFR*. *ASFR* values for each birth cohort may be obtained by subtraction in the following manner: $ASFR_{25-9} = CFR_{30} - CFR_{25}$, where the subscripts are either exact ages or age ranges. The most difficult part of the Census Bureau method is the blending of the historical cumulative and age-specific fertility with projected age-specific, cumulative, and total fertility in such a way that there are no serious trend dislocations. Jacob S. Siegel describes the 1967 projection procedure as follows:

Table 7-2. Number of Children Ever Born Per 1,000 Women at Five Year
Age Intervals For Birth Cohorts of Women, Five Year Birth Cohorts 1880
to 1949

	Cumulative Births per 1,000 Women to Specified Age					
Birth Cohort of Women[1]	*20 years*	*25 years*	*30 years*	*35 years*	*40 years*	*50 years*
Five Year Cohorts:						
1945–1949	373					
1940–1944	457	1,521				
1935–1939	465	1,722	2,588			
1930–1934	407	1,557	2,531	3,032		
1925–1929	299	1,264	2,177	2,741	2,987	
1920–1924	277	1,062	1,892	2,462	2,752	
1915–1919	248	910	1,603	2,107	2,385	2,464
1910–1914	269	890	1,480	1,951	2,223	2,304
1905–1909	305	1,000	1,566	1,955	2,209	2,288
1900–1904	300	1,106	1,754	2,158	2,388	2,469
1895–1899	(NA)	1,146	1,909	2,385	2,646	2,731
1890–1894	(NA)	(NA)	2,000	2,575	2,909	3,018
1885–1889	(NA)	(NA)	(NA)	2,681	3,102	3,244
1880–1884	(NA)	(NA)	(NA)	(NA)	3,258	3,436

NA—Not Available.

1. For technical reasons, the birth cohorts of women are based on the fiscal year
preceding the calendar years by which the birth cohorts are identified. For
example, the birth cohort of 1940 includes women born July 1, 1939, through
June 30, 1940. See Pascal K. Whelpton and Arthur A. Campbell, *Fertility Tables
for Birth Cohorts of American Women*, Vital Statistics–Special Reports, Selected
Studies, vol. 51, no. 1 (Washington, D.C.: U.S. National Office of Vital Statistics,
1960).

Source: U.S. Bureau of the Census, *Current Population Reports*, series P–23,
no. 36, April 16, 1971, Table 5.

    a. Initial projections of the age-specific birth rates for these cohorts
were obtained by linear interpolation between the current age-specific
rates for 1965 and those for the cohorts reaching childbearing age, or age
14, after July 1965 (i.e., born after July 1951). This step would tend to
effect smooth juncture between the latest observed rates and the projected
rates.

    b. The initial age-specific birth rates from step *a* were arranged by co-
hort and summed to obtain initial estimates of "remaining fertility" for
each cohort now in childbearing (i.e., the difference between cumulative
fertility in 1965 and completed fertility for each cohort).

    c. The results in step *b* were added to the cumulative rates for each co-
hort through 1965 to obtain initial projections of completed fertility for
each cohort.

    d. The initial projection of "remaining fertility" for each cohort in step *b* was adjusted upward or downward by an arbitrary factor so as to change the initial projection of completed fertility into the terminal completed fertility rate for each series or at least to move the initial projection in that direction. . . . The particular margins chosen were dictated by the desirability of keeping the adjustments within bounds so as not to do too much violence to the initial projections of remaining and completed fertility and to avoid discontinuity in the projections, by the need to maintain the rank order of completed fertility rates [of the various fertility series] . . . , and by the desire to assure a sufficiently wide range in the rates from one series to another.

    e. Adjusted age-specific birth rates and adjusted cumulative fertility rates to each age and each year were derived by adjusting the initial age-specific rates, obtained in step *a* and grouped by cohort in step *b*, by the same factors cited in step *d*, and combining the adjusted age-specific rates with the cumulative fertility rates through 1965. The completed fertility rates so derived correspond to those obtained in step *d* [12].

This technique was modified in 1970, when it was felt that the *ASFR*s in the various fertility series did not diverge rapidly enough in the first few projection years. Accordingly, a graphic technique was used for the early part of the trending [13].

The earlier projections had different assumptions regarding mean age at childbearing for each of the fertility series, but this was simplified to one age pattern beginning with the 1971 projections.

Target *TFR* values, with one exception, have been judgmentally stipulated on the basis of *CCFR* levels attained by various birth cohorts in the past. The exception is the "E" series (recently renamed Series II) fertility rates, which trend to a *TFR* level which, if maintained indefinitely, would result in a stationary population size for the United States in the absence of foreign immigration.

Tables 7–3 and 7–4 summarize the historical cohort cumulative fertility and period age-specific fertility rates underlying the 1972 Census Bureau projections. The results of the blending of the "E" series rates from the historical rates are also included for illustrative purposes.

The Census Bureau methodology described above may be used to create projected fertility rates for states and local areas. However, there are some problems that are not serious at the national level which become increasingly menacing as the focus of attention shifts down through the state level to the local level. One problem has to do with the estimation of *ASFR*s and *CFR*s for intercensal dates. The national estimates are relatively precise because the nation is comparatively closed to migration and vital statistics data can aid in setting control values for age-sex–specific population estimates for

Table 7–3. Estimates and Projections of Cumulative and Completed Cohort Fertility Rates, by Birth Cohort of Woman, Selected Birth Cohorts, 1900 to 1960 (Rates represent cumulative live births per 1,000 women up to age indicated. Rates below heavy lines are based in whole or part on projected fertility.)

Series and Birth Cohort of Woman	Up to Age 20	Up to Age 25	Up to Age 30	Up to Age 35	Up to Age 40	Completed Cohort Fertility Rate	Mean Age at Childbearing	Median Age at Childbearing
All Series								
1900	274.9	1,098.0	1,807.4	2,254.4	2,502.3	2,580.0	27.1	26.2
1905	314.3	1,053.3	1,645.6	2,026.1	2,260.6	2,343.2	27.0	25.5
1910	281.0	916.1	1,476.5	1,909.8	2,188.3	2,268.0	27.6	26.8
1915	240.1	856.1	1,498.2	1,985.5	2,251.7	2,331.2	27.9	27.4
1920	272.9	1,034.5	1,826.6	2,390.7	2,695.2	2,777.0	27.7	27.2
Series E								
1925	280.0	1,165.9	2,047.7	2,622.2	2,892.7	2,953.4	27.3	26.7
1930	377.4	1,449.3	2,414.6	2,965.8	3,169.0	3,207.5	26.3	25.7
1935	447.8	1,703.5	2,658.5	3,067.6	3,207.4	3,238.5	25.4	24.7
1940	486.8	1,690.7	2,410.4	2,723.6	2,843.5	2,873.1	24.8	23.9
1945	417.2	1,304.4	1,921.0	2,205.7	2,322.5	2,350.6	25.1	24.2
1950	338.0	1,047.6	1,622.7	1,914.0	2,027.9	2,054.6	25.6	24.9
1955	287.8	989.0	1,589.7	1,887.8	1,998.7	2,024.0	25.8	25.2
1960 and later	271.7	1,037.2	1,663.5	1,968.3	2,076.3	2,100.0	25.8	25.1

Source: U.S. Bureau of the Census, *Current Population Reports*, series P–25, no. 493, December 1972, Table A–4.

Table 7-4. Estimates and Projections of the Total Fertility Rate and Birth Rates by Age of Mother, for the Total Population, 1950 to 2005

Series and Year (calendar year)	Total Fertility Rate[1]	Central Birth Rates by Age of Mother							
		10 to 14 years	15 to 19 years	20 to 24 years	25 to 29 years	30 to 34 years	35 to 39 years	40 to 44 years	45 to 49 years
Estimates									
1950	3,029.6	0.9	78.9	192.8	164.9	100.9	52.1	14.4	1.0
1955	3,520.5	1.0	90.3	236.3	187.0	114.9	58.3	15.4	0.9
1960	3,654.9	1.0	90.9	257.0	196.8	112.3	56.6	15.5	0.9
1965	2,922.4	0.9	73.4	194.0	161.4	94.7	46.3	12.8	0.7
1968	2,459.5	1.0	66.8	168.7	135.4	74.3	35.5	9.7	0.6
1969	2,405.8	1.0	67.2	162.7	135.2	71.5	33.8	9.1	0.6
1970	2,428.2	1.1	69.4	163.4	138.3	71.6	32.8	8.5	0.5
1971	2,251.8	1.1	66.0	150.6	130.0	65.8	29.0	7.3	0.4
Projections Series E									
1972	2,000.0	0.5	56.3	135.4	116.4	58.8	25.8	6.4	0.4
1973	1,900.0	0.5	51.2	130.0	111.3	56.2	24.4	6.1	0.4
1974	1,921.5	0.6	51.7	132.6	112.3	56.4	24.3	6.0	0.4
1975	1,942.6	0.6	52.2	135.2	113.3	56.7	24.2	6.0	0.4
1980	2,042.6	0.6	53.8	148.1	118.4	58.1	23.6	5.7	0.3
1985	2,095.8	0.6	53.8	153.1	123.6	59.4	23.0	5.4	0.3
1990	2,106.6	0.6	53.8	153.1	125.3	60.7	22.4	5.2	0.3
1995	2,103.2	0.6	53.8	153.1	125.3	61.0	21.8	4.9	0.2
2000	2,100.5	0.6	53.8	153.1	125.3	61.0	21.6	4.7	0.2
2005 and later	2,100.0	0.6	53.8	153.1	125.3	61.0	21.6	4.6	0.2

1. These total fertility rates differ slightly from those published by the National Center for Health Statistics. These rates are the sum of single year of age central birth rates which are based on births adjusted for underregistration and numbers of females adjusted for net census undercount. The rates for 1969 through 1971 have been estimated on the basis of vital statistics data from selected States.

Source: U.S. Bureau of the Census, *Current Population Reports,* series P-25, no. 493, December 1972, Table A-3.

rate denominators. State and local age-sex–specific population estimates usually must be based on interpolation for intercensal years
between past censuses and are estimated with even less precision in
periods after the latest preceding census and before the forthcoming
census. Uncertainty as to denominator values means that the resulting fertility rates must be somewhat suspect.

Perhaps a more serious problem is the migration "contamination"
effect we have referred to from time to time. This factor can influence historical cohort data and projected cohort fertility as well, because the cohorts are not truly local cohorts. Indeed, the women are
classified by year of birth, but a horde of new suburbanites is not the
same as a group of "native" rural women of the same age; each has
had a different upbringing and outlook on life and on desired ultimate family size. Any attempt to blend historical into projected
fertility should really involve stratification of the population into
two groups (if the area is expected to change its character): One
group would be the original population, and the other would be the
successor population. The problem here is that it is virtually impossible to sort out the historical data for the groups, let alone to project them. This writer presently knows of no existing local projection
methodology that satisfactorily handles the cohort fertility projection problem.

New York State Period Fertility Method. The fertility projection
method described in this section represents something of a compromise between the overly simplified techniques described in the first
part of this chapter and the empirical and conceptual dilemmas inherent in the use of cohort models for local areas. The method is a
variation of the period *ASFR* technique which the Census Bureau
used immediately before going over to cohort fertility models.

"Period" data are data for a given year or other comparatively
short length of time. Period fertility rates would be, for instance, the
*ASFR*s reported in 1970 and their derivative *CFR*s and *TFR*. As
such, they represent an "synthetic cohort" that cuts across true birth
cohorts. Period data are affected by time-related events, and therefore present a slightly distorted picture of the past and the present to
the analyst who wishes to project the future. For example, economic
conditions in a given period could be so bad that numerous women
delay having children, but eventually the children will be born.
Cohort analysis may suggest that what is happening is indeed a delay,
whereas period analysis only indicates a serious drop in *TFR* values,
leading the analyst to think that the short run *TFR* is a portent of
TFR values to come. For this reason, period data should be used
with caution.

The model to be described was used in the New York State regional and county demographic projection series of 1974 [14]. The fertility projection technique was influenced by the observed county variation in fertility timing patterns for the counties in New York State (see Figure 7–1, above). Study of the normalized *ASFR* patterns resulted in the selection of six model normalized patterns that were associated with county "character" types—i.e., "suburban," "college," "rural," and so forth. These patterns are presented in Table 7–5. The pattern we have labeled "A" was found to be typical of rural counties in New York State, pattern "F" represents counties with large concentrations of college students, "E" approximates suburban patterns, and the remainder are interstitial types.

The model normalized *ASFR* patterns are readily transformed into usable *ASFR* values by multiplying each vector element by a scalar quantity which is a *TFR*. As an illustration, we can transform pattern "C" into *ASFR*s resulting in a *TFR* of 2.1 children per females as follows: $2.1 \times 0.08 = 0.168; 2.1 \times 0.325 = 0.685; 2.1 \times 0.3 = 0.630; 2.1 \times 0.19 = 0.399; 2.1 \times 0.085 = 0.178; 2.1 \times 0.02 = 0.042$. The calculated *ASFR* values sum to a *TFR* of 2.102, as would be expected. The system provides considerable flexibility for the user, particularly if even more intermediate patterns were added. All that is needed to operate the system is for the analyst to identify the model normalized childbearing pattern that is closest to the pattern empirically observed for each county at the benchmark date. The chosen pattern is either maintained for future projection dates, or other patterns are selected for future dates according to the judgment of the analyst. *TFR* values are also selected for each projection period and can easily be blended with benchmark *TFR*s. The pattern selections and *TFR*s are filed with other operating parameters in the computer and calculations of the type outlined above are carried out for each county at each projection period to create the *ASFR*s to be used to calculate births.

Table 7–5. Normalized Age-Specific Fertility Rate Distributions Used in 1974 New York State Demographic Projections

Age	A	B	C	D	E	F
15–19	0.110	0.080	0.080	0.060	0.060	0.100
20–24	0.370	0.350	0.325	0.315	0.300	0.250
25–29	0.260	0.290	0.300	0.330	0.360	0.370
30–34	0.160	0.180	0.190	0.190	0.180	0.180
35–39	0.080	0.080	0.085	0.085	0.080	0.080
40–44	0.020	0.020	0.020	0.020	0.020	0.020

Source: New York State Office of Planning Services.

Two problems are inherent to this technique. The major problem has to do with the fact that cross-sectional or period fertility rates such as are created by this method are often unrealistic when they are examined in terms of cohort fertility. The difficulty in reconciling the two ways of measuring and projecting fertility was apparent in the description of the Census Bureau method in the preceding section. The main defense of the New York technique in light of this criticism is to cite the fact that local areas do not have "true" cohorts because of migration. Therefore, net migration may well impose empirical "cohort" discontinuities that are just as severe as distortions created by the use of period fertility rates. This writer suggests that if the New York model is used, the analyst would be well advised to have computer edits of the created "cohort" CFRs made so that cohort discontinuity magnitudes could be spot-checked, and corrected if necessary.

A lesser problem is related to the fact that there is a wide range of TFR values for the analyst to use. However, empirically, there are certain biological limits to the rates. Useful limiting fertility values may be obtained from a paper by Louis Henry [15] on high fertility populations. Henry's data suggest that the TFR should not exceed 11.0 and that no individual annual ASFR should exceed 0.6. Particular care must be taken for ASFR values for age groups 35—39 and 40—44, and age group 45—49 if it is used. These groups are increasingly affected by the onset of sterility, so "impossible" ASFRs should be avoided. Upper limits for the respective age groups would be 0.41, 0.235, and, perhaps, 0.06. These ASFR constraints are for annual values and the model rates are often five year values. The reader may work out a table of safe TFR values for his own set of normalized rates; the patterns from the New York projections appear to be realistic so long as the TFR scalar does not exceed 8.1—a very unlikely circumstance.

Fitting Mathematical Functions to to Fertility Rates

An approach to the problem of modeling fertility rates for projection purposes that has not, to this writer's knowledge, been attempted at the state or local level, is the use of mathematical functions. The main advantage to the use of such functions is their parameterization, which readily permits the computation of smooth curves over all childbearing age groups. Growth curve functions also have the potential of being able to project incomplete cumulative fertility for cohorts. Unfortunately, there are also some disadvantages to such models. These will become apparent as our discussion proceeds.

Keyfitz discusses three techniques for graduating the "net maternity function" (which is the product of the *ASFR* and the proportion of a birth cohort of women who survive to each childbearing age group) [16]. Since mortality rates for women of childbearing age tend to be low in developed countries, we may assume that the techniques are useful for modeling *ASFR* values alone. The models advanced by Keyfitz are the normal, the exponential, and the incomplete gamma functions. All require the use of the zero, first, and second moments about the origin, with the zero moment equated to the net reproduction rate—or the *TFR*, in our variation. Details on the fitting of these curves are in Keyfitz's book. What is important for the analyst is not so much the fitting of curves to historical data; the real concern is to be able to project the curves for realistic applications. Realistic projections are possible only if the parameters are meaningful in demographic terms. The *TFR* has meaning, as does the mean age at childbearing, which is also the mean interval between generations. The second moment about the origin—the variance—poses greater interpretive problems in that it has no demographic meaning. The analyst is advised to compute the moments of his historical *ASFR* data to determine their relationships before attempting any projections that depend on trending or otherwise modifying moment values.

Keyfitz also presented a diagram locating some empirical net fertility functions on the Pearsonian standardized moment plane. All of the distributions fall into the Pearson Type I curve area, and Keyfitz suggested that the "empirical straight line $\beta_2 = 2 + 2\beta_1$ would pass close to all points . . ." [17]. (In the Pearson plane, $\beta_1 + \mu_3^2/\mu_2^3$ and $2 + \mu_4/\mu_2^2$, where μ_n, $n = 1, 2, 3, 4$, are moments about the origin. All curves in the Pearson system can be located on points, lines, or areas on a plane where β_1 is one axis, and β_2 is the perpendicular axis.) Setting aside this intriguing apparent regularity, we shall consider only the fact that Keyfitz's examples all fall within the Type I area. This fact would seem to open the possibility of using that distribution as a model fertility function. Indeed, such has been the case.

Romaniuk and Mitra have been exploring the modeling of *ASFR*s using the Pearson Type I—or beta distribution of the first kind, as it is also called [18]. Romaniuk [19] argues that the Type I distribution is an especially attractive *ASFR* model because it can be fitted using three parameters, each of which can be interpreted demographically. The demographically meaningful parameters are the *TFR*, the mean age of fertility, and the model age of fertility. The *TFR* is actually used as a scalar in the same fashion as in the New York model described above. This leaves the mean and the mode to determine the shape of the normalized *ASFR* distribution density.

The Pearson Type I model used by Romaniuk is outlined below with each of the elements defined; the derivation of the model is not presented here, so the interested reader should refer to Romaniuk.

$$ASFR \text{ at } x = F \cdot \left[\frac{\left(1 + \frac{x}{a_1}\right)^{m_1} \left(1 - \frac{x}{a_2}\right)^{m_2}}{\sum\limits_{x=-a_1}^{a_2} \left(1 + \frac{x}{a_1}\right)^{m_1} \left(1 - \frac{x}{a_2}\right)^{m_2}} \right] \tag{7.1}$$

where F is the TFR; x is age, $\alpha \leqslant x \leqslant \beta$ where α and β are respectively initial and terminal ages of childbearing, and A and m are parameters with $(m_1/a_1) = (m_2/a_2)$;

$a_1 = M - \alpha$, where M is modal childbearing age;

$a_2 = \delta - (M - \alpha)$, where $\delta = \beta - \alpha$;

$m_2 = \dfrac{a_2 \left[(a_1 + a_2)\right] - 2v}{(a_1 + a_2)(v - a_1)}$, where $v = A - \alpha$, and A is the mean

age at childbearing;

$m_1 = (a_1 m_2)/a_2$.

Thus, if α and β are stipulated in advance as Romaniuk suggests, then the only values to be defined are F, A, and M. In principle, the beginning and final ages of childbearing would be parametric values that would vary slightly from case to case. Romaniuk has simplified the distribution from four to essentially two parameters by stipulating unchanging values of α and β over all cases. These stipulations were based on experimentation with Canadian fertility data, and the respective age values are 17 and 50.

Aside from the usual problems of translation from period to cohort rates, the model has some limitations imposed by the quality of local fertility data. Typically, birth data by single year of age of the mother are not easily obtained for counties and other small areas. This means that historical $ASFR$ data in five year age groups usually must be used to help the analyst stipulate mean and modal values for the projections. The comparatively small number of five year groups in the childbearing age range means that calculated mean values may be imprecise. In addition, modal point values cannot be directly measured, so a formula such as Mean − Mode = 3(Mean − Median) must be used. Assuming that mean and median age values calculated from the grouped data are tolerably valid, the analyst may be able to proceed with his investigation. If everything works, the Pearson Type I model has an advantage over the New York method in that there is great flexibility in the shape of the normalized pattern in addition to the flexibility in the *TFR* value selection. Care must still be taken to avoid generating impossibly high *ASFR* values.

Another function that has been used to represent age-specific fertility is the Gompertz curve, which we treated in Chapter Three. Murphy and Nagnur [20] used the Gompertz curve and the related Makeham curve to fit empirical Canadian period and cohort cumulative fertility rates by single years of age. They indicated that the function did not accurately predict completed fertility when fitted to incomplete cohort *CFR* data. They also note that the Gompertz function "does not seem to appear well suited for use with the cohort-translation method of estimating fertility." Furthermore, as was mentioned in Chapter Three, the Gompertz function has the property that the maximum value of its first derivative (or modal point in the distribution density) is at a point equal to 36.8 percent of completed fertility. Examination of the empirical curves in Figure 7–1 indicates that this relationship does not hold for either Monroe County or Nassau County. It follows that, to the extent that empirical *ASFR*s diverge from the relationship, the Gompertz model will yield unsatisfactory results. We therefore submit that the Gompertz function lacks the flexibility to project *ASFR* patterns for small areas where such patterns vary considerably.

Fertility Component Models

One final approach to projecting fertility bears mentioning even though it has seldom, if ever, been used for local areas. That approach is to reduce age-specific and cumulative fertility rates into their components.

One component is the progression of women from one parity status to the next, where "parity," in demographic parlance, means the number of live-born children a woman has had at any given time in her life. Every woman can be assigned a parity status and every woman begins in parity status zero. She can only proceed to higher status levels or remain in her current status. It is possible to gather data at the national level that indicates the proportion of women in given birth cohorts who are at given parity statuses and it is also possible to put together tables indicating both age-specific and lifetime rates of transition from one status to another. Further refinement might be added by taking age at marriage into account as well as intervals between children of different birth orders.

Parity models require highly refined data that seldom can be assembled for local areas. Even if the required data were assembled, many of the data "cells" would contain very few cases, which implies considerable random variability and lack of precision. At the national level, experimental Census Bureau models using parity progression techniques which were tested in the early 1960s apparently have not yet worked well enough for use in official projections [21].

Another component model was developed by Whelpton and Campbell at the Scripps Foundation [22]. It is a cohort fertility model similar to the current Census Bureau technique. It differs in that it stratifies birth cohorts of women by age at first marriage and then treats cumulative fertility of married women of each birth cohort. Once the marital *CFR*s are projected, the rates are adjusted to include all women and are transformed into *ASFR* values to be used for multiplication by the population to compute births in the usual manner.

To conclude the discussion of fertility projection methodologies, the observation must be made that there is no technique in the population projection literature that is free of potentially serious defects where application is intended for local areas. The three obstacles—the lack, or poor quality of data; the effects of local "character" resulting in a wide range of possible patterns; and the contamination effect of net change in the population through migration—are very difficult to surmount. In fact, they doom all of the proposed methods to partial failure. The analyst is advised to weigh these obstacles against the needs of his client, with due attention being paid to the analytical utility of the models and the amount of skill and time required to set them up and run them. The choice of model must, of necessity, be a compromise.

NOTES TO CHAPTER SEVEN

1. *Demography*, Cumulative Index, vol. 1–10 (1964–1973), vol. 11, no. 2, pt. 2 (1974).

2. Illinois Bureau of the Budget, "Uniform Demographic and Economic Data: 1970–2000," Summary (Springfield, Illinois: 1973).

3. Genesee–Finger Lakes Regional Planning Board, "Regional Population Distribution and Projections"(Rochester, N.Y.: 1971).

4. Pennsylvania Office of State Planning and Development, "Pennsylvania Projection Series: Population and Labor Force," Report no. 73 (Harrisburg, Penna.: 1973), p. 1.

5. James D. Tarver and Therel R. Black, *Making County Population Projections—A Detailed Explanation of a Three-Component Method, Illustrated by Reference to Utah Counties* Bulletin (Technical) 459 (Logan, Utah: Utah Agri-

cultural Experiment Station in Cooperation with Oklahoma State University Research Foundation, 1966), pp. 77–78.

6. U.S. Bureau of the Census, *Current Population Reports*, series P–25, no. 326 (1966).

7. U.S. Bureau of the Census, *Current Population Reports*, series P–25, no. 493 (1972).

8. Therel R. Black, Jewell J. Rasmussen, and Frank C. Hachman, "Population Projections: Utah and Utah's Counties," Economic and Population Studies, Utah State Planning Program (Salt Lake City, Utah: 1967).

9. Wisconsin Bureau of State Planning, "Wisconsin Population Projections" (Madison, Wisconsin: 1969), pp. 5, 11.

10. Kentucky Program Development Office, "Kentucky Population Projections: 1975–2000," vol. I (Frankfort, Kentucky: 1972).

11. Temple University Office of Research and Specialized Studies, "The Population of Pennsylvania: Projections to 1980" (1963).

12. U.S. Bureau of the Census, *Current Population Reports*, series P–25, no. 381 (1961), pp. 26–27.

13. U.S. Bureau of the Census, *Current Population Reports*, series P–25, no. 448 (1970), p. 6.

14. New York State Office of Planning Services, "Demographic Projections: for New York State Counties to 2000 A.D." (Albany, N.Y.: 1974).

15. Louis Henry, "Some Data on Natural Fertility," *Eugenics Quarterly* 8, 2 (1961):81–91.

16. Nathan Keyfitz, *Introduction to the Mathematics of Population* (Reading, Mass.: Addison-Wesley, 1968), ch. 6.

17. Ibid., p. 160.

18. S. Mitra, "The Pattern of Age-Specific Fertility Rates," *Demography* 4, 2 (1967):894–906; S. Mitra and A. Romaniuk, "Pearsonian Type I Curve and Its Fertility Projection Potentials," *Demography* 10, 2 (1973):351–365.

19. A. Romaniuk, "A Three-Parameter Model for Birth Projections" (Paper Accepted for Population Association of America Meeting, New Orleans, 1973).

20. Edmund M. Murphy and Dhruva N. Nagnur, "A Gompertz Fit that Fits: Applications to Canadian Fertility Patterns," *Demography* 9, 1 (1972):35–50.

21. U.S. Bureau of the Census, *Current Population Reports*, series P–25, no. 286 (1964).

22. Ibid.

Chapter Eight

Projecting Population by Age and Sex: The Migration Component

INTRODUCTION

It generally holds true that the smaller in area and population a national subarea is, the greater will be the impact of migration in determining the direction and magnitude of its population change. The impact of net change through migration is particularly intense where individual birth cohorts and age groups are concerned. Therefore, if state and local population projections are to be used by persons or agencies concerned with particular age-related client groups, such as persons of college age or retirement age, then the projection analyst should take special pains to see that the migration projected by his model has the most realistic age detail possible.

The present chapter discusses the various techniques known by the writer to have been used for projecting migration by age and sex for states and local areas since the 1950s. The methods vary in their sophistication, but even the more advanced methods are less than ideal solutions to the problem of creating realistic age detail in migration projections. This is because the subject of age-specific migration has been ignored by most demographers.

Our discussion begins with methods that assume straightforward extension of recent migration experience. Then we move on to a number of trending techniques, and finally consider some methods that are more analytical in nature.

METHODS ASSUMING CONTINUATION OF RECENT MIGRATION RATES

Cohort-Survival Method

The cohort-survival method is not a pure migration technique; it combines the effects of mortality and net migration so as to project changes in age composition. Although the technique had been used on a few occasions during the first half of this century, it was formalized in the early 1960s by Hamilton and Perry [1]. We shall rely on the Hamilton-Perry article in this presentation. Using their notation, cohort-survival rates for each age group are obtained as follows:

$$P_x^7 = (P_{x-10}^6 \times P_x^6)/P_{x-10}^5 \tag{8.1}$$

where P_x^7 is the population in age group x in 1970; P_x^6 is the population in age group x in 1960; P_{x-10}^6 is the population in age group $(x-10)$ in 1960; and P_{x-10}^5 is the population in age group $(x-10)$ in 1950. The formula is more easily understood if it is rearranged:

$$P_x^7/P_{x-10}^6 = P_x^6/P_{x-10}^5 \tag{8.2}$$

The relationships can be extended to the populations aged 0–4 and 5–9 in the later year by comparing these persons to reported births in the area during, respectively, the second half and the first half of the intercensal decade. Cohort-survival rates for males in King County, Washington (Seattle and environs), for the decades 1950–1960 and 1960–1970 are graphed in Figure 8–1.

The major justification for using a ratio that contains the joint effect of mortality and net migration on cohort change for population projection purposes is that, according to Hamilton and Perry, it embodies the best possible assumption that can be made if there is to be only one set of projections. That is the assumption of no change in demographic component rates. "After all," they say, "the events of the near future are organically and functionally tied to and dependent upon the events of the recent past" [2]. They perceive the main weakness of using the recent past to forecast the near future as being the possible inclusion of unusual events such as economic depressions or wars in the model. Should the analyst be aware of such disruptive factors, they counsel him to use a broader or perhaps a more "normal" base period. They did feel that the decade 1950–1960 was normal enough to serve as the basis for projecting 1960–1970, and our King County example, at least, bears this out because the rates for the two decades are similar.

More specific assumptions underlying the model are: (1) relevant population definitions such as areal boundaries do not change during the projection period; (2) the age-specific mortality and net migration rates do not change from the baseline decade to the projection decade; and (3) census enumeration error effects in the two calibration censuses hold for the projection date census. The final point is

Figure 8–1. Census Survival Ratios, King County, Washington, Males, 1950–1960 and 1960–1970

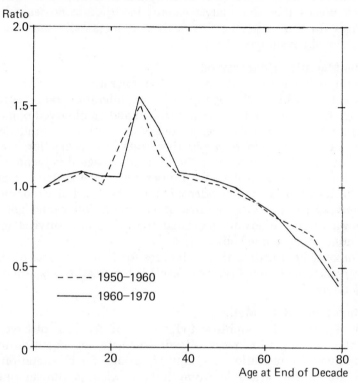

Source: Calculated from U.S. Census Bureau data.

in reference to the fact that all censuses contain systematic enumeration errors that are necessarily built into the projection rates, and if the errors continue to hold in the future, the projection will be free of such bias when compared with the future enumerated population.

Hamilton and Perry state that if the above assumptions hold, then the projection formula is "exact," not requiring explicit adjustments for migration and mortality. Furthermore, it "has built into it the *local* combined mortality and migtation rates of the base decade. . . . Hence, there is no need to adjust for differences between mortality of the local area and that of the state or nation as is necessary in the use of United States Census survival rates in estimating net migration in local areas" [3].

What Hamilton and Perry are really proposing is a baseline set of projections against which alternative projections can be evaluated. But even mortality rates are not static, and rates of net migration are potentially extremely changeable. Taken in isolation, the cohort-survival technique is of limited analytical use. It is also inflexible, which means that the analyst cannot incorporate postcensal trend changes. In this writer's opinion, these defects more than outweigh the claimed advantages.

Net Migration Rate Method

Another means of extending recent migration behavior into the future is to obtain the age-specific net migration rates, either by taking the difference between a survived and an observed population or from responses to the census query as to place of residence five years previously, and to apply these rates for projection purposes without modification. About the only advantage this technique has over the cohort-survival method described above is that the analyst would be able to independently vary the mortality component. Otherwise, the freezing of rates of net migration would appear to have all of the disadvantages listed for the cohort-survival method and none of its claimed advantages.

The only justification this writer sees for fixing any rate of component change at recent historical levels is for creating a baseline set of projections.

Directional Rates Method

A slightly more sophisticated means of freezing observed age-specific net migration rates is to disaggregate net migration into its components—inmigration and outmigration. Such migration flow data are readily available from the U.S. Census Bureau only for states, state economic areas, and for standard metropolitan statistical areas of more than 500,000 population in 1970. For other cases, published information on age-specific inmigration, which is available for many areas, must be compared to estimates of five year net migration in order to estimate age-specific outmigration which is otherwise obtainable only from special tabulations by the Census Bureau. This technique was used by the staff of the planning region surrounding Rochester, New York [4].

The basic migration assumption used by the Genesee–Finger Lakes staff was that the Rochester area would maintain the attractiveness to the rest of the United States that it had in 1965–1970 (a period of considerable growth). Accordingly, the ratio of inmigrants to the national population, by age and sex, was obtained for 1970 and held constant. The ratio of estimated outmigration by age and sex to the 1970 regional population was also calculated. Presumably, it was assumed that outmigratory propensity is a constant, regardless of economic conditions. In the projection calculations, the inmigration ratio was multiplied by national population projections from the U.S. Bureau of the Census and the outmigration rates were multiplied by the surviving regional population at every projection year.

As the projections went farther into the future, the net number of inmigrants declined. This was because the net inmigration assumption had the region growing more rapidly than the nation as a whole and, as a consequence, the base for the fixed outmigration rates was growing more rapidly than the base for the fixed inmigration rates. Hence, the projected numbers of outmigrants were growing more rapidly than the projected numbers of inmigrants, and the gap between the two numbers was thereby narrowing. The analysts who did the projections felt that the decline in net inmigration was more realistic than the result of projections of unconstrained growth rates because "if every area's growth were projected as proportional to its own size, the projections would soon lead to gross inconsistencies between areas with the sum of the parts adding up to substantially more than the whole" [5].

This method of projecting migration is a variation of the method used by the U.S. Bureau of the Census to project state populations which we shall discuss at the end of this chapter. A few remarks can be made regarding the use of this technique at the local level, however. In the first place, if one is not projecting every state or planning region or county in the country, there is no real need to control local migration to a national population or migration value. This is because the local area is very small relative to the whole, and it can safely be assumed that if the area is "competitive" or "attractive" to a certain degree, it will attract migrants to that degree. (To assume that a given region such as Genesee–Finger Lakes has an attractiveness ratio applicable to the rest of the country is itself an oversimplification, because inmigrants tend to be attracted in numbers inversely proportional to the distance from their place of origin. Thus, a more theoretically correct ratio would be inmigrants weighted to changes in the "population potential" of Rochester. "Population potential" is a concept from "social physics," and it is the sum of the rest of the national population divided by their distances from the point in question. For a useful introduction, see Isard [6]. The notion of splitting net migration into its elements is a good one, however, just so long as the directional relationships are not frozen.)

TRENDING PAST RELATIONSHIPS

It should now be clear to the reader that this writer is not enthusiastic about the use of fixed rates of component change in population projection models. Having disposed of the most rigid techniques, we can now proceed to a discussion of methods that have some flexibility.

Variations on the Cohort-Survival Method

We shall first consider some variations that provide a little flexibility to the cohort-survival technique that were used to project the populations of Connecticut and of Pennsylvania and its counties in the early 1960s. The Pennsylvania projections shall be treated first.

Pennsylvania, 1963. The population projections created at Temple University for the State Planning Board of Pennsylvania [7] were based five sets of age-sex–specific cohort-survival ratios—1940:1930, 1950:1940, 1960:1950, 1950:1930, and 1960:1940. In each case, the rates were reduced to five year values by taking either the square or the fourth root, depending whether a ten year or a 20 year observation was used. No attempt was made to sort out the "true" five year rate in terms of cohort-specific components of the manifest ten year and 20 year values (see Chapter Two).

Eight alternative sets of projections were derived from the five sets of cohort-survival ratios. These alternatives are: (1) direct use of the 1950:1940 ratios; (2) direct use of the 1960:1950 ratios; (3) direct use of the 1960:1940 ratios; (4) for each age-sex group, the highest individual ratio from the five basic sets; (5) the lowest of the five basic age-sex–specific ratios; (6) the difference, positive or negative, between each 1960:1950 and 1950:1940 ratio is added to the 1950: 1960 ratio to project 1970:1960; (7) the same as (6), except only positive differences are used—negative differences are recorded as no difference; and (8) same as (7), only negative differences are taken and positive differences are ignored. The report also mentioned that an analyst could use other combinations of the historical ratios, such as averages, if he saw fit.

Although the 1963 Pennsylvania projection model provides some flexibility within the context of the cohort-survival logic, and although local "realism" has been incorporated by use of empirical experiences of each county, the options are still constrained. That is because an area is limited to using its own history as models for the future. This writer is of the opinion that this alternative cohort-survival technique should not be recommended for use in population projections because there are better methods available.

Connecticut, 1962. Population projections for the state of Connecticut for the period 1960–2000 were based on trended cohort-survival ratios [8]. Cohort-survival ratios were calculated for each of the eight decades between 1880 and 1960. These age-sex–specific ratios were then fitted to a trend line using the linear least squares method. Each age-sex–specific trend line was extended so as to project the cohort-survival ratios out to the 1990–2000 decade.

One serious problem emerges when cohort-survival ratios are trended. That problem has to do with the fact that mortality rates in the United States declined for many decades prior to 1950. Since 1950, however, declines in mortality have been slight. Any cohort-survival method that uses pre-1950 data, such as the Connecticut and Pennsylvania techniques discussed in this section, runs a real risk of implicitly continuing a downward mortality trend that may not exist in the future.

Otherwise, this writer feels uneasy about the use of a regression line to "trend" what may well be erratic behavior of the age-sex group data over periods of wars, depressions, booms, and other influential outside events. Perhaps such a trending would make sense as a baseline projection that could be compared to a zero migration assumption projection and to a "best guess" projection. In light of these criticisms, the trending technique used in the Connecticut projections cannot be recommended.

Migration Ratios

The methods discussed below relate the migration of subareas to the migration of larger areas. Provision is also made for trending the relationship of the part to the whole.

Penn Jersey Cohort Ratio Method. The Penn Jersey cohort ratio method was devised as a means of projecting net migration by age, sex, and race for subareas of a metropolitan region [9]. In order for the method to become operational, it is necessary to have appropriately detailed census data for all areas for two consecutive census dates, as well as birth data by sex, race, and subarea for the intercensal period.

The concept of the model may be sketched using the original notation:

$$\,_t^s A_x = (\,_t^s P_x)/(\,_t^r P_x) \tag{8.3}$$

where A is the proportion of the region r population P age x at time t that is in a subarea s. The cohort may be measured from the following census as

$$\,_{t+10}^s A_{x+10} = (\,_{t+10}^s P_{x+10})/(\,_{t+10}^r P_{x+10}) \tag{8.4}$$

The ratio of cohort change may be designated ${}^{s}R_{x+10}$:

$$
{}^{s}R_{x+10} = ({}_{t+10}{}^{s}A_{x+10}) / ({}_{t}^{s}A_{x}) \qquad \cdot \tag{8.5}
$$

Alternatively,

$$
{}^{s}R_{x+10} = \frac{({}_{t+10}{}^{s}P_{x+10})/({}_{t}^{s}P_{x})}{({}_{t+10}{}^{r}P_{x+10})/({}_{t}^{r}P_{x})} \qquad \cdot \tag{8.6}
$$

The R values may be interpreted as the ratio of change due to net migration in a subarea cohort to change due to net migration in the equivalent regional cohort. The last formula indicates that we are dealing with the ratio of two cohort-survival rates—the ratio of the subarea rate to the regional rate. If the assumption is made that census enumeration errors and mortality rates are consistent over time and within all parts of the region, then the observed ratio must be the result of differences in net migration. An example using the city of Seattle and King County, Washington, for the period 1960–1970 is shown in Figure 8–2.

The formula used to calculate five year ratios, based on the assumption that

$$
{}_{t+5}{}^{s}P_{x+5} = ({}_{t}^{s}P_{x} + {}_{t+10}{}^{s}P_{x+10}) / 2 \quad ,
$$

may be written

$$
{}^{s}R_{x+5} = \frac{({}_{t+5}{}^{s}P_{x+5} + {}_{t+10}{}^{s}P_{x+5})/({}_{t}^{s}P_{x} + {}_{t+5}{}^{s}P_{x})}{({}_{t+5}{}^{r}P_{x+5} + {}_{t+10}{}^{r}P_{x+5})/({}_{t}^{r}P_{x} + {}_{t+5}{}^{r}P_{x})} \qquad \cdot \tag{8.7}
$$

R values for ages 0–4 and 5–9 may be calculated as above, when intercensal birth data are entered into the appropriate terms. In this instance, it is helpful to know that

$$
{}_{t+5}P_{0-4} = ({}_{t,\,t+5}B + {}_{t+10}P_{5-9}) / 2 \quad ,
$$

Where B denotes births.

Regional projections are made using a cohort-component technique of the conventional form. Once the regional projection has been made, subareas are projected as follows:

$$
{}_{t+5}{}^{s}P_{x+5} = [\,({}_{t+5}{}^{r}P_{x+5})/({}_{t}^{r}P_{x})\,] \cdot {}_{t}^{s}P_{x} \cdot {}^{s}R_{x+5} \quad , \tag{8.8}
$$

where $(t+5)$ is the projection year. Once all the age-sex-race cohort

Figure 8–2. Penn-Jersey Model Ratios, Seattle and King County, Washington, Males, 1960 and 1970

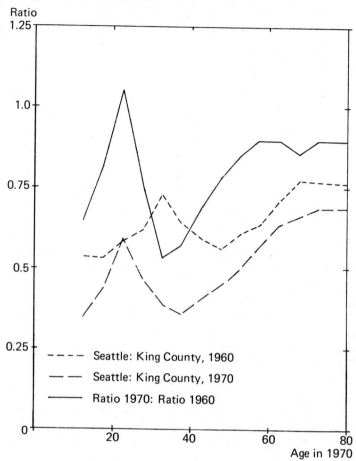

Source: Calculated from U.S. Census Bureau data.

populations are calculated for all subareas at the projection date, it is necessary to adjust the resulting subarea populations so that they sum to the regional values.

It is possible to trend R values. For example, if all $R = 1.0$, then each subarea cohort would change at exactly the same rate as its regional equivalent, and subarea variation would cease. Having R values trend toward 1.0 therefore is one likely projection scenario. If data were available for a number of decades, then it might be possible to obtain two or three sets of R values for each subarea over time, and trend these values in some manner. The analyst should bear in mind that the whole cohort ratio system depends on constant boundaries, so such lengthy time series may not easily be obtained for submetropolitan places such as census tracts.

The basic defect of the cohort ratio method is that the ratios are difficult to interpret and, consequently, are difficult to trend. Taken in isolation, this defect would not be critical; the seriousness is in relation to alternative projection techniques. For instance, it is possible to calculate age-sex-race–specific net migration rates using the same data base required by the cohort ratio method. Net migration rates are inherently more understandable because they provide a cleaner measure of the key element of population change for smaller areas. Future net migration can be manipulated with much greater control, given this knowledge. A preferable alternative technique would be to project populations of subareas using cohort-component methodology and then reconcile cohort subtotals to independently projected regional cohort totals, as in the case of the cohort ratio method.

The only real advantage of the cohort ratio method over the cohort-component technique, which uses explicit migration rates, is that the former method requires less demographic sophistication on the part of the analyst than does the latter if very simple assumptions are made regarding R value trends. If subarea population "character" changes are required, then the reverse is the case; these changes are much more easy to handle using net migration rates directly than through tinkering with R values.

Proportional Net Migrants Method. A population projection method proposed by Tarver and Black [10] for the state of Utah is similar in its effect to the cohort ratio method, although its approach is different. Age-sex–specific net migration values were computed for the state and each county for the decade 1950–1960. Then five projection scenarios were proposed: (1) net migration into Utah would double the 1950–1960 amounts in 1960–1970 and 1970–1980; (2) The amount of net migration would remain at the 1950–1960 level; (3) the net amount of migration would be zero—positive and negative values would be equal; (4) there will be net losses in 1960–1970 and 1970–1980 equal to the net 1950–1960 gain; and (5) there would be zero migration for each age-sex group in each area—that is, population change would be through natural increase. Scenarios (1), (3), and (4) involve manipulation of the 1950–1960 migration values.

Net migration relationships between age groups for each county population are maintained to a considerable degree with this technique; the migration "character" of each county changes little. Net migration magnitudes are scaled to changes in the scenario total for each area-sex group by the following formulas:

$$A(+) = (\Sigma |n_i| + D)/(\Sigma |n_i|) \qquad (8.9)$$

$$A(-) = (\Sigma |n_i| - D)/(\Sigma |n_i|) \qquad (8.10)$$

where $A(+)$ and $A(-)$ respectively refer to adjustments to positive and negative net migration values, n_i, for each age group, and D is the difference between the area-sex group overall net number of migrants stipulated for the projection period minus the calculated 1960–1970 value. The vertical lines mean that absolute values—minus signs disregarded—are to be manipulated. Once the adjusted values are computed for the state, then the same adjustment is made across all counties within the same sex-age group, where D represents the difference between the cohort county sum and the state control value for that cohort. In brief, net migration is trended at the state level, and the counties are collectively moved along with that trend while maintaining their relative contributions to the state total.

Whereas this method preserves county-specific net migration age patterns, it is otherwise limited in its flexibility. There is no provision for counties to change their recent relationship to statewide population growth.

MIGRATION RATE PATTERN TYPES

Earlier in this chapter we referred to the migration "character" of an area's population, but we have not provided any explanation as to what the term means. We shall do this in the present section. First we present a typology of net migration patterns, and then we shall indicate how to make the typology operational in a population projection model.

Empirical Net Migration Forms
Demographers have known for many years that migration—like mortality and fertility—is age-related. The peak migratory ages are from the late teens through the early thirties—the stage in the life cycle when people leave their parental households to seek education, work, and marriage. Migration rates become progressively lower for persons beyond their late twenties or early thirties until the age of retirement, when there is a lesser spurt of migratory activity. Persons in the age range 0–17 tend to be dependents, and their migration behavior reflects that of persons 25 or 30 years older.

Given these general age parameters, there is considerable variation in detail at the local level, particularly when one considers the inmigration and outmigration flow patterns that underlie manifest net migration patterns. This writer has proposed a typology of net migration patterns that is based on two possible dimensions of each directional age pattern [11]. The dimensions are magnitude and timing. Inmigration patterns and outmigration patterns may be dichotomously classed as being either high or low in magnitude and as being either early or late in terms of the timing of the modal or peak age at migration. Thus, we posit four conditions that may be found in a given area: two each for its inmigrants and for its outmigrants. It follows that the number of possible combinations of conditions that shape net migration patterns is 16, of which four cancel, leaving 12 combinations of interest. These may be further simplified and associated with commonplace "character" labels as follows:

1. Unattractive areas should be characterized by heavy, early outmigration and low inmigration, no matter what its timing. This is either a depopulating area or an area which is growing because of a slight excess of natural increase over net [out] migration. Often, but not always, such areas are *rural*.
2. Areas very attractive to mature adults but very unattractive to young adults such as semirural counties or incipient suburbs would have high, early out and high, late in patterns. We call this category *exurban*.
3. Some areas are attractive for all groups. Outmigration of either timing pattern would be low. Inmigration would be high due to attractiveness, and early because there are proportionally more migrants who are younger. . . . Such an area would probably include colleges, jobs, and suburbs. We shall use the term *metropolitan*.
4. There are areas that are attractive enough that outmigration is low (no matter its timing), yet tend to select older inmigrants. Late selection might be due to peculiarities of the local job market or, more likely, because high housing costs restrict inmigration to those who can afford it—typically persons who have had the time to be launched on a career. These characteristics suggest an area that is *suburban*.
5. Finally, there are areas which are sociologically and economically attractive to young persons, yet unattractive to older persons. These areas would be expected to have early inmigration and late outmigration patterns. Such are currently the characteristics of *central cities* [12].

A sixth possible pattern might also be suggested. It is really a separate phenomenon that may be appended to all of the abovementioned types save, perhaps, the rural or heavy net outmigration type. This additional migration type is *retirement* migration, which may be observed in selected counties—particularly in Florida and Arizona.

All six net migration types are illustrated in Figure 8–3. The underlying inmigration and outmigration patterns are also shown so that the reader may compare the explanation above with the empirical data. The state economic areas are the following places: "California—*A*" is the 1960 San Francisco-Oakland SMSA; "New Jersey—1" is a cluster of nonmetropolitan counties in the northern part of the state; "Arizona—*A*" is Phoenix and its surrounding county; "Oklahoma—9" is a group of counties in the southeastern corner of that state; "D.C.—*A*" is the entire District of Columbia; and "Connecticut—*A*" is Fairfield County, near New York City.

Net migration patterns are not always empirically found in their "pure" form. Sometimes, they are "contaminated" by the presence of special migratory subpopulations such as military personnel, college students, and institutional residents. When making projections, it is often wise to separate such populations from the "civilian" population of the area. This means the civilian population must be assigned a migration pattern that is not directly observable. An example is presented in Figure 8–4. Net migration rates by age and sex calculated using the forward census survival method for the decade 1960–1970 are shown for Otsego County, New York. The upper part of the figure contains the observed net patterns which vaguely resemble the center city migration type. But Otsego County is a county of farms and small towns—which also contains two colleges. The presence of the colleges affects the net migration pattern. There is a positive shift around age 20, when the students arrive, and a negative reaction around age 25, when they depart. Note that the zigzag is more extreme for females. This is because one of the colleges is a state teachers college which attracts more females than males.

The lower part of Figure 8–4 contains a "corrected" set of migration rates for the civilian population. The correction was indirect, because of the lack of precise census data at the time the analysis was made. Actually, many useful data series are not available in published form for counties and other small areas, so the analyst may have to resort to making reasonable estimates of the desired values. In this particular case, ratios of Otsego County's population by age and sex to the corresponding New York State groups were obtained and then the ratios were trended by interpolation for the college age groups. These trended ratios were then multiplied by the state population to produce estimates of the county noncollege population in 1960 and 1970. The census survival method was again used to obtain the revised migration estimates presented in the figure. The revised migration rates indicate that Otsego County's noncollege population has an exurban net migration pattern.

Figure 8–3. Examples of Migration Pattern Types, Selected State Economic Areas, 1955–1960 and 1965–1970

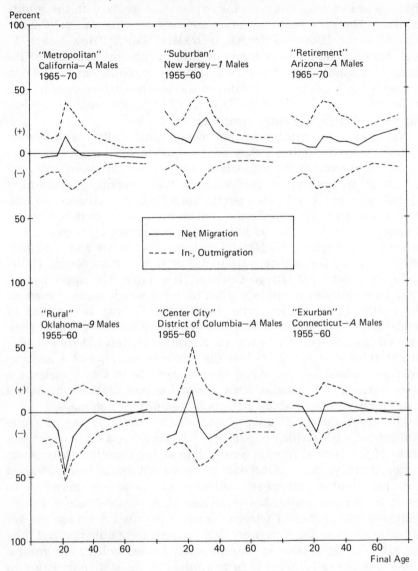

Sources: U.S. Bureau of the Census, *U.S. Census of Population: 1960,* Subject Reports, *Mobility for States and State Economic Areas,* Final Report PC(2)–2B (Washington, D.C.: Government Printing Office, 1963).

_____ , *U.S. Census of Population: 1970,* Subject Reports, Final Report PC (2)–2E, *Migration Between State Economic Areas* (Washington, D.C.: Government Printing Office, 1972).

Figure 8–4.   Age-Specific Net Migration Rates, by Sex, for Otsego County, New York, 1960–1970, Resident Population and Population Less Inmigratory College Students

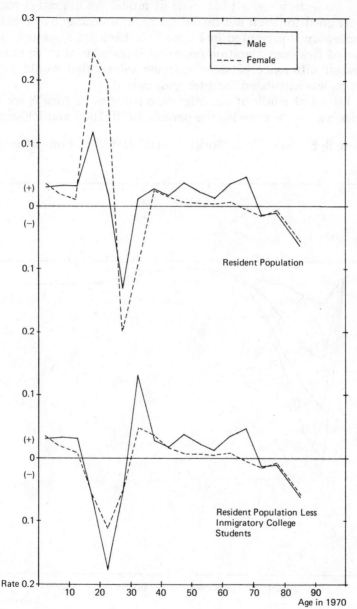

Source: Calculated from U.S. Census Bureau data.

New York Net Migration Projection Technique

The net migration rate typology described above formed the basis for the migration component of the 1974 New York State demographic projection series [13]. Sets of model net migration patterns were designed for each net migration type; an example of sets in the rural category is presented in Figure 8–5. Each set represents a rigid pattern of five year migration rates that is scaled to the "amplitude," or greatest difference between extreme values, that would result if migration was calculated for a ten year period.

An historical study of net migration patterns of New York State counties was made covering the periods 1950–1960 and 1960–1970.

Figure 8–5. New York Model "Rural" Net Migration Patterns

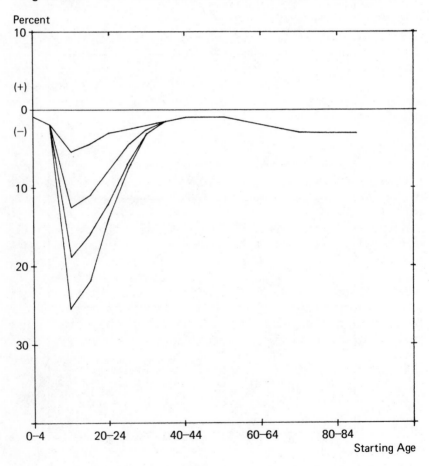

Source: New York State Office of Planning Services.

The net migration type for each sex for each decade was observed, as were the "amplitudes" and the crude, sex-specific net rates. Then a projection scenario was developed that included, for each five year period between 1970 and 2000, sex-specific net migration types, amplitude values, and crude net rates. During the projection sequence, the computer would call up the designated pattern set and multiply it by the population being projected. The calculated age-sex-specific net numbers of migrants would then be summed across all age groups and divided by the total starting population for the sex group in order to calculate a crude net migration rate. This rate would then be subtracted from the target rate in the scenario. The difference then became an algebraic scalar that was added to each value in the model set of age-sex-specific rates so that a new, altered set of rates would be obtained. The revised set, when multiplied by the same population, would produce the desired net migration values. In other words, the adjustment procedure permits the line of zero net migration to move up or down relative to fixed pattern rate sets. So long as the adjustment is not great—say less than 10 percent—the resulting net migration values are fairly realistic. Otherwise, an "unrealistic" migration rate set is probably being used, because the sets were derived from empirical net migration data and are scaled to observed lines of zero net migration.

The main advantage of the technique we have been describing is that it offers more flexibility than previously discussed methods in terms of altering the character of an area's migration over the course of a projection scenario. That is, suburban areas can be changed to exhibit metropolitan or central-city-like migration patterns, while exurban areas can realistically suburbanize.

There appear to be two disadvantages. One is that, within migration types at least, flexibility is limited. Perhaps only four or five sets of rates are available in the present form of the model. A possible solution to this problem would be an interpolation routine that would permit calculation of a greater variety of intermediate sets. A second disadvantage is that the projection results are controlled to crude net migration rates. We have observed earlier that crude rates—past, present, and future—are subject to alteration by variations in the age structure. To the extent that this is true, the calibration of the model is suspect.

Refinements to the Migration
Typology Technique

The migration typology technique is presently in a relatively unrefined stage of its development. Research is being done in this area, but no solid results can be presented at this time. Instead, we shall sketch some of the possibilities opened by the typology.

In the first place, directional rates of migration for small areas may be better understood. If inmigration and outmigration rates by age and sex can be related to each other and to net rates over time, then the way is paved to projection of net migration by its component flows. This in itself is no guarantee of greater accuracy in projections. Indeed, the accuracy might even fall off a little. The advantage would be analytical, allowing the administrator or planner to gauge the population "turnover" and its possible resulting social dislocation, given variations in the model parameters.

A second refinement of the technique would be to key the net migration of the nonlabor force age groups to that of the labor force age population. This would permit the model to be linked to employment projections and it would also lessen the distortion of age structure variation in the parameter specification process. A variation on this refinement strategy would be to relate only young dependents to the labor force age population and project the migration of the population of retirement age population separately. These steps serve to complicate the model, but they should be given serious consideration if they enhance the validity of the results.

LINKING MIGRATION TO ECONOMIC CHANGE

We briefly suggested in the last section that net migration models could be linked to projections of employment. This was done to a limited extent in the OBERS projections discussed in Chapter Four. The techniques dealt with in this section are more elaborate than the OBERS model linkage in that greater age detail is obtained.

1967 Utah Model

The 1967 population projections for the state of Utah and its counties made use of three projection methods [14]. One method was the conventional cohort-component method, where the migration component was comprised of unmodified observed 1950–1960 age-sex-specific net rates for each county. The second method involved the projection of jobs in ten employment categories for each county. These projections were adjusted for dual jobholding and aggregated across all categories in order to obtain a set of projections of the civilian labor force. A population–labor force ratio was used to translate workers into total population for each county. The resulting county populations were then adjusted to an independently derived state control total. The third method was called a "synthesis," and we shall now discuss it in some detail.

The concept is basically the same as that used for most models that seek to interface economic and demographic modules. That is, the employment base (persons of labor force age) is calculated in two ways, and the results are compared. One calculation involves a natural increase (no migration) projection of the population. The second calculation is a projection of employment that is translated into an employment base projection by accounting for dual jobholding and unemployment and then multiplying the result by the reciprocal of the labor force participation rate. If the employment base value from the economic model is larger than the employment base resulting from natural increase, then there will be net inmigration; if the value is smaller, then there will be net outmigration. The ratio of the economic to the natural increase employment base is the value that drives the age-specific net migration submodel. The Utah method may have differed from the scheme just outlined in a few small details, but the reader is best served by understanding the standard approach.

What is unique to the Utah method is the procedure used to translate the employment base migration ratio into age-specific net migration rates. A linear regression model of the form $Y = bX$ was used, where apparently the value of the intercept where $X = 0$ is zero. Y represents age-specific net migration rates over all counties for a given age group, and X is the total county migration rate, or the employment base migration rate—it is not clear which was actually used in the Utah projections. The value of the coefficient, b, is the ratio to be applied to the total migration rate for a county in order to turn it into the particular positive or negative age-specific rate for that county. These ratios for all age groups are presented in Table 8–1 along with an index of explained variation.

In practice, the regression model provides the analyst variations on two patterns of net migration rates—actually, there is only one pattern, but it can be regarded as a positive subpattern and as a negative subpattern. There is apparently no option for some age-specific rates to be positive and for others to be negative, as is often the case empirically; once again, we find ourselves confronted by a quite rigid age-specific migration pattern model. The technique also suffers in that the averaging process used to determine the age-specific ratios is likely to produce discontinuities between empirical age-specific net migration patterns for certain counties and their projected patterns.

Table 8—1.   Regression Estimation of Age-Specific Migration Relative to Total Migration Rate, Utah, 1950—1960

Age at End Of Period	Ratio: Age-Specific Migration to Total Migration Rate	Coefficient of Determination (r^2)
0—4	0.317	0.36
5—9	0.795	0.62
10—14	0.930	0.94
15—19	1.098	0.88
20—24	2.080	0.96
25—29	2.059	0.90
30—34	1.235	0.55
35—39	1.173	0.71
40—44	0.850	0.54
45—49	0.700	0.74
50—54	0.558	0.59
55—59	0.466	0.51
60—64	0.440	0.42
65—69	0.389	0.50
70—74	0.386	0.40
75+	0.352	0.25

Source: Therel R. Black, Jewell J. Rasmussen, and Frank C. Hachman, "Population Projections: Utah and Utah's Counties" (Salt Lake City, Utah: Economic and Population Studies, Utah State Planning Program, 1967), Table 20.

1973 Pennsylvania and Illinois Models

A somewhat simpler migration rate translation technique was used in the 1973 Pennsylvania and Illinois projection models [15], although the economic projection models were more complex than Utah's. The Pennsylvania and Illinois methods both work off an economic base model developed by the National Planning Association which trends basic and nonbasic industrial employment of labor market areas relative to larger contextual regions. Since this study does not concern economic forecasting, we shall focus on the net migration component of these models.

Once employment has been projected, overall net migration is determined by the labor force supply-demand model sketched above. Age-specific net migration patterns were assumed to remain fixed in their 1960—1970 form, adjusted to five year durations. These rates were multiplied by the population being projected and the numbers of migrants were adjusted to the labor force—difference control totals by a method analogous to the proportional net migrants method described above.

Once again, we encounter a case where local age-specific net migration patterns have been preserved at the expense of permitting the analyst to allow the patterns to change in the future. So long as labor market areas are being projected, this defect's impact is slightly lessened because net migration patterns tend to be fewer and less variable in such areas than is the case for counties. (For example, central city and suburban patterns are seldom encountered.) In any event, an effort should be made to incorporate greater age pattern flexibility in models of this kind.

CENSUS BUREAU DIRECTIONAL FLOW METHOD

Since 1966, U.S. Bureau of the Census projections of state populations have made use of a directional flow model of migration [16]. The method used to project the population of the Genesee–Finger Lakes Planning Region that was discussed earlier in the chapter is a variation on the Census Bureau technique.

The Census Bureau had formerly used net migration rates in its state projections, but it was felt that there were defects in net rates that could be overcome by using directional migration data. The logic behind this decision is as follows:

In a number of earlier reports of the Bureau of the Census presenting projections of state population, in which a component procedure was used, assumptions concerning future interstate migration were expressed in terms of "net migration," stated either in terms of rates or absolute levels.

The use of net migration rates requires a choice of type of rate. The manner in which the rates are used suggests that the rates should represent probabilities in which the population exposed to the risk of migration is used as the base in determining the rates. There is a problem in expressing such a rate for net in-migration. The conventional procedure has been to use as the base the population at the beginning of the period for each state affected, regardless of whether it had a net in- or out-migration. Another major problem in the use of net migration rates is that if one assumes the continuation of past trends in the rates, in-migration states automatically receive larger and larger numbers of net in-migrants, while out-migration states contribute fewer and fewer out-migrants, as the base population of specific age groups in the latter states becomes smaller as a result of out-migration. The inconsistency of the situation is obvious, since, under these circumstances, the net in-migrants and the net out-migrants become heavily unbalanced, and the computed net migrations require progressively larger adjustments to make them balance out to zero (or to a national control total representing net immigration from abroad).

These considerations suggest the use of gross figures on in- and out-migration starting with out-migration rates [17].

The solution was to take the age-sex-race–specific outmigration rates for each state from the previous census' question on residence on the intercensal midpoint date, and apply those rates to derive outmigratory populations for each projection period. The numbers of outmigrants from the states were pooled into national age-sex-race groups and then redistributed to the states on the basis of their inmigratory shares of the outmigration pool reported in the census data. In this way, each set of rates was based on an adequate "at risk" population. Also, the problem of reconciling migration flows was solved because the inmigrating populations comprise the outmigration pool—nothing more nor less. Lastly, the runaway growth situation is prevented: a population gains migrants in fixed proportions from the pool, yet loses migrants to the pool in proportion to its size. Thus, the more the population grows, the more it contributes to the pool and the less it receives from the pool relative to its population. Ultimately, the outmigration and inmigration flows tend to balance and the population exhibits rates of net migration that are approximately zero. A variation on this model explicitly trended migration flow rates for all states so that inmigration and outmigration both would be proportional to state size in 50 years.

As we mentioned in our discussion of the Genesee–Finger Lakes method, it is not necessary to take national migration pools into account when projecting areas that are small relative to the nation, so long as the entire nation is not covered in the projections. Judicious scenario writing can readily prevent runaway growth from taking place in the projections.

Basically, the Census Bureau method is a good one for the purpose it serves. Its advantages are noted above. The main defect, as might be expected, is its lack of flexibility. An idealized version of the Census Bureau technique would include provision for modification of the age timing patterns of the migration flows. There would also be provisions for linkages to economic models such as the employment part of the OBERS projection system. It is this writer's understanding that future Census Bureau state projections may have special treatments of migration of college students and military personnel. In the more distant future, linkages to regional economic projection models may be expected.

NOTES TO CHAPTER EIGHT

1. C. Horace Hamilton and Josef Perry, "A Short Method for Projecting Population by Age from One Decennial Census to Another," *Social Forces* 41, 2 (1962):160–170.

2. Ibid., p. 164.

3. Ibid., p. 165.

4. Genesee–Finger Lakes Regional Planning Board, "Regional Population Distribution and Projections" (Rochester, N.Y.: 1971).

5. Ibid., p. 4.

6. Walter Isard, *Methods of Regional Analysis: an Introduction to Regional Science* (Cambridge, Mass.: The M.I.T. Press, 1960), ch. 11.

7. Temple University Office of Research and Specialized Studies, "The Population of Pennsylvania: Projections to 1980" (1963).

8. Connecticut Development Commission "Population: A Demographic Analysis of Connecticut 1790–2000," Technical Report 131 (Hartford: Connecticut Interregional Planning Program, 1962).

9. Albert Chevan, "Population Projection System," Technical Report no. 3 (Philadelphia: Penn Jersey Transportation Study, 1965).

10. James D. Tarver and Therel R. Black, *Making County Population Projections—A Detailed Explanation of a Three-Component Method, Illustrated by Reference to Utah Counties*, Bulletin (Technical) 459 (Logan, Utah: Utah Agricultural Experiment Station in cooperation with Oklahoma State University Research Foundation, 1966), pp. 48–76.

11. Donald B. Pittenger, "A Typology of Age-Specific Net Migration Rate Distributions," *Journal of the American Institute of Planners* 40, 4 (1974):278–83.

12. Ibid., p. 281.

13. New York State Office of Planning Services, "Demographic Projections: for New York State Counties to 2000 A.D." (Albany, N.Y.: 1974).

14. Therel R. Black, Jewell J. Rasmussen, and Frank C. Hachman, "Population Projections: Utah and Utah's Counties" Economic and Population Studies, Utah State Planning Program (Salt Lake City, Utah: 1967).

15. Pennsylvania Office of State Planning and Development, "Pennsylvania Projection Series: Population and Labor Force," Report no. 73, pp. 1–3. (Harrisburg, Penna.: 1973); Illinois Bureau of the Budget, *Uniform Demographic and Economic Data: 1970–2000*, Summary (Springfield, Illinois: 1973).

16. U.S. Bureau of the Census, *Current Population Reports*, series P–25, no. 326 (1966).

17. Ibid., pp. 7–8.

Chapter Nine

Projecting Populations by Age and Sex: The Complete Model

INTRODUCTION

The last three chapters presented a variety of techniques for projecting each of the three components of demographic change. No single method was ideal; the reader must use his own judgment to determine the technique most suitable for his requirements. At this point, we shall assume that methods of determining age-specific rates of fertility, mortality, and migration have been selected, and that matrixes of these transition rates have been established and indexed to the population matrixes they are to be multiplied against.

(A matrix, in mathematics, is a square or rectangular array of numbers in rows and columns. Each number is in a cell, and each cell is identified by its row and column coordinates. The rows and columns represent vectors or dimensions, and a matrix may, in principle, have any number of dimensions. A population matrix may be set up so that columns represent sex and rows represent age. Race could be represented by another vector, as might geographical area and year. To project a population, it is necessary that the population matrix cell values be multiplied by the transition rate values in appropriate cells in transition rate matrixes. If the matrixes and their component rows and columns are labeled or indexed properly, then when one matrix is to be multiplied by another on a term-by-term basis, the cells with the population and the correct coefficient will match, and the desired calculation will be carried out. We shall assume that the analyst either can program computers himself or has a scientific programmer available who has the knowledge to set up a workable computer program.)

Rather than go into repetitious detail in the presentation of a variety of projection models, we shall present one cohort-component computation model that includes most of the features that are likely to be of use to the analyst. Special features that are peculiar to the use of a given component rate technique are not provided. These procedures can be inferred from our discussions above or can be gleaned from the original methodological statements. As was mentioned above, we assume that one way or another there will be appropriate transition rates available at the point in the computation sequence where they are to be used. We might add that some of the procedures to be presented may not be of use in some applications. The analyst is encouraged to study the next two sections of this chapter carefully in light of his requirements and resources with a view toward deleting unnecessary procedures.

GENERAL DESIGN

A symbolic explanation of the population projection model is presented in Exhibit 9—1. The model is a basic cohort-component computation model with several special features that potentially can add precision to the results of the computation.

A noteworthy feature of the model is the "inflation-deflation" procedure which has recently been incorporated in the Census Bureau's national projections [1]. The objective of the procedure is to produce censuslike results for individual age groups and, to achieve this end, age-specific census coverage errors are mimicked. Specifically, the undercounted (and occasionally overcounted) age-sex-race groups are adjusted ("inflation") so that a "true" population is obtained. The various projection operations are carried out and, as a final step, the projected population is readjusted ("deflated") so that it appears as it might if a census were taken. This procedure may seem odd at first, but the reader should bear in mind that certain age groups are more prone to census error than are others. Very young children are usually undercounted and to let this undercount persist in the projection recursions would mean an eventual understatement of adults. If census fidelity is not desired, the analyst may choose to "inflate" the population in the first recursion and then let the population remain "true" for the remainder of the projections.

There appear to be two problems associated with the "inflation-deflation" procedure. One is that the projected behavior of true birth cohorts becomes a little difficult to track with precision over time. The second problem is that the census coverage error may differ considerably from locality to locality and it is very difficult to measure

☆ ☆

Exhibit 9–1

General Projection Model Design

Listed below are the matrixes that comprise the model. It is to be understood that, unless otherwise indicated, each matrix will have vectors for sex, age, race, and area or place. It is to be further understood that all operations indicated—addition, subtraction, multiplication—are done on a term-by-term basis for cells with identical sex, age, race, and area indexes. That is, Nassau County, New York, white males aged 25–29 at a given date would be survived to ages 30–34 at the next projection date in the model by having their cell value multiplied by a rate in a cell in a survival rate matrix indexed as being, for the purposes of that model iteration, initial date white males aged 25–29 in Nassau County, New York. The regular conventions for multiplication of matrixes do not apply in this scheme, although some computations may in fact lend themselves to that algorithm.

Population Matrixes:

P = census or projection year population,
C = population corrected for census undercount,
A = population after adjustment removing special populations,
S = special populations (military, college, institutional, etc.),
E = survived population,
Q = net number of migrants,
B = births.

Transition Matrixes:

K = undercount correction ratio,
M = survivorship ratio,
N = net migration rate,
F = fertility rate,
R = ratio males at birth,

Subscripts:

t = time, year, by projection increments,
s = special population,
q = migrant population,
l = local population (survived, premigratory),
m = males,
f = females,
i = age group,
g = initial childbearing age,
h = final childbearing age,
a = adjusted rate.

Assumptions:

1. Migration rates have the postsurvival population as the rate denominator.
2. The migration control value has been established and the rates have been scaled accordingly.
3. Survivors are aged one age group increment from their starting age group.
4. N and Q may assume negative values.

Basic Computation Sequence:

(1) $C_t = P_t K$ Initial population is corrected for census undercount.

(2) $A_t = C_t - S_t$ Special populations, if any, are removed.

(3) $E_{t+1} = A_t M_{t, t+1}$ Adjusted population is survived.

(4) $Q_{t+1} = E_{t+1} N_{t, t+1}$ Net numbers of migrants are calculated.

(5) $P_{t+1} = (E_{t+1} + Q_{t+1} + S_{t+1} + B''_{t+1})(1 - K)$

       Final population is determined by adding net migrants, special populations, and births (from the fertility computation sequence, below) to the survived population and then multiplying by the complement of the undercount correction ratio to "deflate" the projection to "census reality."

Fertility Computation Sequence:

(F.1) $_l B_{t+1} = (_f A_t + _f E_{t+1})(0.5) F_{t, t+1}$

"Local births are calculated by multiplying age-specific fertility rates by the mean number of females in each age group during the projection interval.

(F.2) $_s B_{t+1} = (_f S_t + _f S_{t+1})(0.5)_s F_{t, t+1}$

Special population fertility, if any, is calculated in the same manner as the "local" fertility. A special set of fertility rates may be used as is indicated here.

(F.3) $_q B_{t+1} = _f Q_{t+1} \cdot _a F_{t, t+1}$

Calculation of fertility for net migration population. Fertility rates must be adjusted to midpoint of projection interval.

(F.4) $B_{t+1} = {}_l B_{t+1} + {}_s B_{t+1} + {}_q B_{t+1}$

Births for all subgroups are summed by age of mother.

(F.5) $_m B_{t+1} = B_{t+1} R$

Male births are calculated by age of mother.

(F.6) $_fB_{t+1} = B_{t+1} - {_m}B_{t+1}$

Female births are derived from total births and male births.

(F.7) $_mB'_{t+1} = \sum\limits_{i=g}^{h} {_m}B_{t+1}$

Male births are summed across age of mother to obtain total number of male births.

(F.8) $_fB'_{t+1} = \sum\limits_{i=g}^{h} {_f}B_{t+1}$

Female births are summed across age of mother to obtain total number of female births.

(F.9) $B''_{t+1} = B'_{t+1}M_{t,\ t+1}$

Births are survived to persons alive in age group 0–4, or whatever is the first age group, in the projection year. This matrix is part of the calculation in equation (5) of the basic computation sequence, above.

☆ ☆

the local error. As a stopgap, national ratios may be applied, but such ratios may not reflect the true census error for the given locality.

Another feature of the model is that provision is made for what may be called "special populations." A special population is a group of persons that is found in a locality usually by reason of an administrative decision or legislative fiat. Furthermore, persons in these groups have certain peculiarities that tend to distort ordinary population projections. These peculiarities are usually of two forms: (1) there is considerable concentration of the group in only a few age categories, thus disturbing the pattern of age-specific net migration; and (2) the group may exhibit divergent behavior in another demographic process, such as having unusually high mortality rates or unusually low fertility rates. Typical special populations are college students; military personnel and their dependents; and inmates of prisons, reformatories, and hospitals.

The analyst need not worry about special populations that are small relative to the unit being projected. Special projection treatment is indicated only when the presence of the special population becomes manifest in benchmark data and historical trend studies. A good example is the college student distortion of the Otsego County, New York, net migration patterns presented in the last chapter.

Where important special populations are found to exist, they should be pulled out of the projection sequence and given special migration, fertility, and sometimes mortality treatment. Often the future values for special populations are stipulated in advance of the projections and one set of numbers at one date is replaced by another stipulated set at the next projection date. This procedure is necessary in cases where the analyst knows that future institutional populations are already programmed by the agency or organization involved. For example, an increasing emphasis on outpatient treatment may mean declining populations in mental institutions; the projection analyst, in cooperation with appropriate officials, can then set up a file of future institutional populations that can be read into the population projections at the appropriate date.

A third special feature is the treatment of the sex ratio at birth. In most populations, the number of male births exceeds the number of female births. The ratio of male births exhibits some systematic variations. For instance, the ratio is lower for black populations in the United States than it is for white populations. Also, the ratio tends to decline with advancing age at motherhood. Most population projections apply a single sex ratio to births, or perhaps race-specific ratios. The procedure exhibited here allows for sex ratios by age of mother as well. Often the lack of available data or the variability of such local data that do exist make the inclusion of this refinement unnecessary. In this case, the calculation sequence described in the exhibit should be altered. Beginning with equation (F.5), the equations should be replaced by:

$$B'_{t+1} = \sum_{i=g}^{h} B_{t+1} \qquad (9.1)$$

$$_mB'_{t+1} = B'_{t+1} R \qquad (9.2)$$

where R is a vector with no age dimension;

$$_fB'_{t+1} = B'_{t+1} - {}_mB'_{t+1} \qquad (9.3)$$

and then the sequence concludes with equation (F.9), as before.

A few other features are worth noting. One is the timing of the net migration calculations. This may vary depending on the nature of the historical migration data used to calibrate the projections and on the judgment of the analyst. Rates of net migration vary with selection of the denominator in the rate calculation, and no convention has emerged among demographers as to which value should serve as the rate base. The model in the exhibit assumes that, since most net migration measures are based on numbers of migrants alive at the end of a given time interval, the migration rate base should be the surviving local population at the end of the interval, and net migration should be projected by multiplying the migration rate matrix by the survived projection population. On the other hand, migration rates are often calculated using the starting population as the base. In this event, the logic should be carried through in the projections, and exhibit equation (4) should be rewritten as either

$$Q_{t+1} = A_t N_{t,\,t+1} \tag{9.4}$$

or

$$Q_{t+1} = P_t N_{t,\,t+1} \tag{9.5}$$

depending on the treatment of special populations and census error. (Strictly speaking, where the "inflation-deflation" procedure is used, the migration rates should be calibrated in their design so that census error is accounted for.) Where net migration rates are based on the initial population, it is possible (but not recommended, because of the special handling of migrant fertility) to combine equations (3) and (4) in Exhibit 9–1 as

$$E'_{t+1} = A_t \left(M_{t,\,t+1} + N_{t,\,t+1} \right) \tag{9.6}$$

and equation (5) in the exhibit would be rewritten

$$P_{t+1} = \left(E'_{t+1} + S_{t+1} + B''_{t+1} \right)(1-K) \tag{9.7}$$

The reason for the fertility rate adjustment of the migratory population in (F.3) has to do with the treatment of fertility in the basic population. Assuming that the projection period is five years, fertility is best treated as if it occurred at the midpoint of the interval. Exhibit Equation (F.1), for reasons of notational simplification, does not make the point as clearly as it might. Accordingly, we may elaborate as follows:

$$B_{i;\,t,\,t+1} = \left({_f}A_{i,\,t} + {_f}E_{i,\,t} \right)(0.5) F_{i;\,t,\,t+1} \tag{9.8}$$

where i represents an age group. This is the computation carried out in the exhibit in the next section. From a logical standpoint, the "local" female population aged i in the interval $(t,\,t+1)$ and the resulting births should be calculated

$$\tag{9.9}$$

$$B_{i;\,t,\,t+1} = \left({_f}A_{i-1,\,t} + {_f}A_{i,\,t} + {_f}E_{i,\,t+1} + {_f}E_{i+1,\,t+1} \right)(0.25) F_{i;\,t,\,t+1} \quad .$$

However, the numerical results are usually very close to those obtained from (9.8), so the additional computation may not be worth the effort. Births for the net migratory females must also be projected and then added to or subtracted from the basic births in order to fully account for the migration effect. A shortcut formula would be

$$B_{t+1} = (\,_fA_t + \,_fE'_{t+1})\,(0.5)\,F_{t,\,t+1} \tag{9.10}$$

but this would tend to understate births for groups with net inmigration because not all births to inmigrants would be included; the reverse would hold where there was net outmigration.

Where net migration is kept separate, fertility for migrants also must be computed for the projection period midpoint population for each age group. This may be done in one of two ways: One solution would be to obtain the arithmetic mean of the net number of migrants in each postprojection age group and in the age group preceding it. The results are multiplied by the regular fertility rate vector or by a specially selected vector, if the analyst assumes that fertility of the migrating population is different from the nonmigrating population. The alternative method is to obtain mean values between the postprojection age group's fertility rate and the rate for the preceding age group. Then the rates are multiplied by the vector of the calculated net number of migrants. Again, special fertility rates could be used. The example in the next section uses the second method, but the results of both methods are equivalent, and the choice of procedure is up to the analyst.

COMPUTATION EXAMPLE

A numerical example of the model described in Exhibit 9–1 is presented in Exhibit 9–2. The population projected in the example is the female population of Otsego County, New York, which is projected from 1970 to 1975. The starting population is taken directly from the 1970 U.S. Census, and it is "inflated"—or adjusted—for undercount using a national white female adjustment ratio [2]. A local ratio—if obtainable—could be substituted. Note that two of the ratios make a downward adjustment to the population. A further adjustment is then made by subtracting an estimated number of females in the county who migrated into the county to attend college.

The final adjusted population is then multiplied by a vector of survival rates used in the 1972 Census Bureau national projections [3].

Note that the population vector and the rate vector are not conformable, so the two final age groups must be consolidated before being survived. The survived population is then multiplied by a vector of net migration rates that, presumably, has already been adjusted so that the amount or rate of migration generated agrees with the stipulation in the projection scenario. In practice, some iterative adjustments might have to be carried out, but these would differ depending on the procedure used to select the rates, so no example is provided. The net migration chapter indicates how some of these adjustments might be made. The rates used in the example are the New York State system's exurban set with an "amplitude" of 40 percent. The rates are in their raw, unscaled form.

Once the net numbers of migrants have been calculated, the fertility sequence (described below) is run and the resulting surviving female population aged 0–4 in 1975 is entered as a single cell vector. The stipulated college inmigrant population in 1975 is also entered as a vector. Next the vectors of the survived population, the survived births, the net numbers of migrants, and the new special population are added across age groups to provide an initial 1975 population. If the analyst wishes to "deflate" this population to census form, the population vector is multiplied by the complement of the "inflation" vector.

In the fertility sequence, the special population of college students and the basic population are prepared for multiplication by fertility rates by adding the values of starting and final populations for each age group (not cohort group). Then the fertility rates are applied. In this example the rates used are New York pattern "B" scaled to a *TFR* of 1.9 (see Chapter Seven for details). It was assumed that the college students would have lower fertility than the general population, so the rates were arbitrarily taken to be one-tenth of the basic fertility rates. Finally, the numbers of births were reduced by one-half to complete the averaging process introduced when the beginning and final populations were added. This adjustment could also have been made to the summed populations prior to the rate multiplication. In either case, the result is the number of births calibrated to the population at the midpoint of the projection interval.

In order to project fertility for the migrant population in an analogous way, the midpoint fertility experience must be captured for the final age group populations. Since there is no beginning population of migrants in the same sense as for the other categories, the age-specific migration rate has to be adjusted to the midpoint condition. This was accomplished by obtaining the mean fertility rate of each final age group and that of the preceding age group. Note that this

☆ ☆

Exhibit 9–2

Example of Cohort-Component Population Projection Computation

A. *Basic Computation Sequence from Exhibit 9–1: Otsego County New York Females, 1970 to 1975*

Starting Age	P_t	K	C_t	S_t	A_t	Mt, $t+1$	E_{t+1}
–(0–4)						0.982188	
0–4	1,969	1.020	2,008		2,008	0.997241	2,002
5–9	2,323	1.022	2,374		2,374	0.998528	2,371
10–14	2,451	1.009	2,473		2,473	0.997810	2,468
15–19	3,666	1.005	3,684	1,510	2,174	0.996649	2,167
20–24	3,409	1.011	3,446	1,498	1,948	0.996013	1,940
25–29	1,551	1.028	1,594		1,594	0.994799	1,586
30–34	1,225	1.020	1,250		1,250	0.992589	1,241
35–39	1,273	1.008	1,283		1,283	0.988883	1,269
40–44	1,507	1.001	1,509		1,509	0.983307	1,484
45–49	1,625	1.005	1,633		1,633	0.975232	1,593
50–54	1,540	0.997	1,535		1,535	0.965217	1,482
55–59	1,439	1.013	1,458		1,458	0.948579	1,383
60–64	1,486	1.027	1,526		1,526	0.921060	1,406
65–69	1,212	0.989	1,199		1,199	0.878601	1,053
70–74	1,067	1.004	1,071		1,071	} 0.662675	1,988
75+	1,822	1.059	1,929		1,929		

P_t	=	Starting population
K	=	Census undercount correction
C_t	=	Corrected population
S_t	=	Special population
A_t	=	Adjusted population
$M_{t, t+1}$	=	Survivorship rates
E_{t+1}	=	Expected population
$N_{t, t+1}$	=	Net migration rates
Q_{t+1}	=	Net numbers of migrants
fB''_{t+1}	=	Survived 1970–1975 female births
P_{t+1}	=	Projected population
F	=	Fertility rate
R	=	Sex ratio

☆ ☆

Exhibit 9–2. continued

A. continued

$N_{t,\,t+1}$	Q_{t+1}	$_fB''_{t+1}$	S_{t+1}	$\Sigma(E, Q, B, S,)_{t+1}$	$(1-K)$	P_{t+1}	*Final Age*
		1,654		1,654	0.980	1,621	0–4
0.010	20			2,022	0.978	1,978	5–9
0.010	24			2,395	0.991	2,373	10–14
−0.180	−444		1,600	3,624	0.995	3,606	15–19
−0.135	−293		1,580	3,454	0.989	3.416	20–24
0.030	58			1,998	0.972	1,942	25–29
0.030	48			1,634	0.980	1,601	30–34
0.030	37			1,278	0.992	1,268	35–39
0.030	38			1,307	0.999	1,306	40–44
0.030	45			1,529	0.995	1,521	45–49
0.030	48			1,641	1.003	1,646	50–54
0.030	44			1,526	0.987	1,506	55–59
0.025	35			1,418	0.973	1,380	60–64
0.015	21			1,427	1.011	1,443	65–69
0.010	11			1,064	0.996	1,060	70–74
0.010	20			2,008	0.941	1,890	75+

Exhibit 9–2. continued
on pages 212 and 213

B. *Fertility Computation Sequences from Exhibit 9–1*

Nonmigratory, Nonspecial Sequence

Starting Age	A_t	$E_{t+1}*$	$A+E$	$F_{t,\,t+1}$	$F(A+E)$	$_lB_{t+1} =$ $0.5\,[\,F(A+E)\,]$
15–19	2,174	2,468	4,642	0.152	706	353
20–24	1,948	2,167	4,115	0.665	2,736	1,368
25–29	1,594	1,940	3,534	0.551	1,947	974
30–34	1,250	1,586	2,836	0.342	970	485
35–39	1,283	1,241	2,524	0.152	384	192
40–44	1,509	1,269	2,778	0.038	106	53

*By final age

Migratory Sequence

Starting Age	Q_{t+1}	$_aF_{t,\,t+1}$	$_qB_{t+1} =$ $Q \cdot F$
10–14	−444	0.076	−34
15–19	−298	0.408	−122
20–24	58	0.608	35
25–29	48	0.446	21
30–34	37	0.247	9
35–39	38	0.095	4
40–44	45	0.019	1

Special Sequence

Starting Age	S_t	$S_{t+1}*$	ΣS	$_sF_{t,\,t+1}$	$F(\Sigma S)$	$_sB_{t+1} =$ $0.5\,[\,F(\Sigma S)\,]$
15–19	1,510	1,600	3,110	0.0152	47	24
20–24	1,498	1,580	3,078	0.0665	205	102

*By final age

B. *Fertility Computation Sequences from Exhibit 9–1*

				Aggregation Sequence					
Final Age	$_lB_{t+1}$	$_qB_{t+1}$	$_sB_{t+1}$	ΣB_{t+1}	R	$_mB_{t+1}$	$_fB_{t+1}$	$M_{t,\,t+1}$	$_fB''_{t+1}$
15–19	353	−34	24	343	0.5154	177	166		
20–24	1,368	−122	102	1,348	0.5129	691	657		
25–29	974	35		1,009	0.5167	521	488		
30–34	485	21		506	0.5141	260	246		
35–39	192	9		201	0.5061	102	99		
40–44	53	5		58	0.5111	30	28		
							Σ1,684	0.982188	1,654

includes age group 45—49, which was not included in the earlier fertility calculations. This group was included because group members were aged 40—44 at the start of the period and half of the group was assumed to have remained under age 45 at the midpoint of the projection interval. By a similar logic, the final 15—19 age group was 10—14 at the start, but half of them were 15 or older at the midpoint. As we mentioned above, the migrants could have been averaged instead of the rates, with the same result.

Once all the births have been calculated, they are summed by maternal age group. Then the birth values are multiplied by a sex ratio vector, and male births are obtained. These are subtracted from the total birth vector in order to arrive at female births. Female births are then summed across age groups and the result is multiplied by the value in the survival rate vector that survives births to age group 0—4. This final result is then entered in the appropriate part of the basic computation sequence described above.

EDITS

Besides generating projected numbers of persons by age, sex, and other categories, it is desirable that a population projection program is written so that other data can be printed out in the form of special edits. There are two basic kinds of edits of interest to the analyst that go beyond the edits necessary for the programmer to check the content of data files and the working of the computation procedure. These are validity edits and special publication edits. Each will be discussed in turn.

Validity edits are edits of data that are indexes of whether the model is generating realistic data that conform to the intent of the projection scenario. For example, the projection routine may call for separate projection of planning regions and their component counties. The reason for doing this is that the planning region may correspond to a job market, and thereby serves as a useful control, whereas the component counties may each have unique fertility and net migration patterns and should be projected individually. To make sure that there is approximate agreement between the fertility, mortality, and migration transition rates for the region and the aggregated transition experiences of the counties, a special edit is needed to sum numbers of births by age of mother and deaths and migrants by sex and age across counties and to divide these values by the appropriate aggregated population denominator values. These rates may then be compared to the rates used for projection of the region and major discrepancies can be located and corrected.

Another useful validity edit would be graphic displays of population pyramids for each population beginning with the census benchmark and extending through each projection date. If the pyramids remain grouped by individual state, county, or region, it is possible for the analyst to easily detect unwanted bulges or depressions in the age structure that result from improperly assigned migration rate patterns or from the presence of undetected special populations in the benchmark population. The alternative to a population pyramid edit is for the analyst to scan the tabular data output for such errors; this is very time-consuming and many errors are likely to pass undetected.

Yet another validity edit that can be recommended is a summary of projected population changes for each unit. This summary might include total population; totals for each sex and race; numbers of live births and deaths by each category; net numbers of migrants by category; crude birth, death, and net migration rates by category; and perhaps some refined measures such as net migration rates by broad age groups. Such edits may serve as a basis for quick comparison with historical data series so that trends could be inspected and anomalous results noted and corrected.

Publication edits are those edits intended for dissemination to the public in one form or another. Typically, these include projections of the population values by each age, sex, race, and geographic category being projected. In addition to this basic information, other data such as the information noted in the preceding paragraph might be released for the official projections. The level of detail released in projection publications varies and depends on the needs of potential users of the data as well as on the policies of the issuing organization. Quite often, simple numbers of persons in each age, sex, race, and place suffice for most users. These data could be printed and sent out as a general projection publication, whereas special edits could be Xeroxed from computer printout in response to the occasional requests for such data.

SUBMODELS

Once the basic projections by age and sex have been created, it is possible to generate projections of age- and sex-related population characteristics such as households, families, labor force, persons by occupation or industry, and persons by educational attainment. Each of these projections may be made by multiplying the projected population by vectors of age-specific characteristic rates that are trended for each area or that are ratios to trended national data. In each case, care must be taken so that "impossible" happenings—such as rates of greater than unity—do not occur. The main advantages for making such projections are twofold: first, the results are consistent with the basic population projections; and second, the projections are relatively easy to make.

The main disadvantage with subprojections is that they are "marginal" rather than "structural." By "marginal" we are referring to the fact that trended age-sex–specific characteristic rates are used to create the projections. Such rates seldom reveal much about the factors that operate to change these rate values over time. A "structural" model, on the other hand, would be an attempt to mimic the processes that underlie the manifest trends. Such structural models can be extremely complicated, and they often are forced to rely on linkages that are not well documented by data or that are poorly understood. As a consequence, they can be very useful analytical tools at best, and at their worst their complexity may deceive the user into believing that the model is precise, when in fact its functioning may be propped up by guesswork.

If there are few limitations in staff and budget, it is always useful to explore the use of structural modeling if for no other reason than to gain insight into the dynamics of the process being projected. Otherwise, "marginal" models may generate useful and often fairly valid results. They are probably better than ignoring the population's age structure, which would be the case if numbers of households or labor force participants were trended outright. They also are probably better than no special projections at all.

NOTES TO CHAPTER NINE

1. U.S. Bureau of the Census, *Current Population Reports*, series P–25, no. 541 (1975).

2. U.S. Bureau of the Census, *Estimates of the Coverage of the Population by Sex, Age, Race*, PHC(E)–4 (Washington, D.C.: Government Printing Office, 1974).

3. U.S. Bureau of the Census, *Current Population Reports*, series P–25, no. 493.

Chapter Ten

Practical Considerations

INTRODUCTION

The present chapter is intended to bring together some of the practical information that was scattered throughout the previous chapters and add new information that may be of use to the projection analyst or supervisor. It is also intended that this chapter provide a framework or context to which the reader can relate the previously discussed techniques. To this end, the three following sections trace the projection creation procedure in approximately sequential fashion. Issues are raised that are likely to be confronted during the course of projection creation, and suggestions are made as to how they may be resolved. The final two sections are devoted to questions of projection validity and future methodological developments.

CHOOSING THE MODEL

The choice of the projection model or technique to be used in a particular project almost always involves a series of compromises that ideally should result in the best possible projections, given the constraints encountered. In other words, the "best" model under one set of circumstances might not be the best model if the circumstances changed. We shall now consider some of the most important factors in model selection.

Needs of the Users

The primary goal of any population projection effort is to satisfy the needs of the potential users of the projections. If there is more than one client, it may be difficult to evaluate the needs so that the best compromise can be made regarding projection methodology. Sometimes, these needs are well defined and sometimes they are not. For instance, one agency may be greatly interested in forecasts of the total number of persons aged 65 and older in a given county for the year 2000. Another agency may want projections by age and sex, but isn't sure if it wants race detail as well.

A more serious problem is that some needs are so specialized that they might strain the resources of the projection team. One example that comes to mind is education. Education planners at the primary, secondary, and postsecondary levels collectively need age data by single year of age for ages less than 30. On the other hand, most other users can get along with data in the standard five year age groups. One solution is to project by single years of age for one year projection intervals and aggregate the results by five year groups for ages 30 and older. But to do so requires five times the effort otherwise expended to collect data and to specify parameters and 25 times as many numbers are generated than in five year projections. These increases may not be excessive if only one unit, such as a state, is projected. However, if many units such as counties were projected, the extra data might overwhelm the analyst. Another solution would be to project by five year groups and then interpolate to obtain single year data. Unfortunately, erratic shifts in the age structure might not be accurately described using an interpolation procedure. A third option would be to ignore the specific needs of the education planners and provide them with the five year projections used by all the other agencies. Each option has its advantages and disadvantages, but there would seem to be no completely satisfactory solution.

The issue often becomes a question of generality versus specificity in terms of demographic characteristics, geographical detail, or both. Great demographic or geographical detail implies a great deal of resource expenditure in creation of the projections. Simplistic detail in both categories is not acceptable to many users. The typical solution is to compromise by leaning toward detail in one area at the expense of the other: Statewide projections can go to single year detail if only a few states are being projected; county, city, town, or census tract projections are feasible by five year age, sex, and race detail if the number of counties to be projected is not excessive. (This writer has found that if proper attention is to be devoted to the analysis of historical data, and if careful projection parameter assignments for each demographic change component are to be made, there are limitations to the number of units the analyst can conscientiously handle. That maximum amount varies by individual, but it probably is not much greater than 100 in most cases.) Accordingly, it might be a good idea for the analyst or project director to educate potential users as to what needs may be satisfied and what needs (or perceived needs) are unrealistic given the available data, money, technology, and personnel.

Availability and Quality of Data

The projection analyst must eventually face the problem of assembling and analyzing the data that form the basis of his projections. The best time to consider the availability, format, and quality of the data is very early in the project; certainly a data inventory should be in hand by the time negotiations with potential users begin. Knowledge of the available data, if nothing else, should allow the analyst to avoid making commitments to do the impossible.

Questions of data availability and quality seldom have clear-cut answers. Most of the data used in projections comes from censuses, so we shall briefly consider some problems associated with U.S. census data. One obvious constraint is that the user must deal with data generated by the questions on the census schedules. It is a good idea to look over the census schedules to learn what was asked. While scanning the schedules, the analyst should observe the sampling detail used to obtain the items. (Most respondents fill out a relatively short schedule which asks basic questions such as date of birth, sex, and race. The more esoteric questions such as field of vocational training or foreign language spoken in the parental home were asked of population samples.) The smaller the sample, the larger will be the minimum population of an area required for a given level of reliability of the data. In other words, detailed data are likely to be unreliable for small areas. Often such data cannot be released for very small areas because of Census Bureau confidentiality rules, a further restriction to detailed small area projection of nonbasic demographic characteristics.

Another consideration when evaluating census data availability is its format. All published data are in the form of cross-tabulations. But not all such tabulations are published, and not all published tabulations are published for all areas. The most detailed tabulations are published for the United States as a whole and the least detailed tabulations are for very small areas, such as city blocks or census tracts. Special tabulations may be purchased from the Census Bureau, and public-use sample tapes are available for obtaining special tabulations for states and metropolitan areas. The former option may prove to be expensive and the latter requires the use of special computer programs and relatively lengthy—and therefore costly— computer runs. Another problem associated with the public-use sample tape is that, even at the state level, the number of cell entries may be too small to be useable if the population is stratified into more than a few subcategories.

Comparisons between censuses often run afoul of definitional changes. Sometimes these are conceptual changes such as "housing units" and "dwelling units" which mean almost the same thing, yet create data that are different—just how different is something that cannot always be determined. Perhaps more vexing to the projection analyst are boundary changes. State and county boundaries are relatively permanent, while municipal boundaries are often changeable. Boundaries of special analytical units such as census tracts that are supposed to be fairly permanent are sometimes changed drastically between censuses. Most population projections are made for places with stable boundaries because historical data series can be assembled for them and because there is some assurance that the projections will be meaningful for future use.

Personnel

The population projection project supervisor must consider his personnel resources if a decision is made to do projections in-house. Indeed, the availability of suitable personnel may be a major consideration to go in-house rather than to bring in consultants. A consultant likewise may not choose to bid for a job involving population projections unless he knows his staff can do the work.

It almost goes without saying that it takes a well-trained demographer or an experienced projection analyst to carry out a sophisticated projection project. Nondemographers, with a little effort, should be able to master the mechanics of the techniques presented in this book, but it may take six months or a year of working with population data before they are truly at ease with the subtleties of population analysis. An example would be persons with a background in economics. This writer's impression, based on his review of population projections, is that economists who lack training or experience in population analysis tend to rely heavily on the use of ratios of parts to wholes and on regression techniques when dealing with demographic data. Nothing is wrong with either technique if properly used. Unfortunately, both techniques can be quick ways of empirically covering up analytical ignorance of what determines observed relationships. A person with experience in demographic analysis, on the other hand, is more likely to disaggregate data in order to try to explain what underlies the observed relationships because he has a better theoretical grasp of underlying relationships and because disaggregation is a procedure that demographers have found to work well when tackling demographic problems.

A rule of thumb is that the projection methods that project only population totals can be handled by persons with a bachelor's degree in economics, sociology, engineering, or equivalent nonacademic experience. (An exception would be a "humanistic" sociologist or economist who lacks training in mathematics or statistics.) Cohort-component models are best left to persons who have a masters degree in sociology, economics, or statistics and also have a concentration in demography, or who have equivalent nonacademic experience.

Part time availability of a computer programmer who writes scientific programs is recommended if a number of areas are to be projected using cohort-component methodology. A well-done set of population projections requires special historical studies as well as the projection model itself, so there are several programming jobs to be done. It is possible to combine the projection analyst and the computer programmer in the same person, although this might not be a wise decision; often analyst-programmers spend less time than they should doing analytical work because of their programming chores. This writer believes that if the budget permits, it is best to have specialists in each role.

THE PROJECTION SCENARIO

The most critical part of the projection process is the selection of the projection scenario, which is the set of assumptions specified for each population for each projection interval. This is critical because the selection determines the population values generated by the model; the scenario *is* the forecast, for practical purposes.

For very simple, single function projections of the kind discussed in Chapters Three and Four, the selection of the methodology is tantamount to the selection of the scenario. The only additional conscious decision needed is the specification of the number of base period observations to which the parameters are fitted, a decision which can affect the results obtained.

If the population model has its migration component determined by, or interfaced with, an economic model, attention must be paid to the explicit and implicit assumptions that obtain for that model. The analyst and the project director must be confident that the economic model's assumptions are acceptable. Ignorance is a poor defense against criticisms that might be leveled at the resulting population values.

The remarks below are addressed to the situation where cohort-component models are used for purely demographic forecasting. That is, we assume that the specification of fertility, mortality, and migration parameters is not directly linked to economic or other variables. The linkage, if it exists, is mediated by the judgment of the analyst. Most population projections are of this type.

Historical Studies

The past cannot be ignored if the future is to be predicted. By the same token, the future should not be completely determined by the past, so far as population forecasts are concerned. The job of the analyst, then, is to make as complete a study of past demographic trends as time and other resources permit, for the purpose of gaining insights regarding each area that is to be projected. This familiarity should serve to improve the quality of judgmental parameter assignments.

Historical mortality studies should be keyed to the intended mortality methodology. If national mortality projections are to be used as a basis for the local projections, the analyst would be well served if he compared local and national life tables over two or three decades. Systematic differences or trends in these differences (should they exist) are difficult to ignore if it appears that distortions in projection results could occur if they were not accounted for.

Fertility studies should also relate the local experience to a larger context. Subareas could be related to regions and regions could be related to national trends. It is recommended that the effect of age structure be removed in so far as this is possible. *ASFR*s and *TFR*s should prove to be the most useful measures in most instances, but it may not be possible to obtain extensive time series of these data for smaller areas. Data for periods around three census years should be sufficient for the analyst to relate local fertility to the larger context. They should also permit useful analyses of changes in the age patterns of fertility.

Census survival techniques permit the estimation of decade net migration for counties and other small areas as far back in time as the basic population data by age and sex are available. Net migration—at least for those portions of the population that are in the labor pool ages—serves as a useful index of economic conditions. It summarizes the net effect of plant openings and closings, shifts in the composition of the occupational structure, and all other economic changes. It also masks the individual economic effects, so a detailed analysis requires the basic economic data. In any event, changes in net migration over time are a barometer of the past economic climate and projection parameters regarding net migration are therefore summary statements about aggregate future economic conditions. Attention also should be paid to the age-specific net migration patterns for clues as to the "character" of the county or region and how it has evolved. Such study should allow the analyst to avoid unrealistic assignments of age-specific migration patterns in the scenario.

Consultation with Local Experts

There are two good reasons for consulting with local experts and officials, such as planners, when undertaking a forecasting project. In the first place, such persons are more likely than the projection analyst to have an intimate knowledge of the locality regarding likely short run social and economic events. Such events would include the likelihood that suburbanization would extend into a neighboring county within the ensuing five or ten years, or the possibility of a corporation closing the local plant. Local information is usually not as useful so far as purely demographic events are concerned. This is because the projection analyst usually has access to the same data and is often in a better position to place that information in a proper context.

Local information may fall off in quality when it comes to an assessment for long range prospects. This is because the local person is not as likely to be as disinterested as the outside analyst; it is hard for local people to avoid getting at least a partial "chamber of commerce" attitude—particularly for areas that have experienced growth for several decades.

The second reason for local consultation is political. This writer has found that persons at each level of government tend to perceive the higher governmental units as ramming unwanted things down their throats—and this definitely includes population forecasts. Local consultation provides the opportunity for local persons to have some say on the forecast outcome and this opportunity tends to lower the level of natural resentment.

Choice of Analytical Control Unit

It is seldom a good idea to project larger units by aggregating the projections of the individual component units. This practice usually results in an aggregate projection that is on the high side of independent projections of the larger unit.

On the other hand, the largest unit may not be the most appropriate control unit. This is particularly so if it is known that the economy of the large unit is not well integrated and that one component exerts a dominant, yet changing, influence on the whole population.

A case in point is New York State. This writer always felt uneasy using trended statewide population component data as controls because of the effect of the weight of New York City events on these component values. The city comprises about 40 percent of the state's population, but that proportion has been decreasing for some time. The city is also socially and economically different from the rest of the state. Statewide data, taken over time, reflect changes in the character of this dominant element as well as the erosion of its dominance. The question becomes one of how to sort out these effects in the past so that likely future events can be specified.

One attractive potential solution to the control unit problem is to use the job market area as the control unit. Job market areas are economically distinct units that may be approximated by *SMSA*s, planning districts, *BEA* regions, *SEA*s, or other such multicounty groups. Within a state, different job market areas can be experiencing varying economic growth; Rochester and Buffalo represent two New York State job market areas whose economies moved in different directions during the 1960s. Once job market projections have been made and their statewide aggregation compared with historical data to see if the results were reasonable, counties can be projected so that their aggregate populations equal the job market control totals.

Age-sex–specific county population values must sum to corresponding control area values and statewide values in the projection report. This agreement can be accomplished by forcing the element data to sum to the control total. It also can be accomplished by letting the control total be an approximation and then juggling the component county projections until their aggregate value closely agrees with that total. Thus, the published age-sex values of the control unit would be the sum of the component county age-sex group values. This latter approach has merit because county parameter values for demographic change components remain known at all times. The forcing routine would tend to alter these values implicitly. Special computer edits, on the other hand, permit the analyst to observe the aggregate control unit fertility, mortality, and migration rates that result from the combination of the separately projected county component change values (see Chapter Nine for a discussion).

Assumption Specification

All projections are predicated on assumptions. Usually these are very general assumptions such as that there will be no wars, economic depressions, or natural catastrophies. These assumptions are common to virtually all projections. Then there are specific assumptions that determine the projection outcome. Sometimes the word "parameter" is used in a loose sense to refer to such assumptions. This section deals with the specification of detailed assumptions, which is the heart of the scenario process.

Once historical and comparative studies have been made and local experts have been consulted, it is time to write a projection scenario. Ultimately, the "written" form of the scenario may be a listing of the net migration types and levels, fertility rates, and mortality rates that move each population through each projection interval. If migration is determined by the output of an economic model, that component may be eliminated from the scenario. The exact form of the detailed scenario will vary depending on the type of fertility, mortality, and migration component models used. If the models are ratios of local to national component rates, then each ratio or its functional form must be stipulated. If a "New York" type model is used, then the scenario must specify in detail the fertility and net migration patterns as well as total fertility and crude net migration control values.

It may be helpful for the analyst to write out an intermediate level scenario for the purpose of clarifying his thinking with respect to the broad concepts that underlie the detailed assumptions. This document may be made public or may be suppressed at the discretion of the project director; in any event, a skilled analyst can recreate most of the detailed and intermediate assumptions from the projection results, so there is little reason to strive for secrecy.

An intermediate level scenario may be expressed in something like the following terms: Planning Region X will continue to experience lower mortality rates than the nation for the remainder of this century. Present differences will be maintained until 1990, and convergence to national levels shall begin in the 1990–1995 interval and continue until equality is attained in 2040. Fertility will decline from its present status of being higher than national levels to reach lower than national levels over the period from the present until 1995 as the region suburbanizes. In 1995, the *TFR* will be 0.95 that of Census Bureau Series II and shall remain at that relative level. Net migration will be positive, with peak rates occurring in the interval 1980–1985. Rates will then fall off to zero net migration by the year 2015. Thereafter, the rates become fixed at the zero net level. County C is assumed to suburbanize first. Its *TFR* is already 0.95 of the national level, so that ratio will drop to 0.9 for the interval 1975–1980 and increase to 0.95 by 1985–1990. Mortality levels will be identical to those of the region. Net inmigration shall peak in 1975–1980 and cross over to slight net outmigration by about 1990, when it is assumed that the county reaches a saturation point in terms of dwelling units (exact timing must be verified by special edit, but capacity is assumed to be 245,400 households). And so forth for all control areas and component units being projected.

Having sketched the intermediate assumptions, it is not very difficult to establish a trial detailed scenario consisting of exact specifications for a computer run. And when the trial projections emerge from the computer, their reasonableness can be evaluated in terms of the scenario. For example, certain areas may be shown as having population decline when the intent of the scenario is for the population to grow very slightly. In this case, it will be necessary to adjust one or more of the component rate specifications so that the total population value behaves as forecasted.

Alternative Projections

The issue of whether to release one set of projections or several sets usually emerges at some point during the project. There are valid reasons on both sides of the issue. We shall first consider the arguments for multiple projections.

In the first place, any single forecast or projection is almost surely going to be wrong. Therefore, the argument goes, it is a good idea to present a range of forecasts that the analyst judges will encompass the range of reasonably likely empirical outcomes. Typically, this range would include one or two intermediate series as well as high and low series. For a number of years, the U.S. Bureau of the Census had two intermediate series and left it to the user to judge which series was most likely—there being no midpoint series to conveniently settle on. In 1975, the bureau switched to a system of three projections—high, low, and an intermediate series that can be regarded as the most likely outcome. Other variations on the multiple projection theme would include analytical projections such as a no migration (natural change only) series and perhaps a series that would be a continuation of very recent component rate values or trends. The various series should permit the user to put the "preferred" or "most likely" series into a meaningful context.

The argument against multiple projection series is that if funding or the results of planning studies that are tied to possible funding can be based on one of several alternative projections, a "numbers game" can occur; parties on opposite sides of a fiscal issue will use the projections most suitable for support of their views. On the other hand, a single forecast of the most likely future population reduces the room for such a maneuver and thereby helps to eliminate interminable squabbling over which set of numbers is best.

In summary, multiple projections are to be preferred from a technical standpoint, whereas single projections are more practical in a budgetary or fiscal sense. The project supervisor must take stock of the setting in which the projections will be used and then decide which approach is better.

PUBLICATION OF THE PROJECTIONS

Before the final set of projections has emerged from the computer, some thought must be given to how the projections are to be published. Some information on this and related topics is presented below.

Publication Format

There seem to be two elements of central importance regarding the format of the forecast publication. These elements are (1) the budget for publication and (2) the anticipated revision cycle. The project supervisor must weigh these factors.

The fanciest possible format would be a hardbound book. Projections are ordinarily not accorded such treatment unless they are an integral part of a project such as a master plan for a city or region. Most such hardcover publications containing population projection were privately funded regional plans published between the world wars.

Today, forecasts are not considered permanent documents, so a paperback book format represents the highest publication quality that can be expected. At the other extreme would be sheets of paper stapled together. The 1974 New York State publication had five year 1970–2000 projections by age and sex printed one county to a page and the sheets were arranged and stapled together according to planning region [1]. A separate assemblage containing methodological information and statewide summary data was also provided. This regionalized format resulted in economies in printing and distribution: users needing forecasts for only a few counties would be sent only the appropriate assemblages. In their 1972 incarnation, the New York State projections were published in booklets—also one to a planning region plus the statewide summary. Complete sets were sent out in plastic-covered ring binders.

Intermediate format possibilities are pages with holes punched and attachment made with metal clasps such as for a term paper. Another popular format is to bind the pages with cylindrical plastic tooth binders.

The publication should be attractive, because it can enhance the public perception of the issuing organization. On the other hand, if it is likely that the projections are to be revised from time to time, the type of binding and quality of printing should hint at the impermanence of the forecasts. The imprecision of the projections might be emphasized by rounding all projected values to the nearest ten or hundred.

Items to be Included

Obviously, the projection publication must contain the total projected population for each area for each projection year. If the calculations include age, sex, and race detail, these should be included as well. It is also advisable to include the most recent available census data as a reference for the user.

Other "must include" items are statements of general assumptions such as no wars, catastrophies, etc., and statements indicating the nature of the major operational assumptions. These assumptions would include the main component change rates for the primary unit being projected. There should also be a statement explaining the projection methodology used to create the projections.

Ideally, the projection publication should include more. The methodology statement should provide enough information so that an outside technician could approximate, if not exactly reproduce, the results presented in the publication. Tables that summarize the projected population totals for each area are a good idea, as is the extension of the tables to include a few decades' worth of historical data so as to place the projections in context. If potentially unfamiliar areas such as counties are being projected, a map locating each such area should be included.

Special computer edit data may also be published. Such data might include crude rates of fertility, mortality, and net migration— or even rates for selected age groups.

Evaluation and Revision

If a governmental agency is the issuing organization for a set of population projections, it is likely that that agency will have responsibility to follow through on the project by monitoring the accuracy of the projections and by making revisions when necessary.

Projection accuracy can be assessed against estimates and censuses. Ordinarily, national censuses are used for this evaluation. There are some municipal and even countywide censuses conducted between national censuses, but these data are seldom available for enough areas to permit comprehensive evaluations at the regional or state level. Therefore, projection accuracy evaluations are usually based on population estimate data.

State, county, and even municipal population estimates are issued by the U.S. Bureau of the Census and by many states and local areas. Such estimates vary in quality, so the projection analyst should be thoroughly familiar with the data and methodology used to prepare the estimates. This writer believes that it is a good idea to have the population estimation and projection functions combined in the same agency—such has been done in California and Washington—as opposed to having the functions in different agencies, as has been the case in New York State. This opinion is based on the observation that the skills required for population estimation and projection are very similar: they can be possessed by the same individual. The result can be a savings in money because one man is doing what otherwise would be the work of two. Combining the functions also permits the projection analyst to understand fully the likely validity of the esti-mates he is using to evaluate his projections.

How often should projections be revised? The answer is: when necessary and if the budget permits it, but not less than twice a decade. This minimum revision cycle is based on the fact that cohort-component projections are typically based on a five year age-time module beginning with a census. American projections would be for the years 1975, 1980, 1985, and so forth, while Canadian projections might be for 1981, 1986, and 1991. At each projection date, the pro-jection runs the very real risk of being invalidated by an estimate or a census. If, as is highly likely, the projected value differs from the enumerated or estimated value, there is pressure from the users of the projections for a modification that takes the new information into account.

For other years, revision will depend on how well the projection is tracking with respect to estimates and special censuses. That is, a pro-jection using 1970 census benchmark data and a five year module will have projected values for the year 1975. As estimates for 1971, 1972, etc., are obtained, the analyst may be able to assess the likeli-hood that 1975 estimates will agree with 1975 projections. If the prospect of error seems high, a revision may be called for. In rapidly changing demographic circumstances, annual revisions might be necessary. A two or three year revision cycle is more likely to be the norm, however. Where the projections are to be used for budgetary purposes, it is likely that the projection revision cycle will coincide with the budget cycle.

PROJECTION ACCURACY

Assessing the accuracy of population projections is not a clear-cut proposition. Siegel [2] has presented several approaches to measuring accuracy that are worth considering. These include (1) comparisons of the percent difference between projected and enumerated populations—this is the most common measure; (2) comparison of the percent change in the empirical population with the projected percentage change; and (3) using such methods, the accuracy of the projections of change components can be evaluated because, for cohort-component projections, it is these projections that determine the total result, and some components may be projected less accurately than others. He also suggests that length of projection period should be considered, because most projections become increasingly inaccurate the farther out in time they go.

Siegel examined U.S. national projections made over the period 1937–1967 using approaches (1) and (2) above, and he also considered the magnitude of the range between high and low series as a measure of the amount of confidence in the accuracy of the projections held by their creators. The accuracy of subnational projections was not even considered because they "employ a different methodology and their level of accuracy is of a different order of magnitude" [3]. He pointed out that the early cohort-component projections were even less accurate than contemporaneous logistic curve projections, partly because of the need to accurately project each of the three components. "In sum, the cohort-component method . . . has often been found to produce unsatisfactory results. . . . Typically, the greatest source of error [at the national level] has been in the projection of births. Birth rates have fluctuated widely and may do so again. These fluctuations make population projection uncertain, and if *they* are impossible to predict, as well may be the case, accurate population prediction is impossible" [4]. Some additional conclusions are: it is presently unrealistic to build cyclical fluctuations into trend projections; there is little point to proliferating projection series by generating the results of each possible combination of assumptions—three of four series forming a likely range will do; there is little evidence that "refinement of methods contributes to the accuracy of projections. The chief advantage of the more elaborate methods lies not in their greater accuracy but in their greater analytic usefulness and in their providing additional detail . . ."; there remains the "need for achieving as high a level of accuracy as possible in the principal projections" [5].

An earlier test of projection accuracy by Helen White compared state projections made using a variety of techniques [6]. The comparisons were for the years 1940 and 1950, and all projections were tied to 1930 benchmark data. White noted that "[o]ne of the rather interesting results of this study is that the cohort-survival method [based on 1920–1930 change] does not appear to yield definitely superior results. . . . In fact, no one method is clearly superior to all others tested . . ." [7]. Other tentative findings were: independent control totals may not be helpful—especially if the control projection is in error; errors tend to vary directly with the length of the projection period; errors tend to vary inversely with the size of the base population; and errors tend to vary directly with rates of recent net migration.

It should be noted that the projections examined by White were based on extrapolation of the past into the future with a minimum of judgmental input. Presumably, skillful judgmental control of component parameters could have made a difference. We might also note the fact that the period 1930–1950 was one of considerable demographic dislocation that made our Pennsylvania projections in Chapters Three and Four inaccurate beyond 1930, in most cases.

John Hajnal looked at the "prospects" for population forecasts in 1955 and also observed that "much of the elaborate techniques of forecasters is expended in vain; crude methods could have achieved equally good results" [8]. After noting that cohort-component forecasts provide useful detail and have great analytical utility for drawing conclusions from factors inherent to the age structure, he concludes by observing:

> If there is a general lesson to be drawn by this, it is, I think, first that as little forecasting as possible should be done, and second, if a forecast (more elaborate than the [recommended] quick calculation discussed earlier) is undertaken, it should involve less computation and more cogitation than has generally been applied. Forecasts should flow from the analysis of the past. Anyone who has not bothered with analysis should not forecast. The labor spent in doing elaborate projections on a variety of assumptions by a ready-made technique would often better be employed in a study of the past. Out of such study may occasionally come important insights about unexpected possibilities in the future" [9].

The present writer generally concurs with Hajnal. However, the electronic computer was not widely used as a means of calculating projections in 1955. Today, very elaborate projections can be obtained very quickly, so it is possible to "eat one's cake and have it too"—the analyst can do a lot of projecting and a lot of thinking at the same time.

Some observers have suggested that statistical confidence intervals be used in conjunction with population projections. Keyfitz, for example, would like to see forecasts—not projections—be given as probability distributions [10]. Unfortunately, any attempt to arrive at such standards must be based on the error found in previous forecasts, whereas, by its very nature, the future has its unknowable aspects—it is bound to differ in ways that can be foretold from past experience. Both Keyfitz and Siegel suggest that it is possible for the projection analyst to have a subjective, though informed, opinion as to the likely range of empirical outcomes. Keyfitz provided an example in which he specified a 95 percent confidence range about a U.S. forecast, and he encouraged other demographers to do likewise.

The present writer is skeptical about the possibility of creating meaningful statistical confidence intervals and of casting forecasts into probability distribution form. On the other hand, if the forecast is the representation of the analyst's best judgment regarding the direction of change in demographic components, then it makes sense to assume that this same professional judgment can be applied to the stipulation of likely upper and lower bounds for the series.

FORECASTING PROJECTION TECHNIQUES

As a conclusion to this study, we shall attempt to predict or forecast the future of population projection techniques. Undoubtedly, these observations will completely ignore developments from unforeseen directions. We also may place too much stock in recent trends. These are foibles of most forecasters. But, for better or worse, let us speculate.

No major change in U.S. census data—questions asked and the size of the sample being asked—can be expected before 1990, so any U.S. breakthroughs from a data standpoint will have to come from other public records such as the Social Security Continuous Work History Sample, or from surveys such as the Census Bureau's Current Population Survey or surveys conducted by survey research organizations. The main impact of new or improved data should be in the realm of sharpening the analytical understanding of fertility and migration.

The only foreseeable improvement in mortality data would be inclusion of social and economic variables in death certificate data or the use of, say, the decedent's social security number as a means of tapping other files for record-matching purposes. Although this procedure smacks of big brotherism, its practical result would be sets of local and national life tables for socioeconomic groups.

Fertility projections may make increasing use of stochastic or Monte Carlo models at the national level to establish period *ASFR* values. However, until the effect of net migration on local fertility is understood and simulated, we are not likely to see major additions to the ways local fertility may be projected. Improvements in survey-derived data and in theories on fertility levels may yield increasingly accurate national projections which, in turn, may enhance the accuracy of local forecasts.

The projection component that appears to have the greatest potential for improvement is migration. A likely feature of forecasts appearing in the late 1970s will be projections of local directional migration flows by age and sex that go beyond the fixed ratio techniques noted in this study. Such projections should be highly flexible, the model having the capability of being interfaced with econometric models or models of place-to-place migration flows.

NOTES TO CHAPTER TEN

1. New York State Office of Planning Services, "Demographic Projections: for New York State Counties to 2000 A.D." (Albany, N.Y.: 1974).

2. Jacob S. Siegel, "Development and Accuracy of Projections of Population and Households in the United States," *Demography* 9, 1 (1972):51–68.

3. Ibid., p. 51.

4. Ibid., pp. 59–60.

5. Ibid., pp. 65–66.

6. Helen R. White, "Empirical Study of the Accuracy of Selected Methods of Projecting State Populations," *Journal of the American Statistical Association* 29, 267 (1954):480–98.

7. Ibid., p. 484.

8. John Hajnal, "The Prospects for Population Forecasts," *Journal of the American Statistical Association* 50, 270, (1955):310.

9. Ibid., p. 321.

10. Nathan Keyfitz, "On Future Population," *Journal of the American Statistical Association* 67, 338, (1972):360.

Bibliography

Arkin, Herbert and Raymond R. Colton. 1970. *Statistical Methods.* New York: Barnes & Noble.

Barclay, George W. 1958. *Techniques of Population Analysis.* New York: John Wiley & Sons.

Bayo, Francisco and Steven F. McKay. 1974. *United States Population Projections for OASDHI Cost Estimates.* U.S. Department of Health, Education, and Welfare, Social Security Administration, Office of the Actuary. Actuarial Study no. 72. Washington, D.C.: Government Printing Office.

Berry, Brian J. L. 1972. "Population Growth in the Daily Urban Systems of the United States, 1980–2000." In U.S. Commission on Population Growth and the American Future, *Population Distribution and Policy,* Sara Mills Mazie, ed. Vol. V of Commission Research Reports. Washington, D.C.: Government Printing Office.

Black, Therel R.; Jewell J. Rasmussen; and Frank C. Hachman. 1967. "Population Projections: Utah and Utah's Counties." Economic and Population Studies, Utah State Planning Program. Salt Lake City, Utah.

Bowles, Gladys K. and James D. Tarver. 1965. *Net Migration of the Population, 1950–60 by Age, Sex, and Color.* Economic Research Service, U.S. Department of Agriculture. Washington, D.C.: Government Printing Office.

Chevan, Albert. 1965. "Population Projection System." Technical Report no. 3. Philadelphia: Penn Jersey Transportation Study.

Coale, Ansley J. and Paul Demeny. 1966. *Regional Model Life Tables and Stable Populations.* Princeton: Princeton University Press.

Connecticut Development Commission. 1962. "Population: A Demographic Analysis of Connecticut 1790–2000." Technical Report 131. Hartford: Connecticut Interregional Planning Program.

Cowden, Dudley J. 1947. "Simplified Methods of Fitting Certain Types of Growth Curves." *Journal of the American Statistical Association* 42 (240): 585–90.

Croxton, Frederick E. and Dudley J. Cowden. 1945. *Applied General Statistics.* New York: Prentice-Hall.

235

Demography. 1974. Cumulative Index, Vols. 1–10 (1964–1973). Vol. 11, no. 2, pt. 2.

Dorn, Harold F. 1950. "Pitfalls in Population Forecasts and Projections." *Journal of the American Statistical Association* 45 (251): 311–34.

Erie and Niagara Counties Regional Planning Board. 1972. "Regional Population Projections, Erie and Niagara Counties." Grand Island, N.Y.

Gannett, Henry. 1909. "Estimates of Future Population." In *Report of the National Conservation Commission*, vol. II, pp. 7–9. Washington, D.C.: Government Printing Office.

Genesee–Finger Lakes Regional Planning Board. 1971. "Regional Population Distribution and Projections." Rochester, N.Y.

Greenberg, Michael R. 1972. "A Test of Combinations of Models for Projecting the Populations of Minor Civil Divisions." *Economic Geography* 48 (2): 179–88.

Greenberg, Michael R.; Donald A. Krueckeberg; and Richard Mautner. 1973. *Long-Range Population Projections for Minor Civil Divisions: Computer Programs and User's Manual.* New Brunswick, N.J.: Center for Urban Policy Research, Rutgers University.

Hajnal, John. 1955. "The Prospects for Population Forecasts." *Journal of the American Statistical Association* 50 (270): 309–22.

Hamilton, C. Horace. 1965. "Practical and Mathematical Considerations in the Formulation and Selection of Migration Rates." *Demography* 2:429–43.

Hamilton, C. Horace and Josef Perry. 1962. "A Short Method for Projecting Population by Age from One Decennial Census to Another." *Social Forces* 41 (2):160–70.

Henry, Louis. 1961. "Some Data on Natural Fertility." *Eugenics Quarterly* 8 (2):81–91.

Illinois Bureau of the Budget. 1973. "Uniform Demographic and Economic Data: 1970–2000." Summary. Springfield, Illinois.

Isard, Walter. 1960. *Methods of Regional Analysis: an Introduction to Regional Science.* Cambridge, Mass.: The M.I.T. Press.

Kentucky Program Development Office. 1972. "Kentucky Population Projections: 1975–2000," vol. I. Frankfort, Kentucky.

Keyfitz, Nathan. 1968. *Introduction to the Mathematics of Population.* Reading, Mass.: Addison-Wesley.

———. 1972. "On Future Population." *Journal of the American Statistical Association* 67 (338):347–63.

Kuznets, Simon S., with the assistance of E. Douglas Burdick, Edward P. Hutchinson, and David T. Rowlands. 1946. *The Population of Philadelphia and Environs in 1950.* A Report to the Philadelphia City Planning Commission. Philadelphia: Institute of Local and State Government, University of Pennsylvania.

Lee, Everett S.; Ann Ratner Miller; Carol P. Brainerd; and Richard A. Easterlin. 1957. *Population Redistribution and Economic Growth in the United States.* Vol. I. *Methodological Considerations and Reference Tables.* Philadelphia: The American Philosophical Society.

Lotka, Alfred J. 1956. *Elements of Mathematical Biology.* New York: Dover.

Michigan Department of Commerce, State Resources Planning Program. 1966. "Michigan Population: 1960 to 1980." Working Paper no. 1. Lansing, Michigan.

Mitra, S. 1967. "The Pattern of Age-Specific Fertility Rates." *Demography* 4 (2):894–906.

Mitra, S. and A. Romaniuk. 1973. "Pearsonian Type I Curve and Its Fertility Projection Potentials." *Demography* 10 (2): 351–65.

Morrison, Peter A. 1971. *Demographic Information for Cities: A Manual for Estimating and Projecting Local Population Characteristics.* Rand Report R–618–HUD. Santa Monica, Calif.: Rand.

Murphy, Edmund M. and Dhruva N. Nagnur. 1972. "A Gompertz Fit that Fits: Applications to Canadian Fertility Patterns." *Demography* 9 (1):35–50.

Newling, Bruce. 1968. *Population Projections for New Jersey to 2000.* New York: Bruce Newling.

New York State Council of Churches. 1970. *A Graphic Presentation of Population Trends and Projections for New York State, Regions, and Counties: 1870–2000.* Syracuse.

New York State Office of Planning Services. 1974. "Demographic Projections: for New York State Counties to 2000 A.D." Albany, N.Y.

Pearl, Raymond. 1940. *Introduction to Medical Biometry and Statistics.* 3rd ed. Philadelphia: W. B. Saunders.

Pennsylvania Office of State Planning and Development. 1973. "Pennsylvania Projection Series: Population and Labor Force." Report no. 73. Harrisburg, Penna.

Pickard, Jerome. 1959. *Metropolitanization of the United States.* Research Monograph 2. Washington, D.C.: Urban Land Institute.

———. 1967. *Dimensions of Metropolitanism.* Research Monograph 14A. Washington, D.C.: Urban Land Institute.

Pittenger, Donald B. 1974. "A Typology of Age-Specific Net Migration Rate Distributions." *Journal of the American Institute of Planners* 40 (4):278–83.

Pollard, J. H. 1973. *Mathematical Models for the Growth of Human Populations.* Cambridge: Cambridge University Press.

Pritchett, H. S. 1891. "A Formula for Predicting the Population of the United States." *Publications of the American Statistical Association*, N.S. no. 14, pp. 278–86.

Romaniuk, A. 1973. "A Three-Parameter Model for Birth Projections." Paper accepted for Population Association of America Meeting, New Orleans.

Saboia, Joao L. M. 1974. "Modeling and Forecasting Populations by Time Series: The Swedish Case." *Demography* 11 (3):483–92.

Schmid, Calvin F. and Stanton E. Schmid. 1969. *Growth of Cities and Towns: State of Washington.* Olympia: Washington State Planning and Community Affairs Agency.

Schmitt, Robert C. 1953. "A New Method of Forecasting City Population." *Journal of the American Institute of Planners* 19 (1):40–42.

———. 1954. "A Method of Projecting the Population of Census Tracts." *Journal of the American Institute of Planners* 20, (2):102.

Shryock, Henry S.; Jacob S. Siegel; and Associates. 1971. *The Methods and Materials of Demography*. U.S. Bureau of the Census. Washington, D.C.: Government Printing Office.

Siegel, Jacob S. 1972. "Development and Accuracy of Projections of Population and Households in the United States." *Demography* 9, (1):51–68.

Siegel, Jacob S. and Horace Hamilton. 1952. "Some Considerations in the Use of the Residual Method of Estimating Net Migration." *Journal of the American Statistical Association* 28:475–500.

Stanbery, Van Buren. 1964. *Population Forecasting Methods*. Revision prepared by Frank V. Hermann. U.S. Department of Transportation. Washington, D.C.: Government Printing Office.

Statistics Canada. 1970. *The Population Projections for Canada*. Analytical and Technical Memorandum no. 4. Ottawa.

Tarver, James D. and Therel R. Black. 1966. *Making County Population Projections—A Detailed Explanation of a Three-Component Method, Illustrated by Reference to Utah Counties*. Bulletin (Technical) 459. Logan, Utah: Utah Agricultural Experiment Station in cooperation with Oklahoma State University Research Foundation.

Temple University Office of Research and Specialized Studies. 1963. "The Population of Pennsylvania: Projections to 1980."

United Nations. 1956. *Methods for Population Projections by Age and Sex*. Manuals on Methods of Estimating Population, Manual III, Population Studies, no. 25. New York.

_____. 1968. *The Concept of a Stable Population: Application to the Study of Populations of Countries with Incomplete Demographic Statistics*. Population Studies, no. 39. New York.

_____. 1970. *Demographic Yearbook: 1969*. New York.

U.S. Bureau of the Census. 1872. *Ninth Census of the United States: 1870*. Vol. I. *The Statistics of the Population of the United States*. Washington, D.C.: Government Printing Office.

_____. 1952. *Current Population Reports*, series P–25, no. 56.

_____. 1963a. *U.S. Census of Population: 1960*. Vol. I. *Characteristics of the Population*. Part 34, New York. Washington, D.C.: Government Printing Office.

_____. 1963b. *U.S. Census of Population: 1960*. Vol. I, *Characteristics of the Population*. Part 49, Washington. Washington, D.C.: Government Printing Office.

_____. 1963c. *U.S. Census of Population: 1960*. Subject Reports. *Mobility for States and State Economic Areas*. Final Report PC(2)–2B. Washington, D.C.: Government Printing Office.

_____. 1964a. *Current Population Reports*, series P–25, no. 286.

_____. 1964b. *U.S. Census of Population: 1960*. Vol. I. *Characteristics of the Population*. Part 1, United States Summary. Washington, D.C.: Government Printing Office.

_____. 1966. *Current Population Reports*, series P–25, no. 326.

_____. 1967. *Current Population Reports*, series P–25, no. 381.

_____. 1970. *Current Population Reports*, series P–25, no. 448.

_____. 1971a. *Census of Population: 1970 Number of Inhabitants*. Final

Report PC(1)–A1, United States Summary. Washington, D.C.: Government Printing Office.

———. 1971b. *Current Population Reports*, series P–23, no. 36.

———. 1971c. *Current Population Reports*, series P–25, no. 470.

———. 1971d. *Census of Population: 1970 General Population Characteristics.* Final Report PC(1)–B49, Washington. Washington, D.C.: Government Printing Office, 1971.

———. 1972a. *Census of Population: 1970.* Subject Reports. Final Report PC(2)–2E. *Migration Between State Economic Areas.* Washington, D.C.: Government Printing Office.

———. 1972b. *Current Population Reports*, series P–25, no. 493.

———. 1973a. *Census of Population: 1970 Vol. I. Characteristics of the Population.* Part 34, New York. Washington, D.C.: Government Printing Office.

———. 1973b. *Census of Population: 1970 Detailed Characteristics.* Final Report PC(1)–D1, United States Summary. Washington, D.C.: Government Printing Office.

———. 1974. *Estimates of the Coverage of the Population by Sex, Age, Race.* PHC(E)–4. Washington, D.C.: Government Printing Office.

———. 1975. *Current Population Reports*, series P–25, no. 541.

U.S. National Center for Health Statistics. 1964. *Life Tables: 1959–61.* Vol. 1, no. 1. *United States Life Tables: 1959–61.* Washington, D.C.: Government Printing Office.

———. 1966a. *Life Tables: 1959–61.* Vol. 2, no. 33. *New York State Life Tables: 1959–61.* Washington, D.C.: Government Printing Office.

———. 1966b. *Life Tables: 1959–61.* Vol. 2, no. 48. *Washington State Life Tables 1959–61.* Washington, D.C.: Government Printing Office.

———. 1968. *United States Life Tables by Cause of Death: 1959–61.* Vol. 1, no. 6. Public Health Service Publication no. 1252. Washington, D.C.: Government Printing Office.

———. No Date. *Vital Statistics of the United States, 1970.* Vol. II–section 5. *Life Tables.* Washington, D.C.: Government Printing Office.

U.S. Water Resources Council. 1974. *1972 OBERS Projections.* Vol. 1. *Concepts, Methodology, and Summary Data.* Washington, D.C.: Government Printing Office.

Whelpton, P. K. 1928. "Population of the United States, 1925 to 1975." *American Journal of Sociology* 34, (2):253–70.

White, Helen R. 1954. "Empirical Study of the Accuracy of Selected Methods of Projecting State Populations." *Journal of the American Statistical Association* 29 (267):480–98.

Wisconsin Bureau of State Planning. 1969. "Wisconsin Population Projections." Madison, Wisconsin.

Index

About the Author

Donald B. Pittenger is Assistant Chief, Population Studies Division, Office of Program Planning and Fiscal Management, State of Washington. He was formerly Associate Demographer with the New York State Office of Planning Services. He received the Ph.D. degree from the University of Pennsylvania and M.A. and B.A. degrees from the University of Washington. Dr. Pittenger is a co-editor of three introductory sociology readers and has had articles published in *Demography* and the *Journal of the American Institute of Planners.*